Civil War Artillery
at Gettysburg

Best wishes,

[signature]

CIVIL WAR ARTILLERY AT GETTYSBURG

Organization, Equipment, Ammunition, and Operations

Philip M. Cole

CCI

COLECRAFT INDUSTRIES

Since 1981

COLECRAFT INDUSTRIES

Published by Colecraft Industries
970 Mt. Carmel Road
Orrtanna, PA 17353
http: //www.colecraftbooks@aol.com

The author wishes to thank the Gettysburg National Military Park
for providing all the artifacts photographed in this work.

ISBN 0-9777125-0-8

For more information please contact us at:

http://www.colecraftbooks@aol.com

Second edition, first printing.

PRINTED AND BOUND IN THE UNITED STATES OF AMERICA

Cover photograph courtesy of Library of Congress

Contents

Maps on pages 60, 206, 212, 216, 217

Acknowledgments

I have been collecting notes and researching materials on the subject of artillery for many years. When I finally decided to thread this mass of material together into book form, I soon realized the difficulty that would be involved in transforming this information into a readable text. Many collected tidbits of information were often mentioned in the source document as a secondary comment to a greater issue. The information contained in these tidbits, however, was insightful and often led to researching answers to questions raised by the comment. Occasionally, conclusions were arrived at through generalizations. Information between the opposing armies was often similar or slightly variant in details but sometimes supporting facts were available only from one side. To assemble the collection of facts, I was fortunate enough to have two individuals point the way and assist me in translating this wealth of information into its final form.

First, I want to thank author and historian Colonel James "Skip" Wensyel, U.S. Army, retired, for his deep involvement in laying the groundwork for this project. Skip spent many hours reviewing and pointing out the techniques necessary to tie the information together into a readable form. After a major rewrite, he repeated this arduous task to further improve the presentation.

Next, I want to thank author and historian Paul Clark Cooksey for his generous involvement and interest in proceeding with this work at mid-stage. Paul helped to further refine the narrative. He offered his own expertise on the subject and, in the process, we exchanged many ideas. He also helped me discover the format that would clarify and finalize the presentation. In addition, Paul graciously provided research materials and other resources from his collection which further enriched this work.

In addition, I am indebted to the Gettysburg National Military Park, superintended by Dr. John Latschar, and staff for the use of its library facilities and for the cooperation received in the completion of this work. I particularly want to thank the curatorial staff at the Gettysburg National Military Park's Gettysburg Museum of the Civil War. Michael L. Vice, museum curator, and his staff were instrumental in fulfilling my requests for accessing and photographing the park's magnificent collection of artillery projectiles and related artifacts. Mr. Vice's staff included Paul

Shevchuk, museum specialist, Craig L. Blindenbacher, volunteer-in-park, and Elizabeth Trescott, museum technician.

With regard to images printed in this work, I am gratified to have had the services of Bill Dowling, professional photographer, for producing many of the excellent views of projectiles, artifacts, and archival material. Bill was kind enough to rearrange his personal time to attend the hours of photo sessions needed to generate the hundreds of photographs necessary to obtain the final selections.

I wish to thank others who looked over the book in various stages and provided additional facts on the subject, offered opinions or suggestions, edited portions of the manuscript, or shared their private material resources. They include historians James Clouse, Charles Hathaway, and Jack Wise.

I am thankful to the Association of Licensed Battlefield Guides at Gettysburg for access to the wealth of information contained in its extensive research library and innumerable files. I wish to thank the many others that assisted in providing documents, books, microfilms, and archival photographs used in this work. They include library staff personnel at Gettysburg College; Adams County Library, Gettysburg, Pa.; National Archives, Washington D.C., including Michael Music; the U.S. Army Military History Institute, Carlisle, Pa., including Michael Winey.

Finally, I want to thank my best friend and spouse, Diane, for assisting me in this long process and especially the understanding and patience she has shown during participation in social obligations when my inner mind would drift into the preparations surrounding this work.

Author's Notes

Abbreviations used for the photographic sources are as follows:

GNMP: Gettysburg National Military Park
MCMOLL: Massachusetts Commandery Military Order of the Loyal
    Legion
USAMHI: U.S. Army Military History Institute
WDC: Archival photograph reproduced by or artifact photographed by
William Dowling
    AC: Author's Collection

Much of the research included in this book addresses areas either not included or not covered in depth in many other works. Some aspects of artillery operations, for example, such as the structured moves performed in the loading process of an artillery piece, are either skimmed over or not included because they are covered in many other informative books on Civil War artillery.

The amount of research data available on the subject of artillery is often lopsided in favor of the Union experience. Many passages in this work and specifications that describe artillery equipment, ammunition, etc. relate to information gleaned from Northern records. Generally speaking, however, both sides suffered the same problems, although in varying degrees, with regard to artillery technology, weapons, ammunition, and operations.

For convenience sake, the Pickett/Pettigrew/Trimble assault will be called Pickett's Charge.

Any omissions or errors are mine and hopefully do not detract from the totality of this project.

Preface

Confederate Major General George Pickett, when asked what accounted for the failure of the Army of Northern Virginia at Gettysburg, replied, "I think [it was] principally to the Yankees." Hidden in his answer were countless small details of the engagement that added up to defeat for Lee's army. I have always been fascinated with the characteristics of soldiers' environment, the background against which soldiers fought, and seemingly obscure or insignificant details that influenced their ability to fight. Such details quite often influence the outcome of a battle but rarely receive attention. "For the want of a nail . . . the battle was lost." One could ask why some Confederate artillerymen failed to hit their mark during the great July 3rd cannonade that preceded Pickett's Charge and, in the same vein as the famous dictum about the "nail," one could expect the response, "I think it had something to do with the smoke." Artillery smoke—one of the countless details of battle—might very well have influenced the outcome of one of this nation's most important battles.[1]

Soon after the battle of Gettysburg ended, historians began describing this three-day event that would eventually become the most written about battle in American military history. For the most part, when analyzing the reasons for the outcome they focused on generalship, troop strengths, the element of surprise, tactics, etc. Whatever the primary reasons for the outcome, a multitude of secondary or minor influences also contributed to its conclusion.

This work is an examination of artillery and its role in the outcome at the battle of Gettysburg, as well as the many elements that affected its operation and performance in combat. Gettysburg was the last engagement in the American Civil War that featured large-scale artillery operations in open country. This study, however, is not a description of the individual maneuvers and tactics of artillery batteries during the battle, or which batteries were moved where and when. Rather, it takes a different approach and examines the various characteristics of artillery, such as organization, tactics, equipment, and ammunition, making conclusions about the role of each of these characteristics in determining the part that artillery played in the battle's outcome.

This book, then, focuses on the many details of the operation of the artillery branches as they fought at Gettysburg. It examines all the circumstances under which artillery was used in the battle, how men coped with conditions, and the impact of these circumstances on the battle's outcome. Details which, taken separately, may provide no measurable influence on the battle's outcome. Taken together, however, these sometimes inconsequential details may have helped to resolve the issue.

The way each army organized its artillery branch, for instance, represents just one facet that influenced its ability to fight. Each army's artillery organization differed significantly from its enemy's, and each commander would derive some benefit in the advantages of his army's customized organizational arrangement that his counterpart could not. But in the last analysis, the composition of federal artillery batteries and the method used to manage the Union artillery reserve provided organizational advantages over that used by the Army of Northern Virginia.

In addition to differences, both armies faced common problems unique to the artillery branch and both were expected to overcome these difficulties and operate efficiently in battle. Artillery was used in battle in concert with infantry. The combination of two distinct army branches working as one sometimes seriously interfered with battle-line command and control—blurring the line between an infantry officer's responsibility to order artillery about and having artillerymen who were more skilled than their infantry officers in the technological details of their equipment operation and capability.

Operating artillery was not just a setting up, loading, and firing operation. Fields of fire had to be determined and suitable terrain and gun placement had to be chosen. Gun crews had to deal with serious shortcomings typical for the artillery branch during the Civil War period. Many factors were beyond the control of the artillerymen, such as faulty equipment, ammunition that was unreliable, and unskilled men assigned to the battery. Throughout the Civil War, artillerymen had to learn new technologies in weapons and ammunition. The use of rifled guns in place of smoothbores, for example, took place in the midst of the war. The transition was done so rapidly that time did not allow improvements in the safety and effectiveness of new innovations.

Lingering questions and continuing debate regarding the role of artillery and its use at Gettysburg remain. Unless one understands the subtle influences that affected artillerymen and the technology they used, a full appreciation of what these brave men did or did not do would be difficult.

Introduction

. . . And such a scene as it presented—guns dismounted and disabled, carriages splintered and crushed, ammunition chests exploded, limbers upset, wounded horses plunging and kicking, dashing out the brains of men tangled in the harness, while cannoneers with pistols were crawling around through the wreck shooting the struggling horses to save the lives of the wounded men.[1]

It was the action on July 2, 1863, on Benner's Hill on the outskirts of Gettysburg, Pennsylvania, that brought us this graphic description of the damage Union artillery inflicted upon Major J. W. Latimer's Confederate guns. Events such as these during the Civil War illustrated the role of artillery at its best moments and also confirmed its destructive power. Even before Gettysburg the artillery branch already had a well-established reputation for affecting the outcome of battles. In 1862 during the battle of Antietam the term "artillery hell" was coined. It was also artillery firepower that saved the Union army from disaster at the battle of Malvern Hill. It would also play a demanding role in the three-day encounter at Gettysburg.

Many accounts would describe the ferocity of artillery and the accolades it achieved at Gettysburg. On the Union side, Northern guns fought tenaciously on July 1 to hold Seminary Ridge as its infantry withdrew through the town. Artillery, considered incapable of defending itself without supporting infantry, on more than one occasion did just that. On July 2 Colonel Freeman McGilvery's reserve guns rushed to the scene near the Peach Orchard, stubbornly resisted the Confederate assault, and withdrew to plug and hold the line until infantry support arrived. Federal artillerymen fought hand-to-hand with Confederate infantry to help save Cemetery Hill. On July 3 gun crews of both armies stood erect at their vulnerable positions and performed their duties in the midst of raining iron during the greatest artillery cannonade yet unleashed in the Western Hemisphere.

On the Confederate side, Southern guns helped smash the Union line on the ridges west of town on July 1 by their deadly flanking fire from Oak Hill and then into the right of Major General Howard's Eleventh Corps line on the Federal right. Southern artillerymen excelled in aggressively supporting their infantry in attacking the Union defenses. On July 2 their destructive fire pummeled Sickles' Third Corps back from the Peach Orchard and then helped stagger the main Federal line close to its breaking point.

Despite Confederate artillery successes at Gettysburg, the glory gained was greatly diminished by the nature in which the guns were used. Confederate artillery achievements throughout the battle were accomplished in a manner isolated by distance. Southern artillerymen operated at moderate to long range from their opponents. They were not exposed to the close-up confrontation of enemy troops and the corresponding threat of losing their guns to capture. The Confederate effort to sustain the previously earned reputation of its artillery branch was overshadowed by the heroic, exciting circumstances of close encounters between Confederate infantrymen and defending Federal artillerymen. "Double-shotted canister" and the "swinging of rammers and handspikes" would be terms associated only with the Union experience. Narratives on Gettysburg have painted vivid descriptions of the heroic deeds performed by Federal artillerymen and their desperate encounters, and have thrusted names such as Bigelow, Ricketts, Hazlett, and Alonzo Cushing into the limelight. For the Confederate cannoneers, however, previous battles had already soundly established their reputation; after Gettysburg there would be ample opportunity to affirm it.

Horse artillery going into action. This engraving at Gettysburg National Military Park depicts the Sixth Independent New York Battery, First Brigade, Cavalry Corps. (AC)

I

From the Beginning

*A*n important aspect in assessing artillery's role at Gettysburg requires a brief review of the origins of each army's artillery branch from the early days of the war. Each army's artillery branch entered the war with little or nothing in the way of adequate manpower levels, trained officers, equipment necessities, and a reliable organization. The Federal army, however, already had a functioning artillery branch to build upon, even though it was small and modestly equipped.

Commanders, during the early stages, could not foresee themselves handling battle lines of lengths never before experienced. The artillery branches lacked the technological know-how to operate efficiently and could hardly anticipate how to exploit innovations without field testing them, or how to deal with their imperfections of design or manufacture.

The artillery organization, in general, was faulty, particularly in the Confederate army. The Army of Northern Virginia's eventual arrangement of batteries into battalions was slow. The Southern army lacked uniform equipment within single batteries and allowed this to continue even after it had the power to improve this condition. It also suffered with improper staffing and manpower levels varied among same-size units. These factors were stumbling blocks to the Southern artillery branch's evolution and, consequently, this branch did not develop as quickly as its infantry and cavalry counterparts.

The groundwork for the developing artillery branch was yet to be laid. There was a need to establish such details as an efficient chain of command and an organizational structure that fulfilled artillery's role and maximized its army's firepower in battle. In many respects, despite these burdens facing each army, the transition during this relatively brief period to the level achieved at Gettysburg was phenomenal.[1]

Manpower

The prospect of a war was difficult for both governments to suddenly face and neither was prepared to fight. Before the first shot was fired building an army capable of winning battles on a scale unforeseen was a daunting task. With war imminent, the Confederate government was starting from scratch in building an army. The U.S. government, on the other hand, had an established permanent army. As small as the army was, it had trained officers and men, and it had a fixed organizational structure. The industrial North also had more skilled men, such as mechanics, needed to fill the ranks of the artillery branch. While these factors made war preparations easier for the North, it had to switch from a peacetime military force to one that quickly required resources far beyond previous experiences. Just before the war, the entire U.S. army numbered 16,367 men. In the Civil War, the evolution of events became commonplace where commanders would be called upon to control individual armies approaching 100,000 men.

Training the eager but inexperienced officers and men to fight and win battles with an army that was understrength and poorly equipped was a monumental task. To fight competently and at the intensity level of Civil War combat, veteran military commanders could only draw from prior battle encounters and textbooks, both of which would be of limited help for the Civil War experience. Only one person in the military, General Winfield Scott, had the experience of maneuvering a force of more than five thousand soldiers. Most commanders, in fact, had not even participated in basic operations at the lowest level of the battalion or regiment. Textbooks did not take into account the improvements of new weapons, ammunition, and other devices used in warfare; soldiers still had to learn to use the products of new technology.

In addition, no previous combat experience compared to that which Civil War leaders were about to confront. The scale of Civil War battles dwarfed any prior encounters. The Mexican War, for example, lasted a year and a half; the battle theater, although far from home, was comparatively small. That war's total casualties were less than those encountered in three days at Gettysburg. The Civil War, on the other hand, lasted four years, covered almost the entire nation, and involved a million men in uniform at the same time—a manpower level more appropriate for the following century. Quick and absolute victories would be more difficult to achieve. By the 1860s larger armies were capable of bringing forth battles that lasted much longer than wars fought on a smaller scale that allowed decisive and conclusive victories to end the conflict.[2]

Despite the abundance of Northern manpower there still was a desperate shortage of experienced artillery officers to command and train artillery units. This deficiency, due in part to the small size of the peacetime army, was further aggravated when many experienced artillery officers left the artillery branch and transferred into other branches that offered better opportunities. In the swelling numbers of the expanding army, the chance for career officers to advance in the ranks of all branches seemed unlimited. But the other branches offered a much greater promise of advancement, and rapid promotion was common only in the infantry and cavalry. Artillery provided the least hope for elevation in rank, and there were practically no generals in the artillery. In 1862, the Federal War Department ordered the elimination of field officers, major and above, in the artillery as an unnecessary expense. Promotions ceased. Capable officers such as Alexander Hays, John Gibbon, and Romeyn Ayres could only move up in rank by transferring to the infantry or cavalry. Artillerymen's opportunities for glory would be plentiful, but their hopes for advancement were dismal.[3]

Federal Brigadier General Henry J. Hunt made his point when he listed his artillery force at Gettysburg and noted the absence of high-ranking officers to manage it:

> In the Gettysburg campaign, with sixty-seven batteries (approximately 370 guns, 320 of which were on the field, with over 8,000 men and 7,000 horses, and the necessary material pertaining to them), I had in the whole army but one general officer (commanding the artillery reserve) and four field officers. Of the seven corps present the artillery of three corps was commanded by captains, and that of one corps by a young lieutenant. Both brigades of horse artillery were commanded by captains. These facts need no comment, yet those only who were charged with the management of such a force with so little aid can fully appreciate the evils and difficulties to which they led.[4]

Joining the artillery required special individuals willing to overlook the shortcomings of this organization, which desperately needed skilled men more than other branches. Perhaps those that remained in the artillery hoped to imitate the fame and glory of heroes born in the Mexican War. For whatever their reasons, they sacrificed personal advancement for the common good and should be remembered for that sacrifice. Lieutenant John Calef, for example, of the 2nd U.S. Artillery which gained fame for being the first battery to engage the Confederates at Gettysburg, would have to wait twelve years to become a captain. Lieutenant James Stewart, 4th U.S. Artillery, who desperately tried to hold back the Confederate line on Seminary Ridge on July 1, retired in 1879 as a captain. Conversely, many of their counterparts in the infantry or cavalry branches began with no military education or experience, some as privates, some with field rank, and frequently retired as brigadier or major generals.[5]

Equipping

The superiority in Northern resources—manpower, wealth, and manufacturing potential—made it easier for the Federal army to assemble an effective artillery organization. Besides recruiting men for the artillery and teaching them to fight, providing the necessary equipment was an equally daunting challenge. At first, the swelling ranks of each army could not be outfitted fast enough. Some newly arrived artillery units came with horses and harnesses; some came without them. The artillery branch expanded, but early on it was a paltry, hodge-podge mix of obsolete weapons that needed to expand many times as both governments realized that the war would be a lengthy one and to win it would require serious undertakings.[6]

At first, equipping each army's artillery branch with the most advanced weapons was not uppermost in the minds of the commanders in chief. With both sides desperately short of artillery firepower, quantity was of more concern than quality. Supplying each battery with enough guns to match the might of its enemy was a challenge for both armies.

Early in the war, Union Brigadier General William Barry, George McClellan's chief of artillery, described the status of the artillery for the Army of the Potomac:

> When Major-General McClellan was appointed to the command of the Division of the Potomac (July 25, 1861), a few days after the first battle of Bull Run, the whole field artillery of his command consisted of no more than parts of nine batteries or thirty pieces of various and in some instances unusual and unserviceable calibers. Most of these batteries were also of mixed calibers, and they were insufficiently equipped in officers . . . 650 men, and 400 horses.
>
> In March 1862, when the whole army took the field, it consisted of ninety-two batteries of 520 guns, 12,500 men, and 11,000 horses, fully equipped and in readiness for active field service . . .
>
> During this short period of seven months all of this immense amount of material was issued to me and placed in the hands of the artillery troops after their arrival in Washington. About one-quarter of all the volunteer batteries brought with them, from their respective states, a few guns and carriages, but they were nearly all of such peculiar caliber as to lack uniformity with the more modern and more serviceable ordnance with which I was arming the other batteries, and they therefore, had to be withdrawn and replaced by more suitable material.[7]

Colonel Edward Porter Alexander, Confederate battalion commander of artillery at Gettysburg, described the Southern army's condition:

> The variety of calibres comprised in the artillery was throughout the war a very great inconvenience, and materially affected the efficiency of the ordnance service

both in the quantity of ammunition carried and the facility with which it was supplied. At the commencement of the war this variety was often almost ludicrously illustrated by single batteries of four guns, of four different calibres, and it was only after the battalions were well organized in the winter of 1862 that anything was done to simplify this matter.[8]

Without the plentiful resources and foundries to manufacture artillery pieces like those in the North, the Southern government faced great problems in equipping its artillery branch. Its newly formed national army started with nothing, and it lacked the resources to build upon in preparing to fight an extensive war. The Confederacy controlled not one national armory in its territory. Therefore the Southern government had to arm itself quickly if it was serious in establishing itself as a sovereign country.

Professor W. LeRoy Broun, formerly a lieutenant colonel commanding the Richmond Arsenal, described the desperate condition of the Southern war machine:

> At the beginning of the war it must be remembered the Confederacy had no improved arms, no powder-mills, no arsenals, no armories, no cap machines, and no improved cannon. All supplies at first, were obtained by importation, though the blockade subsequently cut off this foreign supply. All arms were percussion-cap lock, and issued to the troops. . . .
>
> When we consider the absence of manufactories and machinery and of skilled mechanics in the South at the beginning of the war, its successfully furnishing ordnance supplies for so large an army, during the four eventful years, is a striking evidence of the energy and resources and ability of its people.[9]

As secession spread, the Confederate government seized the Federal navy yards at Norfolk, Virginia, and Pensacola, Florida. Even though hundreds of cannons were captured, almost none were suitable as field pieces. Ultimately, there were three main sources of arms for the Confederate army: those manufactured in the Confederacy; those captured as a result of operations against Federal armies; and those that were imported.

Private foundries, such as the Tredegar Iron Works in Richmond, expanded or converted from peacetime enterprises to making sorely needed artillery pieces. The rapid transition produced deficiencies in artillery weapons, often beyond control of the foundries. "Bad iron" or inferior raw materials were blamed for barrel failure by some. Confederate chief of ordnance, Josiah

Gorgas, blamed Tredegar's inability to secure high-quality gun iron as the primary cause for the defective cannons. Poor manufacturing methods in casting and shoddy workmanship were also contributing causes. A continuing problem confronting foundries that cast bronze artillery pieces was the inability to obtain a final product in a homogenous form with consistent density of material. Bronze ingredients, tin and copper, had different fusibility characteristics making it difficult to form a perfect alloy. Porosity in a gun barrel, especially in the area where the explosive shock occurred, could prove fatal. Apparently iron plugs were screwed or hammered in the barrel to repair porosity defects before being turned into the finished dimensions. Examples of poor castings showing pitted barrels and plugged defects exist today on the Gettysburg battlefield. One example is the bronze Napoleon gun nearest the Eternal Flame peace memorial.

Frequently the Confederate army was provided with cannons that were of poor quality and dangerous to operate. Unscrupulous manufacturers occasionally tried to cover up flaws with plugs or cement which, if discovered, resulted in their rejection. In the first year of the war, D. H. Hill wrote: "Frequent bursting caused a 'Richmond gun' to be viewed with mingled scorn and apprehension." Secretary of War Judah Benjamin sent a scathing letter to the Tredegar Iron Works complaining about their unacceptable quality: "It is bad enough that our brave defenders should expose their lives to the fire of the enemy under such odds as exist against us, but to furnish them arms more dangerous to themselves than to the enemy is utterly inexcusable." Although improvements were made, concerns for reliable weapons continued to the end of the war.[10]

Without quality control it was difficult or impossible to produce artillery pieces and accompanying ammunition in the uniform dimensions necessary to function accurately. J. W. Mallet, ex-lieutenant colonel of artillery and superintendent of the Confederate States Ordnance Laboratories, described the predicament of the Southern Ordnance Bureau: "As a natural consequence there was serious trouble at the arsenals and in the field, from confusion in regard to ammunition—trouble which was made worse by the gauges in use in the ordnance shops, which were not very accurate and often did not agree among themselves. . . . Orders were sent to Europe for a number of accurately tested steel gauges."[11]

Captured Union guns provided another prime source used to equip the growing number of Confederate batteries; ordnance officers estimate that two-thirds of the pieces in Southern artillery units were captured from the Union army—the 3-inch rifles and the 10-pounder Parrotts in particular. At Harpers Ferry in September 1862, for example, General "Stonewall" Jackson reported the capture of seventy-three guns, boosting the Confederate artillery's growing strength. Just weeks before Gettysburg, the Army of Northern Virginia increased its firepower by capturing twenty-eight fine Union cannons at the battle of Winchester. At Gettysburg, the artillery branch's strength of the Army of the Potomac pitted 6,948 men (Brigadier General Hunt, chief of artillery, said it numbered over 8,000 men), manning about 370 guns; against the Army of Northern Virginia's 6,080 men, operating about 270 guns.[12]

Compared to the North's abundant resources in raw materials and in-place manufacturing facilities, the ability to supply ammunition for Southern artillery pieces was exceedingly difficult. Ammunition had not been produced in the South since the Mexican War. Accumulating stockpiles was just as critical as acquiring the guns. E. P. Alexander described the conditions with regard to perpetual shortages of ammunition:[13]

> Indeed, the limited resources of the Confederacy, the scarcity of skilled workmen and workshops and the enormous consumption, kept the supply of ammunition always low. The Ordnance Department in Richmond were [sic] never able to accumulate any reserve worth mentioning even in the intervals between campaigns, and during active operations the Army of Northern Virginia lived, as it were, from hand to mouth. The great majority of the batteries took the field without having ever fired a round in practice, and passed through the war without aiming a gun at any target but the enemy. The order "save your ammunition" was reiterated on every battlefield, and many an awful pounding had to be borne in silence from the Yankee guns, while every shot was reserved for their infantry.[14]

While the North enjoyed a superior capacity for making artillery pieces and projectiles, there was an even greater difference with the South in production capacity for making gunpowder. In the North many pre-Civil War powder mills were already in place within its territory; existing facilities were due to the high demand for gunpowder's use in civilian development. In contrast, the Southern prewar requirements for gunpowder were almost totally dependent on Northern sources. Initially, Confederate authorities were not even aware that any powder works even existed within the boundaries of Confederate territory. Eventually some production facilities were discovered, but of little consequence. In the states that seceded, the census of 1860 listed only two powder mills: one in South Carolina and the other in Tennessee. One employed three men, the other ten. Confederate procurers had to search within their government's newly allied states for ingredients to make gunpowder and then had to construct facilities to produce it. When the war started, the Confederate Ordnance Bureau secured powder, or some ingredients, through capture at arsenals and importation.[15]

Ironically, the Civil War actually caused a decline in the requirements for gunpowder. Even though the U.S. Ordnance Department alone was purchasing, on average, 5.3 million pounds per year at twenty cents per pound, the military needs did not consume gunpowder in war as did civilian usage of explosives in railway construction and other developmental work. Such work tapered off as resources were devoted towards winning the war.[16]

By the end of 1862, General Lee saw positive improvements in equipping his artillery branch and competing more evenly with the Union army's advantages acquired from its rich resources. Lee wrote: "During the past campaign I have felt, in every battle, the advantages that the enemy possessed over us in their artillery. This arose in part from their possessing more experienced artillerists and better prepared ammunition, but consisted chiefly in better guns. These advantages, I am happy to state, are gradually diminishing. Our artillerists are greatly improving, our ammunition is more carefully prepared, and the efficiency of our batteries increased by guns captured from the enemy."[17]

Ordnance Department

The Ordnance Department was responsible for "procuring and distributing ordnance and ordnance stores to the Army, maintaining and repairing such equipment, and developing and testing new types of ordnance." With regard to development and testing, the Federal Ordnance Department spent huge sums of money to incorporate new technology into weapons and ammunition. Apparently, its developmental efforts did not achieve acceptable results. After the war, the report from the Joint Select Congressional Committee on Ordnance stated:[18]

[The] importance of these inquiries will be appreciated when it is considered that during the late rebellion the purchases, contracts, and experiments made by the Ordnance Department of the army alone for the trial and supply of projectiles of this class cost the United States very nearly, if not altogether, the sum of seven millions of dollars. But more especially will it be felt when it is remembered how at Fort Fisher, Morris Island, and the many battle-fields of the Union, this arm of the service from some cause failed not only to realize the expectations of the people, but did, in fact, largely contribute to the disasters which befel [sic] us.[19]

Further findings of the Select Committee on Ordnance pointed out that communications between the chief of ordnance and his principal assistants on the subjects under investigation were destroyed "under the pretense that the whole of such correspondence was private and confidential." According to the committee, the destroyed documents were the only official written memoranda pertaining to the subjects of the investigation.[20]

The committee also addressed the Federal Ordnance Department's methods of adopting and accepting new advancements in weapons and ammunition. The best inventions were not always necessarily adopted. It was not a coincidence, for example, that some of the inventors of the arms and ammunition approved for use were military officers. The report from the Select Committee on Ordnance criticized this practice: "[A] difficulty that has retarded progress in the science of ordnance has been the fact that prominent officers have been inventors of arms, and have possessed sufficient influence to secure the adoption and retention in service of their inventions frequently without regard to the question of real merit, and to the prejudices of other and better devices brought forward by citizens or developed in other countries."[21]

Overall, the Federal Ordnance Department's performance rating in adopting the best innovations proved disappointing. In February 1869, the Joint Select Congressional Committee on Ordnance delivered its report card on their accomplishments:

The ordnance officers, knowing their positions secure to them for life, have not felt the incentive to exertion and improvement which stimulates men when not in government employ, and they have become attached to the routine and to the traditions of their corps, jealous of innovation and new ideas, and slow to adopt improvements.

. . . These officers, educated to a specialty and proud of their positions, come to look upon themselves as possessing all the knowledge extant upon the subject of ordnance, and regard citizen inventors and mechanics who offer improvements in arms as ignorant and designing persons, and pretentious innovators, who have no claim to consideration. Instead of encouraging the inventive talent of the country, these officers seem to have constantly discouraged it.[22]

In contrast, E. P. Alexander, a colonel at Gettysburg, praised the Ordnance Bureau of the Confederate War Department:

> Its admirable chief, General J. Gorgas, might well have hesitated at the task before him. The emergencies and demands of the war were already upon him, and the immense supplies which it became his duty to provide were of a character which the South had neither the factories nor the skilled workmen to produce. With scarcely a single assistant instructed in the peculiar and technical details which are the first elements of an ordnance officer's attainments, and without even an office organization for the transaction of business. . . .
>
> It is true that the Confederate armies were never in condition to use ammunition as lavishly as the enemy frequently did, but the supply never failed to be equal to the actual emergency, and no disaster was ever to be attributed to its scantiness. Wherever insufficiency was apprehended and economy imposed, in fact the scarcity arose far more from the lack of transportation to carry it with the army than from inability of the arsenals to furnish it.[23]

In 1864, Confederate Chief of Ordnance Josiah Gorgas, in reflecting upon his accomplishments, wrote in his diary:

> April 8th, It is three years ago today since I took charge of the Ordnance Department of the Confederate States, at Montgomery—three years of constant work and application. I have succeeded beyond my utmost expectations. From being the worst supplied of the Bureau of the War Department it is now the best. Large arsenals have been organized at Richmond, Fayetteville, Augusta, Charleston, Columbus, Macon, Atlanta and Selma, and smaller ones at Danville, Lynchburgh [sic] and Montgomery, besides other establishments. A superb powder mill has been built at Augusta. . . .
>
> A cannon foundry [was] established at Macon for heavy guns, and bronze foundries at Macon, Columbus, Ga., and at Augusta; a foundry for shot and shell at Salisbury, N.C. . . .
>
> All of these have required incessant toil and attention, but have borne such fruit as relieves the country from fear of want in these respects. Where three years ago we were not making a gun, a pistol nor a sabre, no shot nor shell (except at the Tredegar

Works) - a pound of powder - we now make all these in quantities to meet the demands of our large armies. In looking over all this I feel that my three years of labor have not been passed in vain.[24]

Once the groundwork for weapons production was underway and with a war in progress, rapid development of new weapons was essential to compete with similar weapons used by each army's adversary or to gain the advantage and magnify the fighting ability of its own forces. The timing was terrible for experimenting with new technology and for presenting untested inventions. Nevertheless, a variety of improvements and innovative new devices to the artillery branch were introduced.

Rifle technology, for example, was introduced on a scale grand enough to finally gain general acceptance and soundly establish its future. There were new weapons that could hit targets at much longer ranges and improved projectiles, such as canister, with increased killing power. There were new devices such as friction primers, which provided a reliable means of igniting the powder cartridge and replaced the less reliable or unpredictable burn rate of slow-match fuses, quills, or portfires. A predictable ignition system allowed the guns to be fired more efficiently in the rate of fire and also in hitting moving targets. Another device was the impact fuse. This invention sped up the loading process on artillery pieces by eliminating the step needed in estimating accurate projectile flight time that was essential for time-fused projectiles to work. Many other ideas were introduced and would become the predecessors of weapons for the twentieth century. Adaptability in using the benefits of these new innovations or learning to work around their shortcomings was crucial for success.

Some innovations or improvisations, however, did not originate from the Ordnance Department. A few contrivances, nevertheless, produced entertaining and interesting experimentations with "artillery." On July 2, 1863, at Vicksburg, for example, First Lieutenant P. C. Hains reported:

> In order to have some means of throwing our shells into the fort, I have directed Captain Patterson, of the pioneer corps, to construct spring-boards for this purpose. I learned that General McPherson was using mortars made of trunks of trees (gum trees being the best) to throw 6 and 12 pound shells, and directed him to make some of these also, shrinking about three iron bands around the mortar. These mortars,

which are said to work admirably for about 100 rounds, will be finished and stuck in the ground in the advanced trenches, so they will only have to throw the shells about 50 or 75 yards.[25]

In the midst of combat then, the battlefield was also a laboratory for trial of invention. Soldiers became proficient survivors or unfortunate victims of these grand experiments. The effectiveness of artillery, more than any other branch of the army, depended upon the technology of the day. No other American war experienced the variety of weapons and ammunition in use at the same time.

Bigelow's 9th Massachusetts battery going forward on July 2. Major General Dan Sickles's headquarters is under tree at right. This sketch was made by Charles Reed, bugler of the battery.
(MCMOLL/USAMHI/WDC)

II

Organization

Command

*B*esides the task of training and equipping the artillery branch, the army needed an efficient command structure to support its associate infantry and cavalry forces. Few factors would be more important than the design of a proper artillery organization to function effectively with other branches during operations. Poor ammunition, faulty cannon barrels, impossible terrain, and many other factors would certainly interfere with fighting battles, but an army with an organization inferior to that of its enemy, that could not muster its firepower efficiently, was prone to defeat.

Organizing the artillery branch, however, was a complex proposition. The combination of inexperienced commanders, working with a force whose size had never been seen on the continent, and the introduction of advanced technology in weaponry and ammunition was a difficult challenge to adjust to rapidly.

For one thing, the purpose and tactical use of artillery was hindered by more technical limitations than other branches. Commanders needed to understand the boundaries of the artillery branch's mobility and firepower and the large assortment of subtle elements affecting the operation of its weapons and ammunition. The use of artillery was characteristically more difficult to grasp than that of other branches.

Finding the best organizational chain of command to manage artillery seemed obvious to infantry commanders. From the perspective of artillery officers, however, the view was quite different. Because of the distinct manner in which artillery fought, blending the artillery force to operate efficiently beside other branches was difficult. The artillery branch was confronted with a peculiarity in its operation that other branches did not have to address: artillery's effectiveness demanded that firepower be dispersed throughout the army in order to protect it.

The infantry and cavalry branches enjoyed the benefit of being managed with their large formations operating intact. In contrast, the characteristic of artillery operations was diffusion. Scattering guns throughout an army prevented the best management of artillery's special needs and attention to technical requirements. In a marching column, for example, artillery batteries traveled scattered throughout the line in case they were quickly needed for action. Disbursed artillery units consequently lost the guidance provided by a centralized artillery command. It was impossible to enforce regulations for straggling, packing of the carriages, and proper care of the equipments and animals. Lack of supervision also promoted a lack of discipline within the artillery units. Even in camp, the artillery branch was so widely spread out that artillery commanders had little opportunity to manage and instill discipline in the men.

Even more scattered than artillery units were the reserve artillery supplies and ammunition for batteries attached to infantry units. Before the battle of Gettysburg artillery supplies were most likely incorporated into the general wagon train of their assigned infantry force and rarely received prompt considerations. This arrangement, however, was remedied a few weeks before

Gettysburg with Special Order No. 129. It said: "The artillery ammunition train of the batteries attached to corps will be organized, and placed under the direction of the commander of artillery of the corps; the surplus will be transferred to the Artillery Reserve." Despite this improvement, rapid maneuvers and changing conditions at Gettysburg placed many Union artillery batteries beyond the reach of their own ammunition trains. Many batteries were forced to use ammunition supplies out of the wagons of the artillery reserve, a force of guns, independent of other units and with its own ammunition supply.[1]

Besides the artillery branch facing problems on the march, managing cannons in a line of battle was especially difficult. Artillery units needed to be positioned where they could protect the entire front. Thus, proper deployment of artillery usually meant strung-out, disconnected groups of batteries that made it impossible for the centralized control of an artillery commander.

The effects of scattering a command, no matter what branch of the army, were aptly illustrated at Gettysburg. On July 2, Union Colonel George Burling, Third Corps, had his infantry brigade temporarily disassembled into regiments and singly disbursed to support others needing emergency assistance. This dismantled force resulted in a brigadeless commander and his staff that were relegated to mere spectators. "My command," he wrote, "now all being taken from me and separated, no two regiments being together, and being under the command of the different brigade commanders to whom they had reported, I, with my staff, reported to General Humphreys for instructions, remaining with him for some time." Major General John Sedgwick also suffered a similar predicament as his tired soldiers of the Union Sixth Corps spilled onto the field and were parceled out to plug holes at different points.[2]

Because of the strewn arrangement, artillery's organization and command structure did not fit well in a large army. The blending of artillery units throughout the infantry was essential for protecting a column on the move or fighting a battle, but this arrangement did not easily form itself into one homogenous fighting force. On the march, for example, each branch aggravated the other by their unwillingness to give up the right-of-way; the loser following behind, eating dust and moaning about the insufferable stops and starts caused by the others ahead.

Transferring infantrymen to temporary artillery duty also irritated the relationship between the two branches. In the artillery branch, no reserve manpower pool existed. Often short of men, artillery units depended on the infantry branch to supply assistance needed to perform the necessary duties. General Hunt eventually tried to remedy the manpower problem. In February 1864 he proposed adding units to the artillery that could readily fulfill artillery duties:

> The force asked for as guards, &c., can best be furnished by assigning to this army two or three additional regiments of foot artillery, from which the details for all purposes can be made by the chief of artillery, and this arm be relieved from its present dependence on the infantry. The duties must be performed and men are required to perform them. It is now done by drawing from time to time regiments from infantry brigades and the assignment of men from regiments to serve as drivers and cannoneers in the batteries, to the injury of both branches of the service and a continual struggle and ill feeling between them.[3]

In battle, blending infantry units with artillery batteries was a disturbing arrangement. Infantry troops, positioned near cannons were uneasy because of the inherent dangers of their own artillery and ammunition, as well as the guns drawing enemy fire in their vicinity. And even though mixing infantry troops with artillery batteries in a campaign promoted cooperation and interdependence, especially in combat, each branch operated with completely different duties and skills required. It was human nature for soldiers to attach themselves to a specific group with common duties, experiences, and trained expertise. Thus, infantry soldiers and artillerymen, except during manpower emergencies, would never allow themselves to completely merge into one indistinguishable unit.

Despite the differences between the artillery and infantry branches, it was easy for infantrymen to establish a quiet admiration and respect for their comrades manning the guns during combat. The infantry troops, ducking behind their protective defense-works during a deafening cannonade, and their infantry officers seemingly disinterested in the surrounding dangers, marveled at these brave men standing in the open, calmly loading and firing, in defiance of the enemy iron flung at them. During the July 3 cannonade, General John Gibbon glanced at Cushing's New York Battery and noted: "My eyes happened to rest upon one of the gunners standing in the rear of the nearest limber, the lid open showing the charges. Suddenly, with a shriek, came a

Colonel Edward Porter Alexander, C.S.A., served as one of James Longstreet's reserve artillery commanders. At the battle of Gettysburg he was assigned the important duty of placing and directing the cannons that would directly confront the opposing Union forces on July 3. (WDC)

shell right under the limber box, and the poor gunner went hopping to the rear on one leg, the shreds of the other dangling about as he went . . . Of course it would be absurd to say we were not scared . . . None but fools, I think, can deny that they are afraid in battle."[4]

With infantry and artillery units operating closely together and interdependently during operations, it was obvious that the army needed a clear chain of command. A regulation was needed defining a chain of command that could control the two branches in combination, smoothly and in unison. The question of who should order artillery about in battle seemed obvious.

There were, however, two distinct theories on the issue. First, those within the artillery ranks theorized its organization as needing a strong centralized command by an artillery officer to successfully apply the principles and objectives of artillery. Such a centralized command needed high-ranking officers to enforce its mission. Shortly after the war, Colonel E. P. Alexander described the evils of managing artillery through an infantry commander and yet also recognized the limitations of an artillery commander in this role:

> The infantry at this period [first year of the war] was organized in divisions; the commanding officer of which had, or was supposed to have, on his staff a Chief of

Artillery, who was to exercise a general supervision over the brigade batteries of the division.

This organization was very inefficient for the following reasons. The brigade batteries depended for their rations, forage, and all supplies, upon the brigade staff, and received from brigade headquarters all orders, and thus acquired an independence of the division Chief of Artillery, which was often fostered by the Brigadier Generals resenting any interference with parts of their commands by junior officers, and took from the Chiefs of Artillery the feeling of entire responsibility which every officer should feel for the condition and action of his command. In action the Brigadier could not give proper supervision both to his infantry and artillery; and the Chief of Artillery with the best intentions could himself manage the batteries but inefficiently, as they were so scattered in position along the line of battle.[5]

Others outside the artillery branch held the second theory on who should control artillery in battle. They objected to centralizing the artillery command in battle to an artillery officer for two reasons. First, as Alexander stated above, it seemed physically impossible for an artillery officer in a centralized command to successfully exercise control over his scattered forces during an engagement. Artillery in combat required the presence of hands-on supervision. Second, and more importantly, an artillery officer was not the one who would ultimately be responsible for the success or failure of the line in which his batteries operated. After all, how could an infantry commander, who had the primary responsibility for protecting a portion of the battle line, be held accountable unless all the units within his jurisdiction responded to his orders? No artillery officer would be asked to share the blame with an infantry commander afterward if the efforts in the action were judged to be a failure.

Sharing the control of a battlefront with both an infantry and artillery commander was out of the question. Splitting control would disunite two powerful forces and create uncoordinated exertions in battle when survival depended upon timing and instant mutual support.

A clear-cut chain of command was imperative to address the unpredictable ebb and flow of the crises experienced in battle and also to allow commanders to properly orchestrate the employment of their forces at the proper moment. This unclouded control was critical for commanders to employ the right sense of timing. Timing was the key to feeding and regulating the proper amount of force onto the field at a critical moment in order to sway the outcome of an action.

Controlling infantry and artillery in a battle line as a unified threat to the enemy, however, was no easy task. Clarity of command and timing the employment of a commander's firepower, for example, were complicated and became more so as the battle progressed. At long range, artillery was the dominant force being employed in the engagement, receiving the attention of the line commander in close cooperation with his subordinate artillery officers. Under this condition, artillery needed no active infantry support. As the enemy approached and the range shortened where small arms could participate, however, the dominant force being employed gradually switched from artillery to the commander's infantry with an increasing need to support artillery units. When artillery and infantry units shared the battle line, understanding and agreement between battery commanders and infantry commanders in transferring their firepower from cannons to small arms was critical. This shift required skillful timing and the complete focus of the commander in orchestrating the artillery/infantry role change.

July 3 at Gettysburg presented an excellent example of the importance of the artillery/infantry role change. When the Confederates breached the Union line at the Angle and crowded into the Union guns, this action illustrated the importance of the Union artillerymen clearing themselves from their infantry support's field of fire so they could blaze away at this crucial moment. A clumsy maneuver could be costly in casualties and a possible loss of position. An awkward move wasted the combatants' ability to fight and had the potential for disaster when a battle reached its critical moments when there was no room for misunderstood direction.

The question of who should direct the artillery in battle defied any solution other than to assign control and firepower to infantry commanders supervising the line. Commanding artillery units on the line by an infantry officer then was a necessity of convenience. This arrangement properly placed all units occupying positions under the singular control of a commander who was responsible for the integrity of his line.

Beyond the battle line, however, artillery units needed additional supervision. Someone with technical skills and knowledge in the school of artillery, for example, needed to train the units, maintain their proficiency, oversee the care of the equipments and animals, pay, promote and discipline men, and supply and provide for their ordinary needs. Even though infantry commanders controlled artillery batteries in battle, they could not perform the administrative and technical duties required by artillery units. Infantry commanders had their own administrative duties to attend to for their infantrymen and, more importantly, did not have the skills needed to administer to this specialized arm. To attend to the administrative needs of the artillery branch both armies created the position of chief of artillery. At Gettysburg, the post was held by Brigadier General Henry J. Hunt for the Army of the Potomac and for the Army of Northern Virginia, Brigadier General William N. Pendleton.

In the early stages of the war, the assignment of duties and the level of authority for the position of chief of artillery were vague and needed to be examined. The specific duties of the chiefs of artillery needed established guidelines for their authority and responsibilities. The title needed a job description. In the Union army a board of officers was created to study the question. In his General Order Number 110 of March 26, 1862, General McClellan specified the duties of the position and explicitly stated the level of its authority:

> The duties of the [chief] of artillery . . . are exclusively administrative, and . . . will be attached to the headquarters of the Army of the Potomac . . . [He] will be required to inspect the artillery . . . whenever it may be necessary, and will be responsible that [it is] properly equipped and supplied. [The chief of artillery] will not exercise command of the troops . . . unless specially ordered by the commanding general, but . . . will, when practicable, be selected to communicate the orders of the general to [his] corps.
>
> All requisitions for officers and men and for supplies for the artillery . . . , other than the regular supplies furnished by the staff departments on ordinary returns, will be sent to the chiefs of artillery . . . ; to whom will also be rendered, in addition to those made to General Headquarters and division commanders, such reports of artillery . . . practice, marches, actions, and other operations pertaining to [this arm] as may be necessary to enable [him] to judge of the efficiency both of men and material.
>
> Officers of the staff at any headquarters may correspond direct with officers of their department or corps serving at subordinate headquarters, and give them, in all matters of routine or administration, all orders and instructions, and call for such returns and reports as the good of the service may require; but they will in no case give any order or instructions which will cause interference with another staff department or corps, or will in any way interfere with the duty of the officer with the commander on whose staff he may be serving.[6]

On the Confederate side, Colonel E. P. Alexander, First Corps Artillery Reserve at Gettysburg, fittingly described the important role of the Confederate chief of artillery as superintendent of the guns in battle: "He visits & views the entire field & should recognize & know how to utilize his opportunities. The chief of each corps only sees his own ground." What Alexander pointed out was the great need for the chief of artillery to act as the primary coordinator for employing its artillery's overall firepower. No other commander would ordinarily have the skills and the opportunity to affect such responsibility.[7]

The chief of artillery's prescribed duties mentioned above were extensive, yet little or no staff was provided to carry them out. General Hunt described this deficiency at Gettysburg: "My rank, brigadier-general, the command being that of a lieutenant-general, gave me a very small and insufficient staff, and even this had been recently cut down. The inspector of artillery, Lieutenant-Colonel Warner, adjutant-general, Captain Craig, my only aide, Lieutenant Bissell, my one orderly, and even the flag-bearer necessary to indicate my presence to those seeking me, were busy conveying orders or messages, and I was alone; a not infrequent and an awkward thing

Brigadier General William N. Pendleton served as chief of artillery for the Army of Northern Virginia. Appraisals of his performance at Gettysburg are usually negative. He oversaw the preparations for the cannonade on July 3.
(MCMOLL/USAMHI/WDC)

for a general who had to keep up communications with every part of a battle-field and with the general-in-chief."[8]

It is safe to say that neither army's chief of artillery enjoyed the thought of an infantry commander controlling "their" artillery in an operation. The Army of Northern Virginia's chief of artillery, General William Pendleton, wrote to General Lee and expressed his feelings on this matter:

> The objections to the brigade batteries and division groups now existing are obvious. Burdened as are brigade and division commanders, they can scarcely extend to batteries thus assigned that minute supervision which they require, and the supply officers, whose chief care lies with considerable bodies of infantry, cannot devote to one or more batteries the time and attention they imperatively need. This is most injuriously experienced in times of pressure. . . . Batteries, besides, permanently attached in this way, can scarcely be assigned elsewhere, whatever the emergency, without producing some difficulty, almost as if a vested right was violated. But, most injuriously of all, this system hinders unity and concentration in battle.[9]

General Hunt mirrored Pendleton's displeasure regarding uneducated army officers' displays of ignorance and their misunderstood relationship of the artillery branch to its army and the "*necessity* of special organization and rules of service to [it]": ". . . Since 1821 our army regulations have became, in successive editions, . . . more and more obscure, . . . and in fact both law and regulations have been so disregarded and perverted in special interests that confusion . . . ensued and no one can learn from our present code alone what the organization of the special arms and their rules of service ought to be, or where they differ from those of the cavalry and infantry. On this point, our experience in Mexico gave us no light. The whole force was small, there was no Chief of Artillery."[10]

Hunt complained: "[There were] no regulations for [artillery's] government, its organization, control, and direction were left to the fancies of the various army commanders." His frustration was clearly expressed in his testimony regarding his role as chief of artillery at the battle Chancellorsville: "I simply had the administration of the artillery, without its military command, of which [Hooker] deprived me at that time. Consequently I did not know all the movements, even of the artillery until the battle was well under way." Hunt's duties were confined to the responsibility for safe passage across rivers and to making reconnaissances during the battle, while the greater part of the artillery moved "without my knowledge or orders." Hunt protested his predicament: "The separation of the duties of command and administration is anomalous; I do not know of any other army in which it exists."[11]

If artillery were to be employed effectively under the direction of infantry commanders, they either needed to have a technical understanding of its use or have a skilled advisor nearby to assist in controlling it. In reality, it was not unusual to have infantry commanders lack the expertise to manage artillery, understand its capabilities, its limitations, and when to use it. Infantry officers' lack of technical knowledge with respect to artillery operations lent itself to bearing resentment toward subordinates who knew the details on handling such matters and, in turn, fostered the artillerymen's lack of respect toward infantry commanders, ignorant of the proper application of artillery. One of the frustrations of an artillery officer was to see infantry commanders shoving batteries in areas they were not supposed to. Adding to the frustration, artillery officers experienced inflexibility in relocating artillery firepower assigned to brigadiers of infantry. Having an infantry officer controlling artillery in the line certainly clarified the chain of command but did not necessarily improve artillery's efficiency.

After the war, Hunt assessed the results of artillery's performance under the control of non-artillery officers: ". . . The efficiency of the artillery was sometimes sacrificed and shows the necessity of regulations securing the command of artillery . . . to the [artillery] officers commissioned to command them, and to attach a proper responsibility to those who in virtue of their rank, misapply them."[12]

Complicating the problem even further was the fine line that existed between an infantry commander controlling a battery and the degree to which he should micromanage the minute details of artillery operations. It was likely that an infantry commander's orders appeared more like interference when his instructions went beyond general directives pertaining to the battery's role. An infantry commander, for example, might want artillery positioned at a specific point in the line; whereas, an artillery officer might see the impracticality of such gun placement because of soft ground, poor field of fire, or improper support. Opinions differed when to open fire, the rapidity of fire, the choice of targets, or any number of points for managing the guns. Ultimately, however, it was the infantry commander's call.

Brigadier General Henry J. Hunt was Union chief of artillery in July 1863. An active leader who was usually in the thick of the battle, Hunt was given high marks for his performance in the battle of Gettysburg but would find coordination between the infantry and artillery one of his greatest challenges. (MCMOLL/USAMHI/WDC)

Furthermore, the administrative and command responsibilities over artillery units by two separate authorities were not always clear-cut and left plenty of room for friction. Conflicts arose regarding overlapping responsibilities in the chain of command or confusion in the assignment of duties which changed from the fluidity of unsteady circumstances.

Artillery officers' acceptance of control by infantry commanders was not total, and the realities of it were different than the directives. Artillery officers had orders that were countermanded by infantry officers and vice versa. No other army branch faced such a relationship.

There is no better example to illustrate the "tug of war" between an infantry commander and an artillery commander than an incident that took place at Gettysburg on July 3, 1863. In this case, it was the quarrel between General Winfield S. Hancock, commanding the Union Second Corps, and Chief of Artillery General Hunt in competing for control of the guns during the cannonade. Although the disagreement occurred in a convoluted way, the incident demonstrated the susceptibility toward misunderstanding the artillery's chain of command.

The conflict began when General Hunt, in "taking command," ordered all batteries to avoid a shooting match between artillery forces and thereby conserve ammunition for the anticipated infantry assault. The temptation to fire

Major General Winfield S. Hancock commanded the Union Second Corps at the battle of Gettysburg. Coordination of the battle with the chief of artillery, Henry Hunt, would prove to be one of the many challenges he faced on that Pennsylvania battlefield. (MCMOLL/USAMHI/WDC)

back at the blazing Southern artillery with a full response, however, was too great for General Hancock on Cemetery Ridge. When the Confederate guns opened, Hancock countermanded Hunt's instructions to hold their fire. Hancock ordered all of the batteries on his front to open in reply. He depended on a full artillery reply to calm and preserve the fighting spirit of his infantrymen until it was their turn to receive the assault. At that point they were helpless and vulnerable to the crash and explosion of the incoming missiles. Hancock also reasoned that by returning the fire, it would create the appearance of a line strongly defended and make an unattractive point of attack.

Captain Phillips, one of the artillery reserve's battery commanders, later said, "The rebels were not doing us any harm and, if they wanted to throw away their ammunition I do not see why we should prevent them." General Hunt soon learned from the smoke and sound on Cemetery Ridge that his instructions to avoid a gun duel were being ignored. Hunt then countermanded Hancock's order to fire and instructed batteries to hold back on their salvos.[13]

Preserving morale for the waiting infantry meant little to Hunt at this defining moment. Saving ammunition was a more valuable option since it would provide positive and measurable physical relief in stopping the enemy when needed at the critical moment. In Hunt's view, the spiritual benefits gained by Hancock "wasting" precious rounds overlooked the physical disability that this tactic was creating—the artillery could not kill approaching enemy infantry with empty ammunition chests. Hunt said, "I wanted a *half* supply of ammunition for the assault after the rebels had exhausted theirs."[14]

Besides General Hancock's desire to engage in the gun duel, Major Thomas Osborn, commanding the Eleventh Corps artillery on the Union right-center over on Cemetery Hill, was also tempted to fire back at the enemy cannons:

> Their fire was exceedingly harassing and did us much damage. Several times my men swung their guns around to answer the fire of the enemy's batteries, which were annoying them so severely. I was often compelled to order them to turn their fire back upon the enemy's infantry, where their work would tell most effectively in deciding the fate of the day. It was hard for my men to have this fire concentrated on them from half the enemy's line, while they were not permitted to reply. The effects of long discipline in the field, and the obstinacy of veteran troops, were put to the utmost test, while more than a hundred guns were playing on them, manned by as old and skilled artillerists as themselves. Yet they were not permitted to fire, but ordered to direct their fire upon a body of troops in no way annoying them at the time.[15]

If the Confederates made it to the Union line in great numbers, when the battle came to close quarters, infantry fighting was where the real damage would come from. The Union guns on Cemetery Hill and Cemetery Ridge, therefore, needed to be ready to stop attackers before they entered the Union stronghold and mingled with the defenders and, as a consequence, neutralize the Union artillery in providing any further assistance.

The Southern artillery fire of the July 3 cannonade, designed to pave the way for the infantry assault, might ruffle the spirit of the Union infantry line, but, if its effects were anything like in prior battles, there would be relatively little physical damage. Hunt knew that gun duels rarely produced any great benefit for the defenders and were often a wasteful use of their ammunition. A pre-assault cannonade was even less of a benefit for the attackers. General Helmuth von Moltke, the Prussian chief of staff, explained the defenders' superiority over attackers: "It is absolutely beyond doubt that the man who shoots without stirring has the advantage of him who fires while advancing, that the one finds protection in the ground, whereas in it, the other finds obstacles. . . . "[16]

The Confederate artillery fire on July 3, however, tested the mental endurance of Hancock's waiting infantry to its limits. Self-control was difficult. The fury begged for a response from the Union guns to eliminate the source that was taunting the men's mortality. The very least that could be achieved by the responding Federal artillery fire was the generation of a smokescreen thick enough to conceal their vulnerable positions.

On the left-center of the Union line, however, Colonel Freeman McGilvery was busy preventing his thirty-nine guns from firing in reply. For his disciplined artillerymen the muted response was working according to Hunt's wishes. But then McGilvery was interrupted with an unexpected change of plans. He reported: "About one-half hour after the commencement, some general commanding the infantry line ordered three of the batteries to return the fire. After the discharge off a few rounds, I ordered the fire to cease and the men to be covered. After the enemy had fired about one hour and a half, and expended at least 10,000 rounds of ammunition, with but comparatively little damage to our immediate line, a slow, well-directed fire from all the guns under my command was concentrated upon single batteries of the enemy of those best in view, and several badly broken up and successively driven from their position to the rear."[17]

The organizational discord pitting the authority of the chief of artillery [Hunt] against an infantry commander [Hancock] had surfaced—and the unfortunate lower-echelon artillery commanders were placed in the middle of the dispute. It was an uncomfortable dilemma for an artillery officer on the line and under a most terrific fire to receive conflicting orders from two squabbling generals. Determining who controlled frontline artillery in the midst of a decisive battle could prove disastrous. This predicament forced officers of lower commands into the uncomfortable position of choosing between conflicting orders at a most inopportune instant. At the moment of choice, their lives were at stake; if they lived, their careers were at risk—a minor point to consider in the scheme of their destiny.

Captain John Hazard, commanding the Second Corps artillery brigade in the Union center, was placed in an even greater predicament than McGilvery's batteries. Although Hunt told him to hold his fire, he was under the direct control of Hancock. How could an artillery captain refuse the direct order to open fire from his corps commander? He didn't. Hazard reported: "The batteries did not at first reply, till the fire of the enemy becoming too terrible, they returned it till all their ammunition, excepting canister, had been expended. . . . The rebel lines advanced slowly but surely; half the valley had been passed over by them before the guns dared expend a round of the precious ammunition remaining on hand."[18]

While Union artillery fire helped stop the assault on Cemetery Ridge on July 3, its overall effectiveness was compromised by confusion over who controlled artillery firepower. That out-of-hand situation contributed to the Army of the Potomac's fate in coming dangerously close to disaster when combat reached its peak in the Union center.

General Hunt assessed the performance of Union artillery during this event. To say the least, he was not happy. As a result of Hancock's "premature" artillery fire from his Second Corps's guns, Hunt viewed the affair as being a waste of precious ammunition early on in the cannonade and made the guns practically unusable at the critical moment. Hunt remarked: "The artillery of his Corps had thrown away in an utterly useless cannonade, every round of its long range ammunition and therefore, it could not open on the advancing troops until they came within canister range of his 12-pound batteries." Even then Hunt remained disappointed by the firepower emanating from the center of the Union line. He said: "Of course [Hancock's] fire was 'feeble' for the rifle-batteries were still ineffective, their canister range being less than half that of the 12 pounders."[19]

Hunt regretfully summarized: "The effective power of our artillery defence was reduced by Hazard's silence to less than a third of what it ought to have been. . . . All experience as well as reason goes to show that [the enemy] would have reached the wall, if at all, in too disordered a condition to have seriously contested the ground."[20]

In the aftermath, the argument between Hunt and Hancock erupted. Hancock deflected Hunt's accusation of wasting ammunition. In Hancock's after-action report, he unjustly wrote: "The artillery of the corps [was] imperfectly supplied with ammunition . . ." The two generals verbally dueled on who controlled the artillery. Hunt said:

[Hancock] charges me with obstructing his operations at the Battle of Gettysburg, to such an extent as to compel him to "threaten force" on his own line, in order to make a battery fire on the enemy. . . . As to the organization of the artillery . . . of active armies, what he says, shows conclusively that he does not understand the proper relations of [this arm] to an army, and the consequent *necessity* of special organization and rules of service for [it]. On this subject ignorance is very prevalent even now. . . ."[22]

Hancock responded:

It is thought to be common sense and much safer, that those commanders, who fight the troops in time of war, and are responsible for success or failure of the operations, should have the same control . . . over the other arms . . . rather than to have them subject to the command of officers, who would not be responsible, whether a battle was lost or won. . . . I would have been held responsible in the event of a loss, while the Chief of Artillery of the army would have had no responsibility in that event.[23]

Hunt addressed Hancock's complaint regarding the "Artillery Captain [who] refused to obey his order to open fire":

I was bothered to death with the complaints, and absurdities of generals, ignorant as horses of the organization of modern armies with a view to their duties, "He had better bring him to trial then, if a General can't command the troops under his orders I can't help him." "But," said Meade, "if the Captain was not a part of his command." "Then," I replied, "It depends on circumstances if the Captain should obey him." Oh! said Meade "a battery Captain must obey a General who gives him an order." I said "the same principles of military command apply to the artillery as to other troops. A general has no more right to order about the batteries of another corp. or division than his own then he has to order about their infantry or cavalry regiment. Let any General undertake to give orders to my battery in violation of my orders, and I will soon teach the Captain who obeys him unless the facts warrant the different action, whether he can obey. If he must obey any casual General who may come along & fancy to give him orders he must by the same rules obey any Colonel, Major or Captain of higher rank who chooses to commence to control him. He will obey at his own peril."[24]

Hunt recommended a solution to clarify misunderstandings with a pitch to redesign the organizational role of the artillery command in battle. He also took the opportunity to point out the main cause of this close brush with disaster on July 3: "The prime fault was in the obscurity of our army regula-

Major General George G. Meade was commander of the Army of the Potomac at the battle of Gettysburg and thus became embroiled in the disagreements within the command structure between artillery leaders and infantry leaders exemplified by the Hancock–Hunt dispute. (MCMOLL/USAMHI/WDC)

tions as to the artillery, and the absence of all regulations as to the proper relations of the different arms of service to one another. On this occasion it cost us much blood, many lives, and for a moment endangered the integrity of our line if not the success of the battle."[25]

The seeds of the Hunt–Hancock controversy continued to sprout even beyond the war's end and enticed the two participants into discussing, once again, the role of the chief of artillery. The disagreement was not so much over the standing order defining the role of who controlled artillery on the front line, but it was the interpretation of orders received by Hunt. In emergencies, expediency was sometimes preferable over following the cumbersome chain of command. After all, Hunt took control of frontline guns on July 2 during the emergency defense at the southern part of the line. General Warren, chief of engineers, also expeditiously grabbed control of Union troops already committed to saving General Sickles's line and, by doing so, saved Little Round Top and then became known as the "savior" of Gettysburg.

The Hunt–Hancock dispute had developed from a chain of events that caused the misunderstanding. It began on July 2 when General Slocum approached Meade to report a gap between his Twelfth Corps's troops and Cemetery Hill. Meade told Hunt (as nearly as Hunt could recollect): "This is your affair. Take the proper measures to provide against the attack, and make the line safe with artillery until it is properly occupied." From Meade's instruction, the assignment now thrust upon Hunt seemed clear. Hunt logically concluded: "This, with his previous instructions, left me no room to doubt his intent as to my duties and powers, and it was under a full sense of the responsibility thus imposed that I immediately assumed the active command of the Artillery and exercised it during the remainder of the battle."[26]

Meade's instruction to Hunt perfectly fit the clause in the regulation that described the duties of chief of artillery. This, in effect, canceled the statement that the chief of artillery "will not exercise command of the troops" and confirmed the exception clause in the regulation: "unless specially ordered by the commanding general, but . . . will, when practicable, be selected to communicate the orders of the general to [his] corps."[27]

In addition, Hunt's active role seemed confirmed on July 2 when General Sickles moved his Third Corps into position, far in advance of the main Union battle line. In the late afternoon, when Sickles's forward move was under attack, Hunt was on the scene with the Third Corps's chief of artillery, Captain George E. Randolph, approving the disposition of batteries. It was the fero-

General Robert E. Lee was commander of the Confederate army at the battle of Gettysburg. The problem of mixed guns in his artillery and the resultant problems of coordinating supplies, ammunition, and artillerymen for that variety of guns was one that plagued him throughout the war. (MCMOLL/USAMHI/WDC)

cious Confederate attack against Sickles forward line on July 2 that resulted in a sequence of events that laid the groundwork for the Hancock–Hunt dispute on July 3. After Sickles moved forward on July 2, the sequence unfolded as such:

> McGilvery's Artillery Reserve brigade [controlled by Hunt] is moved forward near the Peach Orchard to support Sickles.
>
> One of Hancock's Second Corps's infantry divisions, Caldwell's, is sent from the main battle line [south of where the Pennsylvania monument stands today] forward to the Wheatfield to support Sickles.
>
> Sickles falls back in disarray.
>
> McGilvery's reserve batteries fall back to plug the hole left from Caldwell's original position. McGilvery regroups to command the batteries in this sector on July 3.
>
> On the evening of July 2, Caldwell's division [under Hancock] returns to its original position behind, and in support of, McGilvery's artillery [under Hunt].

From these developments, Hancock now correctly assumed he had control of this part of the line—McGilvery's batteries supported by his infantry. His infantry, even though in a supporting role, now occupied ground for which he was responsible. Hunt, on the other hand, was under the impression that he was still acting on Meade's instructions he had received on July 2, and as mentioned above, that he was to take active control of the artillery. When the line was re-established, Hunt did not transfer his assumed authority over the guns to the corps commander [Hancock] who was responsible for protecting this frontage. And Hancock did not expect Hunt to relinquish the command over the guns in question. Proper protocol did not call for the formal transfer of authority. The standing regulation established control of battlefront artillery units by the infantry commander protecting the line, and Hancock had no idea of any conversations regarding Meade's instruction to Hunt.[28]

Hancock later commented on Meade's verbal order to Hunt which gave him active control: "What an indefinite, irregular and insufficient assignment to such an important duty! In well regulated armies high commands are not left to be deduced by subordinates through the operations of logic, but are conferred in orders!"[29]

Bigelow's 9th Massachusetts battery in Trostle's yard on July 2, 1863. This sketch is by Charles Reed, bugler of the battery. (MCMOLL/USAMHI/WDC)

Before the July 3 cannonade opened, there was no hint of controversy. The coordinator for arranging cooperation within the artillery force was General Hunt. He had the opportunity to insure collaboration beforehand on July 3, and he went about the line doing just that. Hunt stated: "At 10 A.M. I made an inspection of the whole line, ascertaining that all the batteries—only those of our right serving with the Twelfth Corps being engaged at the time—were in good condition and well supplied with ammunition. As the enemy was evidently increasing his artillery force in front of our left, I gave instructions to the batteries and to the chiefs of artillery. . . ."[30]

No corps commanders seemed to mind Hunt's riding through their front and instructing the batteries. After all, they had to prepare their own infantry troops. When the Confederate guns finally opened and Hunt could determine the nature of the attack, he rode to the artillery reserve to ready the batteries and returned to the front to observe and replace damaged batteries. He continued to maintain control of McGilvery's guns and instructing their fire, until the fight was over.[31]

Meade's instruction to Hunt, from his July 2 comment involving the gap in Slocum's line, to "take the proper measures and provide against the attack" certainly appeared to be a positive order from the commander in chief to Hunt in giving him tactical control during the action. Hunt viewed the directive as such rather than his issuing orders on behalf of and in the name of General Meade. Hunt said: "I will not command troops in another man's name taking all the responsibility at the risk of having my actions abused and receiving little of the credit."[32]

Hunt's final point, reinforcing his view that he was in an active command of artillery, originates from the communications he received during the July 3 cannonade. Hunt recollected: "I met [Captain Henry H.] Bingham of Philadelphia then of Gen. Hancock's staff who informed me that Gen. Meade's aids [sic] were looking for me with orders to stop the fire of our batteries, and had requested him if he saw me to deliver the orders. As I had already done this and the firing had almost ceased I answered 'Very well.' General Bingham some years after reminded me of this incident which had almost escaped my recollection."[33]

From this exchange with Bingham, Hunt deduced what his duties were at that time and reasonably concluded: "It is curious too that General Meade's order to cease our fire sent to the *Chief of Artillery* and thus recognizing all the batteries on the line as under his command, should have reached him through one of Gen. Hancock's staff officers!"[34]

In looking at the chain of events in total, because of the fast pace of the action, the fluid changes of circumstances, and the absence of written orders, perhaps Hunt misread Meade's seemingly unambiguous words. As the Army of the Potomac pursued Lee's retreat, Meade, apparently having no intention of conveying such tactical control, relayed to Hunt his puzzlement in "how a Chief of Artillery could command all the artillery scattered over such large spaces."[35]

The Hunt–Hancock controversy does not actually illustrate an example of a flawed design in the Army of the Potomac's artillery organization. The operational rules existed. The misunderstanding was a combination of Meade not informing the appropriate commanders of his assignment to Hunt to "take the proper measures and provide against the attack" for Slocum's line on July 2 or

Meade not clarifying the intention and scope of his order to Hunt and when to terminate it. Complicating matters was the participation of two strong-willed characters, Hunt and Hancock, each thinking they were right. This example, however, certainly points out the artillery organization's susceptibility to misunderstanding the chain of command and the gravity of the consequences when two separate branches must interact and operate as one. The affair happened at a climactic moment and the Army of the Potomac almost lost it.[36]

Interestingly, the Confederate chiefs of artillery faced the same dilemma as Hunt in operating with the dual-command nature involving artillery units but found no impediment in the arrangement of its artillery organization. E. P. Alexander commented:

> A theoretical drawback, perhaps, existed in the fact that the Chief of Artillery of each corps really had two independent commanders, namely, his corps commander and the army Chief of Artillery, between whom there might arise conflict of orders. The objection would be very material if the Chief of Artillery should be considered like the Chief of Cavalry as the actual commander of that arm; but it vanishes when he is regarded simply as a staff officer of the Commanding General's, charged with the supervision of that rather peculiar branch of the service, and only giving orders through the corps commander, except in matters of mere routine and report. The original orders directed the organization were not explicit upon this point, but common sense and circumstances soon gave the proper turn to the matter, and not the slightest discord ever occurred.[37]

In judging the implications of the Hunt–Hancock dispute, it is interesting to ponder who made the best choice—Hunt wanting to conserve ammunition during the cannonade for use in the final stage of the infantry assault or Hancock wanting to blast the enemy to calm his men. Each officer's decision was undoubtedly influenced by his role in battle. Hunt's command responsibility, for example, was not directly involved with controlling large numbers of men in a line of battle. His job was not a frontline responsibility except in emergencies. If his responsibility was in a line of battle, like at Gettysburg, his temporary command was in a spread out deployment of loosely packed artillerymen and not subjected to the same psychological concerns that bothered Hancock so much. Hancock, on the other hand, because of his experience as a corps commander, was in a better position to weigh the value of wasting ammunition as the price paid to sustain the psychological well-being of his men. For such emotional benefit, he was willing to take this important risk, even to the point of sacrificing his own life. In fact, that very day he was almost mortally wounded by dangerously displaying his presence on the front line to inspire his men. Here was a corps commander whose responsibility was to command frontline troops. His experience was more attuned than Hunt's to what motivated *his* men. His success as a commander demanded that he be able to compel his men, operating in densely packed formations and under stressful conditions, to respond to his orders and maneuver them in battle. He saw what could happen in battles when a line fled from the front in an uncontrollable panic. He also knew the stigma attached in the aftermath to the commanders who led them.

Brigadier General Francis Walker of Hancock's staff pointed out later that: "Unquestionably it would have been a strong point for us if other things being equal, the limber chests of the artillery had been full when Pickett's and Pettigrew's divisions began their great charge. But would other things have been equal? Would the advantage so obtained have compensated for the loss of morale in the infantry which might have resulted from allowing them to be scourged, at will, by the hostile artillery? Every soldier knows how trying and often demoralizing it is to endure artillery fire without reply."[38]

Thus there is great difficulty in judging the correctness of Hunt's directive to conserve ammunition over Hancock's order to fire away. We'll never know how much psychological value Hancock's blazing guns bolstered the courage of his men to remain on Cemetery Ridge until the contest was decided. We'll also never know how the early response of Hancock's artillery affected the Confederate infantry's resolve before the assault.

★ ★ ★

To summarize, the artillery branches of each army were dogged with organizational problems that posed serious threats to the well-being of their respective forces. Initially, with the inexperience in handling large armies, commanders were uncertain on the best way to organize their forces to achieve results. Artillery's role then, evolved somewhat from theory and, to a greater extent, what worked well through battle experience. Through necessity, the organizational chain of command for an artillery unit was controlled in combat by the infantry commander responsible for the line of battle and was managed administratively by an artillery commander. Artillery's requirements thus created the arrangement of a dual-command relationship which sometimes lent itself to becoming a potential impediment and an easy target for discord.

Some problems were overcome, some faded as they learned, and some remained unsolvable. Although both armies' artillery organizations were not yet fully evolved in the first half of 1863, by then the faults of its organization were recognized and gradually improved. They were maturing to a stage that would remain relatively unchanged for the remainder of the war. When the battle of Gettysburg was fought, two years of confrontation in the field added important elements in learning the pitfalls of artillery management and how to best organize this branch into a powerful force capable of fulfilling its role in battle.

Brigades, Battalions, and Batteries

By mid-1863 each army's artillery branch had established its organization into manageable units for operations. Depending on resources, the organizational structure was arranged either by what the army preferred or by necessity. General Hunt felt it practicable to assign batteries to form a brigade. This arrangement usually had five batteries, averaging thirty cannons each, to form a brigade. One brigade was assigned to each of the seven infantry corps, two brigades were assigned to the cavalry corps, and five brigades went to one general artillery reserve. Each brigade had an artillery officer at corps headquarters performing duties as commander of artillery under the command of the corps commander.

For the Confederate army, forming batteries of artillery into battalions was preferred over the brigade structure. General Pendleton wrote: "It is respectfully proposed that in each corps the artillery be arranged into battalions, to consist for the most part of four batteries each, a particular battalion ordinarily to attend a certain division, and to report to, and receive orders from, its commander. . . ."[39]

For the Confederate artillery, four batteries in a battalion meant, on average, sixteen pieces [guns] and each battalion was assigned to one of the three divisions that made up each of the three infantry corps. One battalion was also assigned to the cavalry corps. In addition, each infantry corps was assigned one artillery reserve, each containing two artillery battalions. This organization was maintained until the close of the war.

The basic unit of the artillery branch was the battery. At Gettysburg a Northern battery usually numbered six pieces; of the sixty-five Union batteries, fifty contained six guns. A Confederate battery usually consisted of four guns; of the sixty-seven Southern batteries, fifty-four contained four.[40]

The organization of artillery batteries, however, evolved differently in each army. Although six guns were preferable, the four assigned to a Confederate unit was more by necessity than choice. Colonel E. P. Alexander described the arrangement: "The batteries were generally composed of but four guns, which is not an economical arrangement; but as no objection was made to it, either at army headquarters or at the War Department, and as the scarcity both of horses and ordnance equipment made it difficult to get, and more so to maintain a six gun battery, it resulted in that few six gun batteries were put in the field, and nearly every one of these was eventually reduced to four guns."[41]

The idea of Union batteries numbering six guns was proposed just months into the war. It was also recommended that batteries be equipped with guns of uniform caliber. Once this proposal was adopted, the Union batteries were almost always equipped with identical weapons. At Gettysburg, there was only one Union battery, Sterling's 2nd Connecticut, with a mixture of guns.[42]

In contrast to the uniformity in Union batteries, Confederate batteries most often contained a mixture of pieces. Some four-gun batteries were equipped with two types, and a few had three different types. Non-uniformity of weapons would prove to be an important impediment in making the Confederate's artillery organization an effective force.

For the Confederate army, mixing guns within the same battery was a natural occurrence as a result of engagements with the enemy when Yankee guns were captured or abandoned on the field. The Confederate artillery branch somewhat depended on subsisting off the Union army by capturing its highly desirable, better quality, Northern-manufactured guns. Such guns were treated as war trophies by Southern artillerymen, and they resisted the idea of trading them for others to achieve uniformity.[43]

But even though experience proved the effectiveness of concentrated fire from batteries with uniformity in guns, the Confederate artillery apparently preferred to have a section (two guns) of rifles and a section of smoothbores. There was a benefit to this arrangement of mixed guns. Having a variety of calibers and ranges provided the flexibility in both range and killing power. A battery of short-range guns only, for example, could not respond to enemy batteries firing from long-range, thus making it unable to participate. On the other hand, it was beneficial to have short-range guns present when fighting was close-up because of their superior killing power over long-range guns. Short-range guns had barrels with a larger bore and fired larger projectiles with deadly effect.[44]

The versatility provided by batteries of mixed guns, however, did not outweigh the benefit produced from batteries composed of guns of the same type. The custom of mixed guns in a battery created a supply nightmare and caused guns to be put out of action for the want of proper ammunition. It was hard enough just to supply artillery ammunition during combat which, more often than not, required traversing terrain without the benefit of roads, over land torn up by battle, and overcoming numerous obstacles including a landscape scattered with slain soldiers, animals, and the wreckage of war.

For mixed batteries, resupplying ammunition depleted in a cannonade was particularly troublesome for artillerymen. The intensity level of gun duels naturally increased the urgency to replenish ammunition. A battalion firing each of its sixteen guns at one round per minute for just ten minutes, for example, would need almost a ton of a variety of projectiles to replenish what it just fired. Trying to replenish an assortment of ammunition for a battery of mixed guns required searching for the right wagon with the right type of ammunition, and doing this during a battle was not conducive to efficient operations. Uniformity of guns within a battery, as in the Union army, made the difficult chore of resupplying ammunition considerably easier. Additionally, uniformity allowed the interchange of like parts, tools, implements such as aiming devices and rammer sponges, and other equipment used to service the gun.

Non-uniform guns in a battery also impaired the efficiency in loading and handling when gun crews had to assist at different pieces. Different models and their accompanying ammunition involved special loading and aiming conditions. Smoothbores, for example, used *fixed ammunition*. [The powder cartridge was attached to the projectile.] Rifled guns had the cartridge bag separate from the projectile; this required each to be inserted and rammed home separately. Safety procedures varied. Diverse guns had different barrel lengths, handling weights, and loading times. Rifled guns were more complex to load than smoothbores. Specific projectiles, even of the same caliber, were required with specific models of guns and all performed with their own characteristics and expectations varied.

Another important drawback for artillery units with mixed guns involved the efficient placement of a battery's pieces. Confederate artillery batteries, which were comprised of both short- and long-range guns, possessed a fundamental flaw in developing firepower especially when used on a broad front. Any range versatility gained by mixing guns, for example, was canceled out by the loss in freedom to position both the short-range and long-range guns to each type's best advantage.

One of the more effective artillery tactics to punish the enemy was crossfiring or oblique firing. For best results then, based upon their range limitations, short-range guns like Napoleons and howitzers in particular, had to be placed differently than any long-range guns in the same battery to participate or achieve the most effective fire. If a site was chosen within the firing limits

Confederate guns on Seminary Ridge. In the Army of Northern Virginia, almost two-thirds of its batteries contained non-uniform artillery pieces. (AC)

Federal guns on East Cemetery Hill. All batteries in the Army of the Potomac, except one, contained uniform artillery pieces. (AC)

of short-range guns, for example, and the long-range pieces were placed with them, the benefit of long-range firepower was misapplied. Furthermore, since the long-range guns had less killing power than the short-range pieces of the battery, the net effect was that a battery under-utilized its long-range assets. At the same time it was less lethal than a uniform battery composed of short-range pieces only.

Lee had to improvise and maximize his firepower, blunted by the use of mixed batteries, on July 3 as his artillery prepared for the grand cannonade. Some Confederate batteries, organized with guns of mixed ranges, were handicapped in their ability to place firepower where the best results could have been achieved. Mixed batteries, kept intact, were either under-utilizing their short-range guns to take advantage of their long-range pieces or vice-versa. Short-range cannons that remained in the main battle line beside the long-range elements of their battery were comparatively limited in their ability to fire obliquely at enemy targets. Had the majority of Confederate batteries been composed with cannons of similar effective ranges, additional options would have existed. Long-range batteries could have been placed appropriately in

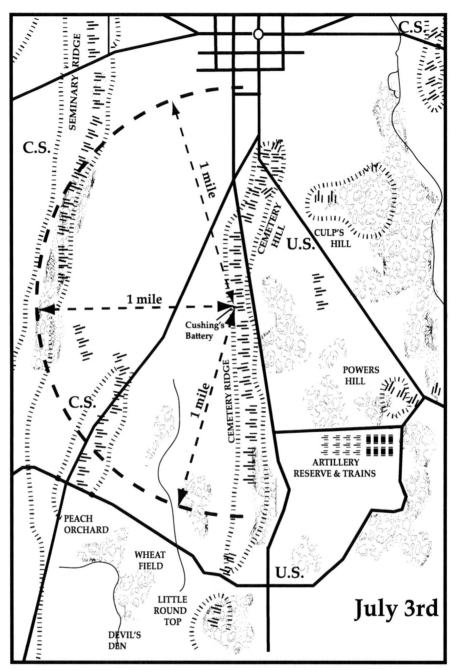

Note the ability of Confederate guns to create a destructive crossfire against Union forces on Cemetery Ridge. All Confederate rifled guns participating in the July 3rd cannonade could employ oblique fire covering a wide area of the Union center. The effectiveness of Confederate smoothbores using an oblique fire against the Union center, however, was limited to guns located within the arc illustrated above.

order to hit the Union targets with a crossfire at the most destructive angle, and not be restricted by any short-range guns in the unit. At the same time short-range batteries could have been placed to achieve the best results within the limits of their ranges.

Theoretically the only way to occupy the best positions for all guns of a mixed battery was to separate them according to range limitations. The breaking up of batteries to establish uniformity in guns, however, was a risky proposition and not a realistic option. A rearrangement would have produced an organizational nightmare by subjecting artillerymen to sudden unaccustomed changes in their operating conditions. Gun crews needed teamwork and familiarity with their officers to conduct operations efficiently. A divided artillery command was not practical.

To remedy this critical problem of non-uniformity, the Confederate chief of ordnance wanted to redistribute these captured guns according to need. In February 1863, the Confederate chief of artillery, Brigadier General Pendleton, recommended to General Lee that batteries "should be rendered homogeneous in armament, as soon as practicable, by interchange of guns with other batteries." In May, with spring operations already underway, little progress had been made in rectifying mixed batteries. With the Gettysburg campaign days away from being launched, Pendleton backed off his proposal temporarily for obvious reasons. He stated:[45]

> . . . Considerable difficulty exists between the armaments of many of the battalions. Some have rifles in excess, others Napoleons. This difficulty dates back to irregular appropriations of captured guns last summer and fall. It has been deemed a less evil to let it remain than to create other difficulties by enforcing an equalization. . . .
>
> It will be observed that in order to give rifles to Major Eshleman, they must be taken from some other battery. To this I have no objection, if the commanding general deems it best, but I cannot recommend it, because the serious changes of armament now in batteries and battalions, that have long used certain guns, must produce regrets and dissatisfaction, which, in a case like ours, requiring the whole hearts of men, it does not seem to me wise to excite.
>
> For the same reason, I cannot recommend the taking of guns from the Second Corps batteries, although the artillery of that corps has now more rifles than that of the First Corps. It seems to me the least evil to let the battalions remain as they are, with such addition as can be gradually supplied.[46]

By the time the battle of Gettysburg took place, almost two-thirds of the Confederate batteries were equipped with mixed guns and approximately half of those mixed batteries were equipped with a combination of short- and long-range guns.

Artillery Reserve

In addition to batteries assigned to infantry units, both armies could draw additional guns from the artillery reserve. Artillery reserves had a special purpose and their disposition depended upon the conditions of combat. General Hunt described the care necessary for deployment of reserve batteries: "The number and kind of these troops as so attached in any given case depend on many circumstances, e.g. the nature of the theater of operations, whether it is wooded and mountainous country, or an open level one."[47]

The commitment of reserve cannons in battle required careful thought in how to employ their firepower efficiently. For various reasons, parts of a battle line might need more guns than assigned under normal circumstances. Easy access by the enemy to a defending line's vulnerable flanks, for example, would require additional guns. The shape of the line, terrain features allowing quick thrusts by attackers, or ground unsuitable for placing adequate numbers of defending infantry troops might also require more than the usual firepower. At other places, fewer guns may be required because of terrain features, obstacles offering defensive advantages, shape of the line, etc. It was also necessary to consider how the enemy perceived its artillery's gun placement. Too few artillery pieces in a line made a zone a tempting point for the enemy to attack. Incorrect placement of guns could also present a lost opportunity for the defending artillery to develop its firepower against the enemy's intentions.

Although it was important to have enough firepower, too many guns could congest or otherwise interfere with fighting effectively. At Fredericksburg, for example, batteries from idle divisions were used to reinforce the reserve for common use of the army, but these extra guns interfered with, rather than helped, the desperate situation. General Hunt explained this misapplication of Union artillery: "The divisions which passed directly into the city—constituting half the army—took their batteries with them although they could not use more than half a dozen of them there. The other fifteen or twenty batteries, more than useless, blocked the streets, made confusion, and, by their losses, swelled the lists of casualties."[48]

The primary importance of the artillery reserve then, when managed properly, was to provide flexibility in meeting the changeable needs of the battle line. Each army's artillery reserve was organized differently. The Union artillery reserve at Gettysburg was one large unattached unit and capable of assignment anywhere batteries were needed. It contained twenty-one batteries totaling 106 guns present on the field. The Union reserve represented almost one-third of the Army of the Potomac's artillery pieces, and it was entrusted with the freedom to attend contingencies that threatened any of its forces.

Under the singular command of Brigadier General Robert Tyler the Union artillery reserve consisted of five brigades—one regular brigade and four volunteer brigades. Four of the brigades contained four batteries each and were commanded by Captain Dunbar Ransom, Lieutenant Colonel Freeman McGilvery, Captain Elijah Taft, and Captain James Huntington. The fifth brigade had five batteries and was under the command of Captain Robert Fitzhugh.

The Army of Northern Virginia's Artillery Reserve, instead of one unit, was broken into three separate reserves—one assigned to each of the three infantry corps. The First Corps Reserve was commanded by Colonel J. B. Walton with ten batteries, the Second Corps by Colonel J. Thompson Brown with eight batteries, and the Third Corps by Colonel R. Lindsay Walker with nine batteries. Each reserve contained two battalions. The combined total of the reserve was only slightly smaller in number of guns than its Union counterpart. It totaled twenty-seven batteries of 101 guns.[49]

A critical distinction between the two armies was the fact that the Confederate artillery reserve had three independent commands *attached* to infantry corps, while the Union artillery reserve contained one commander and one pool of guns independent and *unattached* to any infantry command.

The Army of the Potomac's unattached artillery reserve could prove to be an impediment to an infantry corps commander's needs. The Federal artillery reserve, being organizationally separated from the control of corps commanders, required the close attention of an artillery commander. To make it work, an artillery commander or his representative controlling the reserve batteries had to be highly accessible to all corps commanders and have the authority to release batteries in order to cooperate and meet the contingencies facing the infantry commands on the front line. A Federal corps commander, needing more firepower, for example, had to rely primarily on the chief of artillery to supply reserve guns that were outside the infantry commander's jurisdiction. At Gettysburg, although some reserve batteries were released by orders from Meade or his corps commanders, General Hunt, in fact, was responsible for the disposition of most of them.[50]

Despite corps commanders' lack of immediate control over reserve batteries, there were tremendous advantages that overshadowed any such shortcomings of an unattached Federal reserve operating as a central pool. One advantage of a single reserve, particularly useful at Gettysburg, was the Union's fish-hook-shaped line that allowed easy internal movement of Federal reserve guns from a central location to any part of the field.

An even greater advantage was having an independent reserve that allowed rapid massing of artillery. This unattached firepower streamlined the Union army's ability to move guns around without the characteristic interference created in the chain of command. Certain "niceties," such as the required protocol, had to be observed when guns were "borrowed" from another command. This transaction slowed progress when rapid emergency movement was the key to success. An independent reserve also prevented idle batteries from being "snatched up" by overanxious corps commanders.

Regarding the Army of Northern Virginia's Artillery Reserve, by dividing it up and assigning batteries to each of the army's infantry corps, the arrangement allowed a proportionate number of guns in the reserve to be physically closer to support its corps' front lines. By using this arrangement, the reserve was on location, ready for action as needed, at the direct disposal of the corps commander and thereby equipped with a chain of command, shorter than the unattached and centralized Federal reserve.

With the offensive nature of the Confederate artillery at Gettysburg, the long length of the army's battle line, and the exterior positions of the reserve units, positioning reserve guns at each corps' location was more practical than the method used by the Federals. The accessibility problems presented by using one centralized reserve would have made it difficult or impossible to support the urgent needs of Confederate infantry commands in such a long battle line as at Gettysburg.

A pitfall in the organization of the Confederate artillery reserve, however, was the absence of unattached reserve guns for general use by commanders who needed them. Since each and every gun was assigned either to specific divisions or to a reserve within each corps, Lee's artillery force was compartmentalized and *all* the guns were spoken for. This arrangement created a cumbersome chain of command and was troublesome for the free movement of reserve guns to areas outside each respective corps' line. Consequently, it was more difficult for Confederate infantry commanders to pry batteries from other commands for critical use elsewhere. To do this, General Pendleton, Lee's chief of artillery, had to first consult with corps commanders to obtain permission for the use of that corps' reserve artillery. In other words, when artillery was needed on a broad front, an extra layer in the chain of command interfered with moving guns around during battle. Conversely, on the Federal side, General Hunt could order his entire unattached reserve about instantly and at his own discretion.

The freedom to mass guns of the Army of Northern Virginia's attached artillery was particularly cumbersome to deal with for Lee's planned cannonade on July 3. With a long battle line, moving guns could be difficult, especially during combat when fluid conditions constantly change battle plans and when corps commanders jealously guard the assets that protect their battlefront. Such an undertaking required the necessary agreement from the corps commanders who would provide the guns and the artillery staff to assure cooperation in the exchange and to coordinate their firepower according to plan.

One such difficulty in shifting firepower out of a jurisdiction was illustrated at Gettysburg on July 3. General Pendleton borrowed nine of A. P. Hill's howitzers from Garnett's battalion [Garnett said they were rifled guns.] for use beyond Hill's command with Colonel E. P. Alexander's artillery in the assault of Pickett's division. At the right moment, they were to spring into action with Pickett's infantry. When it was time to bring them onto the field, however, they had disappeared; Pendleton had ordered some to the rear and others had their positions changed to avoid the shelling; and their new location was not communicated to Alexander. This missing firepower gave Alexander a sobering surprise at a most inopportune moment as the infantry columns were put into motion for the assault.[51]

Compared to their Union counterpart, efforts to manage the use of the

Confederate artillery reserve became more complicated when simplicity was needed. The design of the organization stifled the rapid employment of the artillery's reserve firepower when used on a broad front. Colonel E. P. Alexander saw the advantages of a general pool of guns for the Army of Northern Virginia. He said that it was "not that we did not want it, but we could not maintain it."[52]

★ ★ ★

In summary, the Federal artillery reserve had the freedom to react in its entirety to the fluid nature of battle covering the whole front, but the success of its organizational structure was highly dependent on the chief of artillery responding to the urgent needs of infantry commanders. The Army of the Potomac's organizational structure for the reserve proved to be a welcome asset for the defensive tactics Meade used at the battle of Gettysburg. The large pool of reserve guns was used along the entire Federal front and under the close eye of its overseer, General Hunt. Hunt's active participation was magnificent. He seemed to be everywhere when needed and was remarkably useful in distributing reserve guns where they were required and in a rapid manner.

The unattached Federal reserve guns enjoyed the freedom of movement without the jurisdictional headaches associated with attached batteries and without the hindrance of a cumbersome chain of command. In a defensive situation, Meade needed the benefit of a quick response to react to situations produced by crisis management, especially when an attack was in progress.

Union Major Thomas Osborn, chief of artillery, Eleventh Corps, commented: "The artillery reserve proved all that could be expected or even asked of it; without their assistance I do not conceive how I could have maintained the position we held." The artillery reserve prevented the total collapse of the Union line as the decimated ranks of General Sickles's Third Corps were flung back from his advanced line on July 2. The reserve was highly useful in turning back the advancing lines of Pickett, Pettigrew, and Trimble on the third; it also allowed non-reserve batteries to subsist off its ammunition supply, and it kept them operable at critical instants.

Brigadier General Robert Tyler, commander, artillery reserve, wrote of the battle: "I believe it almost unnecessary to speak of the value of the services rendered by the Artillery Reserve during the last two days of this action and the great share it had in the glorious result. The one-hundred and eight guns which were on the field were all in position, their fire being concentrated and felt wherever the battle was hottest."[53]

Had the Federal reserves been structured as the Confederate's, one reserve to each corps, those certain "niceties" or required protocol most certainly would have interfered with the ability, in emergencies, to quickly "grab" reserve guns that belonged to a different corps. To say the least, it would have created great confusion for battery commanders to simply ignore existing instructions and follow the orders of an unfamiliar officer wishing to acquire the guns. Such a slowdown in implementing any emergency movements would have been bothersome or worse.

In contrast to the Army of the Potomac, the Confederate artillery reserve, divided to support each of its three infantry corps, benefited from having it physically close to its assigned corps and under its jurisdiction for rapid use. Comparatively though, its organization provided almost no artillery for the general use of the army and its batteries had much less freedom than the Federal reserve to move about beyond the ground protected by the infantry corps to which it was attached.

Since Lee was on the offensive, the impact created from the more restricted freedom to move reserve guns was less critical than being on the defensive where a quick response was often needed to help save the line. Nevertheless, the freedom to move reserve firepower made it more difficult to participate in large-scale operations like the grand cannonade undertaken on July 3. In this case, at least, the Army of Northern Virginia might have fared better with an artillery reserve organized along the lines of the Army of the Potomac's.

In 1866, Colonel E. P. Alexander critiqued the Confederate artillery reserve's contribution:

> This body, however, not being in intimate relations with the infantry, who always develop the situation, and being invariably put on the march either behind the infantry commands or on same road to itself, was never promptly available on an emergency. Indeed, if the history of the general reserve artillery during its entire existence be investigated it will be found that although excellent in material, and comparatively so in equipment, the service that it rendered was greatly disproportionate to its strength. It resulted, therefore, that although the numerical strength of the Confederate artillery was as great in the first year of the war as ever afterwards, its

weight in the scale of actual conflict is never seen to affect the result, until the second battle of Manassas. For instance, during the Seven Days' battles around Richmond, General Lee's artillery numbered about three hundred guns (nearly four guns to every thousand men), ninety eight of these being in the general reserve; but in the history of the fighting this powerful organization has only left the faintest traces of its existence. Now the wretched character of the ammunition which filed [sic] its chests may well be charged with many of its shortcomings; but an examination of the official reports of the battles will show that scattered and either uncommanded or too much commanded, as it was, there was an entire absence of that ensemble of action necessary to the efficiency of all arms, but peculiarly so to the artillery; and that when fought at all, it was put in only in inefficient driblets.[54]

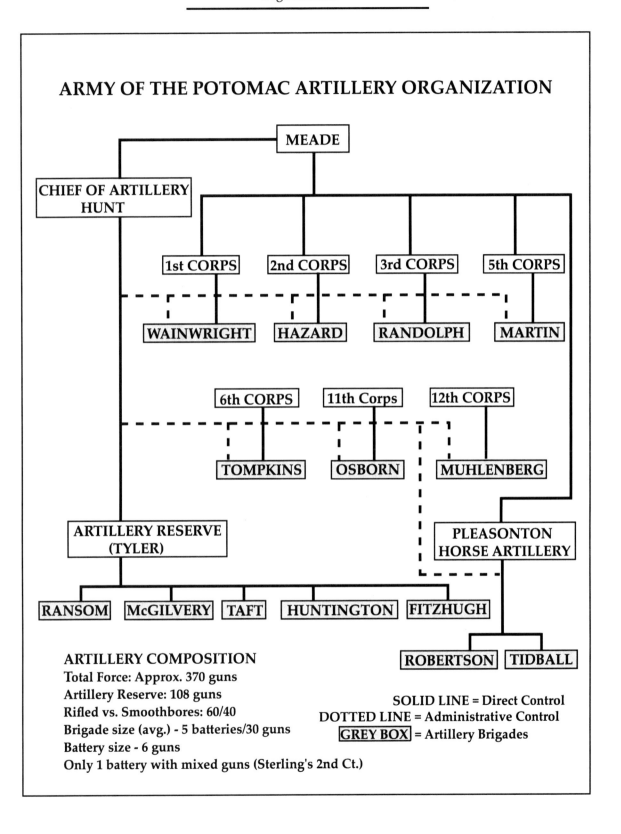

ARMY OF THE POTOMAC ARTILLERY ORGANIZATION

MEADE

CHIEF OF ARTILLERY
HUNT

1st CORPS
2nd CORPS
3rd CORPS
5th CORPS

WAINWRIGHT
HAZARD
RANDOLPH
MARTIN

6th CORPS
11th Corps
12th CORPS

TOMPKINS
OSBORN
MUHLENBERG

ARTILLERY RESERVE
(TYLER)

PLEASONTON
HORSE ARTILLERY

RANSOM
McGILVERY
TAFT
HUNTINGTON
FITZHUGH

ROBERTSON
TIDBALL

ARTILLERY COMPOSITION
Total Force: Approx. 370 guns
Artillery Reserve: 108 guns
Rifled vs. Smoothbores: 60/40
Brigade size (avg.) - 5 batteries/30 guns
Battery size - 6 guns
Only 1 battery with mixed guns (Sterling's 2nd Ct.)

SOLID LINE = Direct Control
DOTTED LINE = Administrative Control
GREY BOX = Artillery Brigades

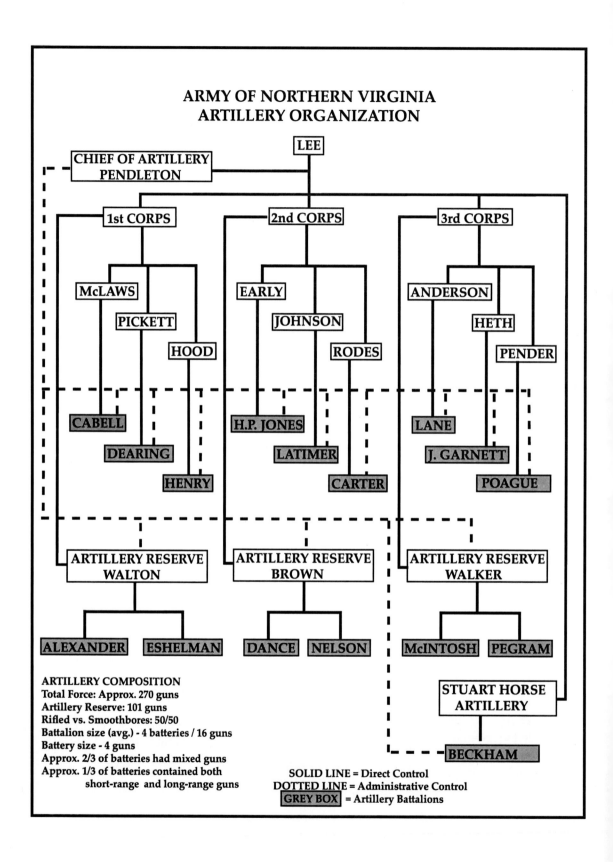

ARMY OF NORTHERN VIRGINIA
ARTILLERY ORGANIZATION

LEE

CHIEF OF ARTILLERY
PENDLETON

1st CORPS
2nd CORPS
3rd CORPS

McLAWS
PICKETT
HOOD

EARLY
JOHNSON
RODES

ANDERSON
HETH
PENDER

CABELL
DEARING
HENRY

H.P. JONES
LATIMER
CARTER

LANE
J. GARNETT
POAGUE

ARTILLERY RESERVE
WALTON

ARTILLERY RESERVE
BROWN

ARTILLERY RESERVE
WALKER

ALEXANDER   ESHELMAN

DANCE   NELSON

McINTOSH   PEGRAM

STUART HORSE
ARTILLERY

BECKHAM

ARTILLERY COMPOSITION
Total Force: Approx. 270 guns
Artillery Reserve: 101 guns
Rifled vs. Smoothbores: 50/50
Battalion size (avg.) - 4 batteries / 16 guns
Battery size - 4 guns
Approx. 2/3 of batteries had mixed guns
Approx. 1/3 of batteries contained both
       short-range and long-range guns

SOLID LINE = Direct Control
DOTTED LINE = Administrative Control
GREY BOX = Artillery Battalions

3-inch Schenkl shell (missing papier-mache sabot).(GNMP/WDC)

III

Artillery Technology

Artillery pieces at the battle of Gettysburg belonged to the class of guns designated as field or light artillery-weapons small enough to maneuver through difficult terrain and keep up with a moving army and its rapid changes. Subcategories of field artillery included mounted and horse artillery. With mounted artillery, horses pulled the equipment while the gun crews walked or sometimes rode on the ammunition chests. Horse artillery required all members to be mounted in order to accompany the rapid moves of the cavalry. Field artillery covered in this work came in a variety of classes. There were smoothbore and rifled guns, muzzleloaders and breechloaders, bronze barrels and iron barrels, cannons and howitzers.

Smoothbores, named for the smooth inside surface of the barrels, were referred to by the approximate weight of solid shot that they fired, or the name of the gun's inventor, or someone associated with its introduction, such as the Napoleon. Rifled guns had spiral grooves adjacent to corresponding raised surfaces, called lands, down the length of the bore to impart a spin on the projectile and stabilize its flight path. Rifling will be discussed in more detail later under "projectile technology." Rifled guns were referred to either by their bore size, the weight of the solid shot they fired, or their inventor, such as the Parrott.

Muzzleloading guns [barrels loaded from the front] constituted all of the artillery pieces at Gettysburg except for two. Muzzleloaders required a loose fit of the projectile in the bore. This fit permitted the transmission of flame from the propellant to ignite the fuse on the front end of the projectile but, more important, it made loading possible. The difference between the bore diameter of the gun and the diameter of the projectile was called windage. Windage for muzzleloading artillery was a necessity and guns could not operate without it. After each firing the ignited powder charge left a heavy film in the barrel which required it to be swabbed or sponged after each shot. Because sponging did not completely remove the residue as firing continued, the film thickened in the bore. This buildup decreased the windage and increased the difficulty in ramming the charge down the barrel. Windage allowance was also needed for the tin straps on fixed ammunition and rust build-up in iron barrels.

Because of windage some of the propellant force was lost through the gas leaking around the projectile. It was, therefore, important to keep the windage as small as possible, consistent with the ease and efficiency of loading, in order to capture the explosive force to attain range. Because of windage, tests proved that projectiles lost about ten percent of their initial velocity, the speed from the barrel, in comparison to balls fired without windage. The stress on

WINDAGE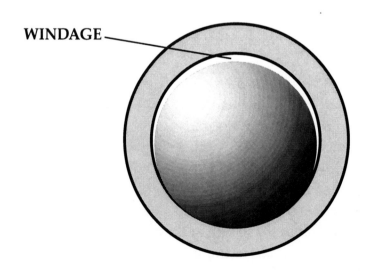

any barrel fluctuated depending on the amount of explosive gas that was allowed to escape in the firing process.[1]

Excepting canister, to be discussed later, muzzleloading *smoothbores* fired round ammunition. The spherical shape precluded designing projectiles that eliminated windage. With the introduction of muzzleloading *rifled* guns, however, windage was overcome *after* loading, by the design of the elongated rifled projectiles which sealed off most of the escaping gas when fired.

Breechloaders [barrels loaded from the rear] were just being introduced to American armies and were few in number. The Army of Northern Virginia had two breechloaders present at Gettysburg, English Whitworths. Breechloading had already been introduced in small arms in the 1820s but it was questionable whether the breechloading principle could be applied to artillery as well or whether a breech mechanism could be made strong enough to withstand the enormous explosive force and shock without great expense and a complicated mechanism suitable for field operations. Efficiency was also impaired in the care and length of time consumed in loading and handling with breechloading mechanisms. But even though breechloading took longer, rapid firing was not often a great necessity anyway since smoke had to drift to allow aiming the next shot.

But breechloaders provided advantages to a gun crew in both safety and efficiency. Standing behind a gun provided some cover for the artillerymen and safety improved substantially with rear-loading. In contrast, muzzleloading a charge down the front of a barrel was by no means a casual affair, particularly in a rifled bore that could hide sparks in the grooves and be possibly overlooked by the sponging step of the loading sequence. Breechloaders also gave access to the rear of the gun for cleaning and inspection. And while muzzleloaders required the projectile to be undersized to be rammed down the bore, breechloading Whitworths allowed a much tighter fit. As a result, the barrel captured more of the exploding propellant gases and sent the projectile much farther.

Despite the advantages of breechloading, there were problems associated with hot gases escaping from the breech mechanism when fired, so some gun crews preferred loading Whitworths at the muzzle. In fact, problems with the Whitworth breech mechanism were never overcome during the war. Most of the time the rear access was locked and the piece was fired as a muzzleloader.

Top view of Whitworth breechloading mechanism. (AC)

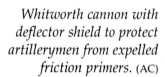

Whitworth cannon with deflector shield to protect artillerymen from expelled friction primers. (AC)

Another potential danger involved the friction primer, the device that ignited the charge. It was inserted in the center of the breech facing rearward. When ignited, the primer's ejection path was rearward of the gun and had the potential to cause severe injury to artillerymen working behind the gun; mortars had the same inherent danger. To prevent injury to a member of a gun crew, some Whitworths were equipped with an attached shield to deflect the primer as it ejected like a bullet. [As of this writing, such a deflector shield can be seen on one of the two Whitworths located near the Eternal Flame peace memorial at Gettysburg.][2]

Bronze vs. Iron

The difference between bronze and iron cannon barrels resulted in unique characteristics in performance and endurance. Cannon barrels were subjected to the tremendous stress caused by the exploding powder cartridges and the abrasion of ammunition. The projectile's hard cast-iron body, scraping or slapping against the bore, subjected the barrel to the punishing effects of friction. The conversion from gunpowder to propellant gas was a tremendous strain. John Gibbon's *Artillerist's Manual* stated that: "In an explosion these gases evolved at a very high temperature, which, of course increases immensely their bulk . . . The volume has been estimated as high as 5,000 times the original bulk; and Gen. Piobert estimates the ordinary maximum pressure of these gases on a projectile at between 2,000 and 3,000 lbs. to the square inch. Figures, however, are merely approximations, and no definite idea can be given of the absolute force of gunpowder."[3]

The stress imparted on a bronze gun versus an iron gun was quite different. Bronze smoothbores were subjected to much less instant stress than rifled iron barrels. Smoothbores, having greater windage, leaked significantly more gas than rifled guns and consequently did not capture the total explosive force of the powder charge. In contrast, rifled iron guns were more efficient. Their projectiles were designed to expand and seal in practically all of the explosive force. Therefore, iron guns needed additional barrel strength to contain the great shock developed from the increased tension and bursting power when the windage was abruptly cut off.

The efficiency in capturing the explosive gas of a smoothbore and a rifled gun is illustrated by comparing the throwing force of their powder charges and the ranges achieved: a Napoleon, for example, threw a 12-pound shot about one mile using a 2½-pound powder charge. A 3-inch Ordnance rifle fired a 10-pound shot about 2 miles using only a 1-pound charge.

Bronze guns damaged differently than cast iron or wrought iron pieces. Bronze guns, made of ninety parts copper and ten parts tin, experienced little external injury with a few exceptions. One such exception, caused after long service or heavy charges, was the bending of the barrel's trunnions. Trunnions were cylinder-shaped protrusions on both sides of the barrel to cradle and secure the barrel in the gun carriage.

Burst Napoleon illustrating the elasticity of bronze. This destruction appears to have been intentional since the projectile's small bursting charge was not powerful enough for such damage.(AC)

Another type of external injury in bronze barrels was cracks that developed from the expansion of the barrel caused by the great internal compression from the explosions. Some barrel bores of the Napoleon found today show that they have expanded over half an inch from their manufactured 4.62-inch diameter—undoubtedly causing a considerable loss in propellant gas pressure. This expansion is found at the muzzle and apparently tapers to normal towards the rear of the bore. Canister, a type of ammunition packed with iron balls, is suspected of causing this expanded-muzzle phenomenon; as explosive pressure and inertia jam and wedge the canister balls outward and as the velocity increases so does the jamming against the surface of the bore.[4]

Bronze guns actually suffered more from internal injuries. High-pressured explosions further increased any existing cavities and imperfections and weakened the barrel. The action of propelling the round ball out of the barrel also caused internal damage. Over time, a depression on the bottom of the bore in the rear of the barrel was formed. This compression of metal was created from the explosive high-pressure gas leaking over the top of the ball (windage) and created a downward force on the projectile which scraped the bottom of the bore and subjected the barrel to injury. As wear in this area increased there was a corresponding "burr" in front of the depression. This burr and the motion imparted on the ball caused the projectile to deflect along the top and then bottom of the bore. The deflections of the ball struck the same points each time the gun was fired and they resulted in creating deeper depressions in the bore (usually three). When the gun was fired, this deflective motion undoubtedly contributed to imparting the easily identifiable "spang" sound of a bronze barrel which reverberated into the distant enemy lines. After long use, the indentations at the mouth of the bore rendered the piece unable to produce an accurate fire and were the chief cause of failure in a bronze gun. There were some remedies used to overcome bore damage caused by deflecting projectiles. Making a longer cartridge, for example, caused the ball to strike at different points. Another solution, using a sabot [a wooden disk] or wrapping the ball in wool or paper reduced the windage which reduced the deflective reaction of the shot.[5]

Cast-iron guns were stronger than bronze pieces, but strength, in this case, also meant rigidity. If iron guns burst, which usually occurred at the breech or muzzle, the barrels shattered like glass inflicting injury or death to their tenders. Bronze, on the other hand, had give to it and was less prone to fracturing than cast iron. Despite the Napoleons' wear from heavy use, George. D.

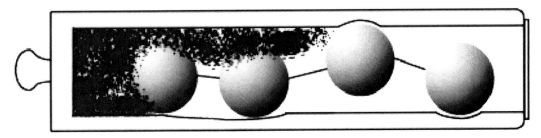

Leaking propellant gas over the top of the ball imparted a downward force and wore a depression at the bottom of the bore causing the ball to bounce out of the barrel.

Ramsay, Union brigadier general and chief of ordnance, stated his confidence in using bronze for gun barrels: "For smooth-bore field guns, bronze is good enough, and the material valuable after the guns become, from any cause, unserviceable, more so than steel. No instance has occurred during the war where they have been so severely tested of the 12-pounder bronze gun having worn out or of its bursting."[6]

Wrought iron guns, in comparison to cast iron pieces, were tougher. Their strength was about double that of cast iron. Wrought iron also had flexibility compared to rigid cast iron. In fact after heavy use the *lands*, the raised portion of the wrought iron rifled bore, sometimes protruded beyond the barrel muzzle.

In determining the useful life of a barrel, frequency of use was most often a factor. Inspecting cast iron barrels, however, did not easily reveal weaknesses inherent in the metal and their life span for safe use was unpredictable. Some artillery experts considered that after 1,200 rounds, iron guns were not safe and that bronze guns were more durable—some barrels having been fired as many as 2,400 times without failing.[7]

The chief problem of an iron gun was rust. Corrosion occurred at the vent, the opening at the rear of the barrel that communicated the fire to the powder charge, and also at the mouth of the barrel, and any location with particularly sharp angles such as the rifle grooves. Rust caused roughness and made it more difficult to sponge or ram the ammunition; removing the corroded metal caused bore enlargement. Rust buildup also changed the windage and interfered with introducing the projectile to the bore.

The vent in any barrel was most vulnerable to wear. Rapid and continuous firing was the chief cause of vent damage. The vent, more than any other part of a gun, was exposed to the hottest temperature achieved in the firing process. It wore quickly from the constant exposure to the corrosive effects of water and the hot gases that escaped through it. The vent wore twice as great in rifled guns as in smoothbores because, as mentioned earlier, ammunition from rifled guns cut off the windage more completely and abruptly and thus captured more of the explosive force to act on the vent. The enlargement of the vent opening resulted in the loss of gas pressure needed to propel the projectile and eventually made the piece unusable.

For better endurance, the vents in many, but not all, bronze guns were made into a separate and replaceable part called a vent-piece. They were made of corrosion resistant copper and were threaded and screwed into the top of the barrel. Some vent-pieces were supplied defective with imperfect threads or were cut too short at the foundry and were blown out in firing, disabling the piece. Cast iron barrels such as Parrotts were also subject to corrosion problems and usually had copper vents. The stronger wrought iron barrels such as 3-inch Ordnance rifles were more resistant to corrosion and did not always use a separate vent-piece.

The condition of an iron gun was determined by the appearance of the vent. *The Ordnance Manual for the Use of the Officers of the Confederate States Army* stated that, "After about five-hundred rounds the vent becomes enlarged to .3 inches and should no longer be used." The ordnance manual for the Federal army suggested that vents of iron pieces be replaced between fifteen hundred and two thousand rounds. To replace vents in barrels not equipped with a removable vent-piece, the Confederate ordnance manual described how to do it: "The vent is filled up by pouring in melted zinc, the vent being closed on the interior by means of clay placed on the head of a rammer and pressed against the upper surface of the bore, and a new vent is bored at a distance of two to three inches from the first."[8]

Although the vent was not a movable part, it was still a vital component that could make the gun inoperable. Sometimes unskilled or excited artillery-

Parrott rifle with threaded copper vent-piece. The vent communicated fire to the propellent charge. It was most vulnerable to wear and a separate vent-piece made replacement easier. (AC)

79

men, for example, forgot to remove the priming wire—the tool used to clear debris from the vent or puncture the powder bag. When the ammunition was rammed down the bore, it bent the priming wire, blocked the vent, and disabled the piece. Guns were also disabled when vents became impacted with fragments of friction primers.

All barrels eventually broke down or wore out for a number of reasons. Besides the damaging effects of exploding powder charges, ammunition also caused barrel damage, particularly in a bronze gun tube. Sometimes the projectile could not withstand the shock of the cartridge explosion and fractured in the barrel. The broken iron fragments produced deep gouges and ridges in the softer bronze bore which interfered with further loading. [Today, this kind of damage is visible at the Gettysburg National Military Park. As of this writing, a good example is one of the two bronze Napoleons located at the Eternal Peace Light memorial.]

Smoothbore vs. Rifled Guns

When General McClellan was in command of the Union army, he believed that shorter-range smoothbore cannons were more suitable than the longer-range rifles in the wooded terrain of Virginia. Wooded terrain would limit the range of rifled artillery below its delivery capability anyhow, and it seemed likely that armies would continue to fight battles within the effective range of smoothbore guns. Even if the range of rifled guns wasn't hampered by terrain, killing enemy soldiers at longer ranges produced little overall benefit to an army seeking a victory. Therefore, the benefit of keeping smoothbores instead of trading them for rifled guns was largely dependent on the advantage of the smoothbores' killing power over the killing power of rifled artillery. An army needed smoothbores at close-range to achieve a breakthrough or stop an attack. McClellan wanted to have two smoothbore guns for every rifled field piece.

By comparison, the range of a rifled artillery piece was at least one and a half to two times greater than that of a smoothbore. The exact ranges, derived for specific artillery pieces from test firings or results listed in ordnance manuals, vary so widely that they are difficult to state absolutely. Each gun performed differently than others of the same model. Variables also included the gunpowder used, weather conditions, and measuring instruments. Generally, for smoothbore howitzers, the effective range was three-quarters of a mile; smoothbore cannons, one mile; and rifled guns, Parrotts and 3-inch, between one and a half and two miles.

At Gettysburg, excepting the howitzers, most of the distances between the two battle lines was within range of all artillery. For most artillery pieces used in the battle, the published ranges, measured at five-degrees elevation, were as follows:

12-pounder howitzer—1,072 yards
24-pounder howitzer—1,322 yards
12-pounder Napoleon—1,619 yards
3-inch Ordnance rifle—1,830 yards
10-pounder Parrott—1,850 yards
20-pounder Parrott—1,900 yards
12-pounder James—1,700 yards
12-pounder Blakely—1,850 yards
12-pounder Whitworth breechloader—2,800 yards[9]

The information above merely provides a comparison of ranges for different artillery pieces at a given elevation and does not necessarily reflect their effective ranges or maximum elevations of use. Gibbon's *Artillerist Manual*, for example, lists the range of a 3-inch rifle gun as being 4,180 yards at sixteen-degrees elevation.[10]

Possessing longer-range rifled artillery was, most certainly, important, but often it was not that important. In 1860 Sir William Armstrong, speaking to the Institute of [British] Civil Engineering, addressed the fascination that long-range guns produced but recognized the realities of the effects that long-range guns contributed in a battle's outcome: " . . . although the public is always captivated by the attainment of long ranges, a great delusion prevailed on the subject; such extreme distances rendering accuracy of aim impossible, so that the fate of a battle, however perfect the weapon might be, could never be decided by firing from them."[11]

Colonel E. P. Alexander was of the opinion "that long range, random shelling is very far less effective than it is popularly supposed to be . . . While an aimed & accurate fire can accomplish almost any result, a random, or an inaccurate one amounts to very little, except where it can enfilade lines." Range might be a valuable factor in achieving a damaging oblique fire, or when cannons were sniping at each other with subdued firing, or at the beginning of a cannonade when the air was clear. When both sides were blazing away, however, and the terrain was covered with dense white smoke, visible range could drop to a mere few hundred yards, negating the advantage of long-range artillery.[12]

It was exciting to ponder the potential benefits of rifle technology for artillery weapons, but the true worth of this technology had to be proven in the field. Until that happened, many artillerymen clung to weapons which they felt were reliable and capable of doing the job. Even though the overall accuracy and increased range of this new generation of guns was spectacular, the overall effect of rifled artillery fire over smoothbore fire was disappointing. One distinguishing characteristic of a rifled barrel was that its bore was smaller than that of a smoothbore. At Gettysburg, the most commonly used rifled barrels had bores with less than half the cross-sectional area of a Napoleon 12-pounder bore, the most common smoothbore cannon. Rifled guns, therefore, produced correspondingly less killing power at close range. The close range ammunition, canister, fired from small-bore rifled guns was insignificant when compared to the damage inflicted by a Napoleon belching it out. The additional killing power provided by the smoothbore Napoleon made this gun a favorite choice over rifled guns by many artillerymen.

In cases where range wasn't a factor, an army "upgrading" its artillery force by overloading itself with a disproportionately high number of rifled guns diminished its capacity to kill at close range. At Gettysburg, over 40 percent of the Union guns were smoothbores, and in the Army of Northern Virginia they totaled close to 50 percent. Although smoothbores were slowly becoming obsolete, they continued in popularity. By the end of the war, the Army of the Potomac's inventory of 12-pounder smoothbores made up almost half the field guns in its service.[13]

Make no mistake, an army could not do without long-range artillery. Each side had to have the capability to toss rounds at enemy targets, respond to their opponent's long-range firepower, and also be able to produce a crossfire that might otherwise be limited if equipped with shorter-range guns only.

By shifting the composition of the artillery force from smoothbores to rifled guns, an army gained the advantage of projecting its firepower at longer distances. But decisive battles were never won by long-range combat. As rifled guns replaced smoothbores, an army sacrificed the qualities it needed most—the killing power of canister fired at short range from a large-diameter smoothbore. That's what was needed to kill, maim, or stop a massed assault close-up, where the battle's success or failure was almost always decided. This close-range capability would be sorely missed by the Union soldiers at Gettysburg on July 3, as the Confederate soldiers stormed the Union works on Cemetery Ridge.[14]

Although artillerymen probably cared less, a final distinct side benefit gained from the transition of bronze smoothbores to iron rifled guns was cost savings. Compared to bronze, iron guns were cheap, making them attractive to government procurers, and they could be turned out in quantity. The average cost of a bronze Napoleon to the Federal government, for example, was approximately $550. A 3-inch Ordnance rifle was produced with an average cost of only $350. A 10-pounder Parrott cost the U.S. government about $180 and a 20-pounder, $380—a tempting cost-saving incentive to convert from bronze to iron.[15]

Access to raw materials also played an important role in the decision and pace which bronze smoothbores were replaced with rifled cannons. Rifled cannon, with a few exceptions, were made of iron. The availability of iron ore was practically unlimited. There were no domestic sources for tin, a required component for making bronze. The supply of copper, the main ingredient of bronze, was also a critical factor, particularly for the Confederacy, in determining the types of guns that could be supplied to meet the future needs of the artillery branch. In early 1862, when the shortage was evident, General Beauregard wrote: "Notwithstanding that there was a scarcity of the materials for making bronze field pieces . . . I issued a call upon the planters for their bells. Already that call has met with a patriotic response from all quarters, and a large number of these bells have been placed subject to my orders . . ." By the end of 1862, General Lee was calling for recasting bronze 6-pounder smoothbores and even 12-pounder howitzers to provide metal for making Napoleons. During the first two months of 1863, Tredegar foundry in Richmond made only seventeen Napoleons because of the short supply of raw materials. To find alternate sources, the government requested that corner posts made from old bronze cannons be pulled from the streets of Richmond. By mid-1863, the foundry had acquired over 80,000 pounds of copper and tin, mostly from outmoded guns. By 1864, the Confederate chief of ordnance suspended the production of bronze cannons altogether because of the deficient copper supply. Instead, banded iron cannons were substituted for the bronze Napoleons.[16]

In contrast, Northern manufacturers, apparently, were sufficiently supplied with enough bronze to cast guns for provisioning Federal arms depots. From the war's beginning to the end of 1863, the U.S. government had ordered an impressive total of 1,113 Napoleons. The last Napoleons would be applied for in 1864. The era of bronze artillery had ended.[17]

Batteries on review. (MCMOLL/USAMHI/WDC)

IV

The Guns, Equipment, and Animals

Smoothbores

Howitzers

Smoothbores included howitzers and cannons. Howitzers were short-barreled guns used primarily for firing hollow projectiles. While their hollow shells needed enough propelling charge to attain a certain velocity to remain accurate, they were also susceptible to fracturing if large charges were used. Consequently, howitzers, unlike cannons, had a powder chamber in the rear of the barrel with a diameter smaller than that of the bore and used compara-tively small charges to deliver their projectiles. The reduced powder chamber made howitzers ineffective when firing a solid projectile, but allowed this short-barreled weapon to be quite effective with lighter ammunition.

Howitzers had some advantages over other artillery pieces: they were lighter than cannons and more easily moved about in action or transported on a march. In hard campaigning the weight of an artillery piece became increas-ingly important as horse teams were reduced in size or became exhausted and yet the animals were still expected to maneuver as if at full strength.

Howitzer fire was greater than cannons. The howitzers' large hollow pro-jectiles fired high into the air, in an arcing trajectory, and, consequently, could hit their targets indirectly behind a ridge or in a protected area not accessible to the flat trajectory of cannon projectiles.

The primary disadvantages of a howitzer included its limited range and the type of ammunition it could fire. Because of its short range, it was mostly restricted to a defensive role or for special service. Since the Confederate army at Gettysburg was not on the defensive, there was no opportunity for its how-itzers to repel any attack. Although they possessed substantial firepower and their presence would appear as a visual threat to enemy troops contemplating an attack, they would otherwise be worthless unless they could be brought up close enough to the enemy to produce any damage.

The Army of Northern Virginia brought one 6-pounder howitzer, twenty-four 12-pounder howitzers, and four 24-pounder howitzers into Pennsylvania; the Army of the Potomac had only two 12-pounder howitzers accompanying its artillery force at Gettysburg.[1]

Although howitzers were a dying breed, they still maintained their pres-ence in the Confederate army throughout the war. In 1865, E. P. Alexander, then brigadier general of artillery, described his view of the howitzers and their application:

> I consider [12-pounder howitzers] the best gun for [the cavalry] service, and would prefer them to anything were I in that arm. Our 3-inch have no shrapnel; their shell are very defective and uncertain, even when they explode at all, and you know the frequent complaint on this head, and their canister is very small and inferior. The Yankees have shrapnel and canister with lead balls, and thus use them very efficient-ly, but our 3-inch are not their 3-inch by a great deal. The 12-pounder howitzer is

12-pounder howitzer. (AC)

lighter, its ammunition cheaper and more abundant; it fires a formidable shrapnel; its shell seldom ever fails, and its canister is but little inferior to that of Napoleons. Where guns have to protect themselves against a charge of either infantry or cavalry, I believe the 12-pounder howitzer superior to the Napoleon and worth twice its number of 3-inch rifles. Is not this gun better adapted to the service of cavalry than a gun whose only recommendation is that it has a very long range and one-half of whose projectiles never burst (and when one does burst it does not make a dozen fragments), and which is very dangerous to our own men when fired over their heads? I have entirely forbidden their use by my battalions over our infantry. I have sent in to Colonel Brown to know what he can give me to replace the 3-inch, if you still desire the exchange. I don't want Parrotts (would rather have mountain howitzers), and prefer 12-pounder howitzers to Napoleons, of which I have enough.[2]

Smoothbore Cannons

After 1857 the basic smoothbore cannon used by the U.S. Army was the Napoleon. Named after Napoleon III of France, it was sometimes referred to as the "gun-howitzer," or the "light 12-pounder." This artillery piece was the

The 12-pounder Napoleon. Most Northern-made Napoleons had the flared front end of the barrel called the muzzle-swell. (AC)

Confederate 12-pounder Napoleon. Note the straight lines of the barrel length, characteristic of Southern-made Napoleons. (AC)

greatest gun in its category. A substantial improvement over the howitzer, Napoleons had a longer range, and their barrels could withstand the explosive force of large charges of powder. They were safe to fire and seldom burst. If they did burst, the bronze didn't shatter like the cast-iron cannon barrels, but stretched to absorb the bursting energy.

Smoothbore cannons were designed as a weapon that could provide greater flexibility by firing not only the howitzers' spherical case shot, shell, and canister, but smoothbore cannons also added solid shot to their ammunition inventory. The trajectory of the smoothbore cannons' projectiles was flat rather than the arcing path characteristic of a howitzer.

In the early stages of the war, then Brevet Major Henry Hunt spoke of the Napoleon:

> The guns, light 12-pounders (the new canon-obusier of Louis Napoleon), are the only ones in our service of that kind. Their firing is very accurate, and with equal mobility, they have much greater power than the 6-pounder. Each is perfectly adapted to the use of all the projectiles known in the service—shot, shell, spherical case, and canister. The fire of one portion of the battery is therefore never sacrificed to that of another, as so often happens in ordinary batteries, where the fire of the gun must often be sacrificed to that of the howitzer, and vice versa.[3]

After the Atlanta campaign in 1864, Brigadier General William Barry, U.S. chief of artillery, observed: "The light 12-pounder has more than ever proved itself to be the gun for the line of battle, where facility of service and effectiveness of solid shot, spherical case, and canister is most required." Compared to their rivals, Napoleons were admired for their killing power, especially at closer ranges. "No column can stand a concentrated fire of six Napoleons by volley or battery, double shotted with canister," wrote Union Brigadier General John Corse.[4]

In the Army of the Potomac, except for two howitzers in Stirling's 2nd Connecticut, the Napoleon 12-pounder was destined to become the exclusive smoothbore used. It was the most commonly used artillery piece at Gettysburg. It also had the distinction of being the last cast bronze gun used by an American army and would mark the end of an era that used bronze artillery.

Rifled Guns

There were six models of rifled guns used at Gettysburg: the 3-inch Ordnance rifle, the 10-pounder Parrott, the 20-pounder Parrott, the James gun, the Blakely, and the Whitworth. One other model, the 4½-inch Ordnance gun, was in the region but never made it to the battlefield. Rifled barrels were longer than smoothbores; a longer bore increased their range by allowing the explosive force more time to react on the projectile and therefore propelled it further.

The 3-inch Ordnance Rifle

The 3-inch Ordnance rifle, invented by John Griffen, was the most commonly used rifled gun. Unlike most rifled guns made of brittle cast iron, the 3-inch rifles were made of extremely durable wrought iron. Making a barrel consisted of wrapping metal sheets around a pile of wrought iron to obtain the

Federal 3-inch Ordnance rifle. (AC)

correct diameter. The mass was then subjected to a welding heat and rolled out in length with the trunnions added later. The cooled result was then machined down to its finished condition and the end product was one of the strongest barrels used in the war.

A remarkable test by the army proved the Ordnance rifle's toughness when it caused one to burst, but only after it was filled with seven pounds of powder and thirteen solid projectiles. There is only one case on record where a Northern-made, 3-inch Ordnance rifle burst. At the Wilderness in May 1864, Ricketts's battery had one of its guns burst and knock off its muzzle. Likewise, there are only a few instances of 3-inch pieces of Southern manufacture bursting. One such occurrence was at Gettysburg. On the evening of July 2, a 3-inch rifle belonging to Captain Reilly's battery in Hood's division burst. This 3-inch gun was made in Richmond undoubtedly of burst-prone cast iron rather than wrought iron; improper manufacturing methods or inferior raw materials may also have caused its uncharacteristic ending.[5]

When accuracy at long range was needed, the 3-inch Ordnance rifle was exceptional. During the battle of Atlanta, a member of Lumsden's Confederate battery declared: "The Yankee three-inch rifle was a dead shot at any distance under a mile. They could hit the end of a flour barrel more often than miss, unless the gunner got rattled."[6]

The Parrott

The next most common rifled gun was the Parrott. It was manufactured in different sizes, from a 10-pounder all the way up to a 300-pounder. At Gettysburg, only the 10-pounder and 20-pounder Parrott models were present; both armies used them. The 10-pounder was, by far, the more commonly used of the two models. At Gettysburg, there were two bore sizes of the 10-pounder Parrott—2.9-inch and 3-inch. The Confederate army used both while the Army of the Potomac used only the 2.9-inch bore size. The 3-inch Parrott rifles, many converted from the 2.9-inch models, would not be delivered for the Union army until 1864. The largest gun at the battle of Gettysburg was the 20-pounder Parrott. Its barrel alone weighed over 1,800 pounds.[7]

Parrotts were made with a cast iron and wrought iron combination. While some artillerymen marveled at the accuracy of cast-iron guns, they introduced

Federal 2.9-inch Parrott rifle. This was the type of Parrott used at Gettysburg. Note the characteristic muzzle-swell of this caliber. (AC)

Federal 3-inch Parrott rifle. Note the straight-lined barrel shape. The 3-inch was introduced to the Army of the Potomac after Gettysburg. (AC)

The 20-pounder Parrott was the largest artillery piece used in the battle of Gettysburg. (AC)

new dangers, as previously mentioned, regarding the brittle barrel's susceptibility to fracturing. To overcome this weakness, the back end or breech of a cast-iron Parrott barrel was overlaid with a wrought-iron reinforcing band to contain the force. Despite this addition, the gun still burst, usually at the muzzle or front end. Barrel failure was unpredictable and continued to be a problem throughout the war.

Parrotts had a mixed reputation during the war. After the battle of Fredericksburg, Captain Richard Waterman, Battery C, First Rhode Island Light Artillery, compared the Parrott with the 3-inch Ordnance rifle: "It may be proper to state that, from the experience of the last nine days, as well as from ten months' active service with the 3-inch gun, I consider it inferior at ranges of from 900 to 1,500 yards to the 10-pounder Parrott gun."[8]

Major General Quincy A. Gilmore, U.S. Army, respected them. He reported: "There is, perhaps, no better system of rifled cannon than Parrotts; certainly none more simple in construction, more easily understood, or that can with more safety be placed in the hands of inexperienced men for use. The enormous and constant demand under which it has been rapidly developed, particularly among the larger calibers, to its present state of efficiency and excellence, gives promise of a degree of perfection that will leave little to be desired at no distant future." Gilmore also recognized that the Parrotts had defects, particularly "their very unequal endurance." Some burst in their early stages of use; others fired thousands of rounds before they became unusable.[9]

Other artillery commanders begged to be rid of the Parrotts. "I would most respectfully recommend that the 20-pounders be taken from the Macon Light Artillery, as it is a good company and deserves better than to have its members wounded and killed by defective guns," advised Confederate Major John Haskell. E. P. Alexander once complained, "The 10-pounder Parrotts in my command I have condemned entirely, and have made arrangements with the Ordnance Department to exchange them all for 24-pounder howitzers, having found it impossible to get satisfactory firing from them, and I hope to be rid of every one when we take the field."[10]

Brigadier General John J. Pettigrew, C.S.A., also deplored the Parrott:

> I regret to say that their performance was execrable—fully as bad as the experiments at Goldsborough led us to fear . . . Half of the shells from the 20-pounders burst

just outside of the guns. They turned over in the air and were perfectly harmless to the enemy. At length the axle of one of these guns broke and it became unserviceable. Then another burst, wounding 3 men, 1 of them mortally. These four 20-pounders were our sole agents for accomplishing the object of the expedition. It was now painfully evident that they were worse than useless. . . . The failure of the effort . . . was owing solely to the utter worthlessness of the 20 pounder Parrotts, which had hung around our necks like a millstone during the march and failed us in the vital moment.[11]

By the end of 1862, General Henry Hunt was fed up with the 20-pounder version and attempted to eliminate them from the Army of the Potomac. He felt that they were "very unsatisfactory, from the imperfection of the projectiles, which, notwithstanding the pains which have been taken to procure reliable ones, are nearly as dangerous to our own troops as to the enemy, if the former are in advance of our lines. In addition, the guns themselves are unsafe. At Antietam, two of [them] and [at Fredericksburg], another, were disabled by the bursting of the gun near the muzzle." At Gettysburg on July 3, one of Captain Elijah Taft's, 5th New York, 20-pounders burst at the muzzle.

While Parrotts had their flaws, they were, nevertheless, easy to operate, they could lose part of the muzzle and keep on firing, they were cheap to make, and they could be produced rapidly and in abundance. Robert Parrott, the gun's inventor, spoke of his creation: "I do not profess to think that they are the best gun in the world, but I think they were the best practical thing that could be got at the time, and I suppose that was the reason for getting them. . . ."

Although Parrotts achieved a dubious reputation, they had the distinction of being one of the three most widely used artillery pieces by either army and were heavily utilized as a necessary means of prosecuting the war. When it was over, they were never used again.[12]

The James Gun, Blakely, Whitworth, and 4½-inch Ordnance Gun

The more exotic artillery pieces used at Gettysburg were the rifled bronze James gun, the iron Blakelys, and the Whitworths. The James gun resembled the Napoleon in appearance. Rifling seemed like a good idea, but the rifling of any bronze barrel, including the James gun, produced poor results as it could

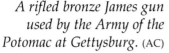
A rifled bronze James gun used by the Army of the Potomac at Gettysburg. (AC)

not be subjected to the same wear as an iron gun. The characteristic of a bronze barrel was incompatible with the ammunition it fired. When a harder, cast-iron projectile was propelled in the comparatively soft bronze barrel, the rifling simply wore down and quickly made the piece unfit. Only the Union army used the James guns [four of them] at Gettysburg.[13]

The English-made iron Blakely guns were formed "with an internal tube or cylinder of cast iron, enclosed in a casing of wrought iron or steel [collars]." Sometimes two or more reinforcing rings were included, with the trunnions being part of one of the rings. Colonel E. P. Alexander described their performance: "The Blakely guns were twelve pounder rifles, muzzle loaders, and fired very well with English ammunition ('built up' shells with leaden bases), but with the Confederate substitute, they experienced the same difficulties which attended this ammunition in all guns. The only advantage to be claimed for this gun is its lightness, but this was found to involve the very serious evil that no field carriage could be made to withstand its recoil. It was continually splitting the trails or racking to pieces its carriages, though made of unusual strength and weight."[14]

General Robert E. Lee described another shortcoming of the Blakely: "We shall be obliged to rely on imported ammunition for the use of the Blakely guns, as its manufacture requires so much expense and time as to prevent its preparation at our arsenals, and, in addition, it consumes so much lead that it is found impossible to supply it without interfering with other demands for that article."[15]

There were at least four Blakely guns present at Gettysburg; all of them were in the Confederate artillery. Their participation at Gettysburg is vague. At least one Blakely was mentioned as participating with Captain R. P. Chew's horse battery and the others were attached to Captain J. F. Hart's horse battery. Neither Chew, Hart, nor their commander, Major R. F. Beckham, wrote battle reports.[16]

Rarest of all the guns at Gettysburg were the two Confederate Whitworth rifles. Made in England, Whitworths had a 2.75-inch bore and a long 104-inch barrel, and weighed close to 1,100 pounds. They fired a shell projectile and also a 12-pound solid bolt with a 1¾-pound powder charge. Whitworths were breechloaders and, with the exception of these two guns, all other artillery pieces at the battle of Gettysburg were muzzleloaders. These pieces were so technologically new that their innovative design revolutionized artillery warfare far into the future and deserve additional description of their use.

Whitworths boasted the longest range, by far, of any artillery piece at the battle. Able to fire over five miles, they could shoot twice the distance of any Union artillery piece at the battle of Gettysburg. Equally impressive was their

The English-made iron Blakely rifle was a 12-pounder muzzleloader. (WDC)

The English-made breechloading Whitworth rifle used by the Army of Northern Virginia at Gettysburg had a range exceeding five miles. (AC)

exceptional accuracy. The *Army and Navy Gazette* of April 9, 1864, described it: "It put every shot into a bull's eye one foot in diameter, at 300 yards." The *Engineer* of April 22, 1864, stated that, "at 1600 yards the Whitworth gun fire[d] 10 shots with a lateral deviation of only 5 inches." Another result showed the amazing precision of the Whitworth. At a range of two and a half miles, the mean deviation of the projectile was just under nine feet. This increased range and accuracy made the Whitworth especially useful in "elegant sharpshooting" to dismount enemy guns. After seeing a firing demonstration, Federal General Hooker found them "unrivaled pieces for accuracy of shooting and length of range."[17]

Long range made Whitworths particularly suited for firing over water. At Wilmington, North Carolina, for example, Major General Whiting counted on his Confederate Whitworth to keep Federal gunboats at bay, as well as support Southern blockade runners. Following the loss of this prized weapon, Whiting lamented: "I have met with a serious and heavy loss in that

Whitworth, a gun that . . . has saved dozens of vessels and millions of money [sic] to the Confederate States. I beg that a couple of the Whitworth guns . . . may be sent here at once. Their long range makes them most suitable for a seaboard position."[18]

Another testimonial was from Major General D. H. Hill, C.S.A.: "You were greatly mistaken in supposing that I was indifferent about the Whitworth. I told you that it was too late to get it, but that it was worth all the guns I had. I had tried the Parrotts, and their shells all burst prematurely."[19]

Although range was the Whitworth's greatest asset, it was a benefit not often required by land armies. Fighting battles over rolling, broken terrain interfered with visibility and concealed enemy targets. In addition, the Whitworth projectile produced limited damage. There was a psychological value, though, in the effects that the Whitworth produced at long range. Major General D. H. Hill, C.S.A., reported that the Whitworth: "Drove entirely off the field near Upperville a Yankee battery of artillery and a large force of cavalry and infantry at a distance of 3½ miles. 'The restorers of the Union' have made their trust so much in their long-range guns that, when they find themselves under the fire of a superior range, they become demoralized and will

Left: *2.75-inch Whitworth case.* (WDC)
Right: *2.75-inch Whitworth shell.* (AC)

not fight. . . . I make this report to call the attention of the War Department to the extraordinary merit of the Whitworth gun in the hands of such a man as Hardaway-the best practical artillerist I have seen in service."[20]

Despite the testimonials in favor of the Whitworth, the commitment to train artillerymen in the use of this gun, the expense to equip a unit and supply it with animals, appeared to have had a low priority. E. P. Alexander described the performance of the Whitworth thus:

> . . . Six breech loading twelve pounder Whitworths were distributed through the army, and often rendered valuable service by their great range and accuracy. They fired solid shot almost exclusively; but they were perfectly reliable, and their projectiles never failed to fly in the most beautiful trajectory imaginable. Their breech loading arrangements, however, often worked with difficulty, and every one of the six was at some time disabled by the breaking of some of its parts, but all were repaired again and kept in service. As a general field piece its efficiency was impaired by its weight and the very cumbrous English carriage on which it was mounted, and while a few with an army may often be valuable, the United States three inch rifle is much more generally serviceable with good ammunition.[21]

No Union Whitworths were present at the battle of Gettysburg. The U.S. government did have some in its arsenal but, in the course of the war, expressed only a casual interest in them. In 1861, fearing a shortage of weapons, a complete battery of six Whitworth guns, along with carriages, three thousand rounds of ammunition, and a machine for manufacturing projectiles, were presented to the U.S. government by a group of patriotic citizens living abroad—a generous gift costing $12,000. The battery's ultimate use, however, was inconsequential. Although they were taken along on the Peninsular campaign, they apparently were viewed as a curiosity rather than as a revolutionary new weapon and that was not sufficient to convince anyone of their worth. For most of their service they remained "cooped up" in the defenses of Washington.

In 1864, Charles Knap testified before a Senate committee: "As a toy it is the most wonderful gun in the world, but it is not fit for actual service for it requires . . . very delicate manipulation and common soldiers in action are not very delicate fellows in handling their projectiles and those guns would be very apt to jam . . . It is a perfect thing to show the state of the art, but for actual service, in my opinion, it is not worth carrying into the field. . . ."[22]

At Gettysburg, the two Confederate Whitworths fired 133 rounds consisting of at least two types, a solid bolt and a shell. Another type, case shot, was made for the Whitworth, but its presence at the battle is uncertain. To produce a Whitworth shell the Confederates bored out a cavity in the bolt. The shell was apparently just introduced prior to the Gettysburg campaign; on May 12, 1863, Colonel Josiah Gorgas of the Confederate Ordnance Department stated: "The Whitworth shells, fabricated at Richmond, are a decided success; they did admirable execution." But with limited space to work with, the shell could not contain enough of a bursting charge to be of much service. Even though Colonel Gorgas was impressed with its initial performance, it is suspected the effects of this shell were minimal since the diameter of the projectile was too small to create an explosive projectile with lethal result.

At Gettysburg, use of the Whitworth shell was uncommon; little information exists regarding its employment in the battle. There are a few examples of relics uncovered afterwards and on display in museums. One such rare Whitworth shell, picked off the field at Gettysburg, is on display at the Adams County Historical Society in Gettysburg.[23]

In addition to all of the types of cannons in use at Gettysburg were the larger cannons, the 4½-inch guns. A big brother to the 3-inch Ordnance rifle, these 4½-inch gun barrels usually fired a 30-pound Hotchkiss or Schenkl projectile and had excellent range [3,265 yards at ten degrees] and great accuracy. Their barrels were monstrously heavy, weighing over 3,500 pounds, and were mounted on siege carriages. One observer considered them to be "more readily moved than the 20-pounder Parrott batteries."

Brigadier General Robert Tyler, commanding the Federal artillery reserve, wrote: "Much to my regret, the two batteries of 4½-inch guns (B and M, First Connecticut Artillery) were ordered to Westminster, to remain with the supply train. I am satisfied that the action of Gettysburg would have demonstrated their extreme mobility and usefulness as field guns, in addition to their already proved excellence as guns of position." Although the 4½-inchers did not make it to the battle, they eventually made it to the battlefield. Today at Gettysburg these grand iron barrels can be seen as location markers for the Union corps headquarters.[24]

Of all the different guns available both armies leaned towards only a few models to equip their artillery branches in significant numbers. Lee consid-

A few Federal 4½-inch, 30-pounder guns were near Gettysburg at the time of the battle, but did not reach the area until they were used to mark Federal head-quarters' sites on the battlefield. (AC)

ered the 12-pounder Napoleon, the 10-pounder Parrott, and the 3-inch rifle to be the best guns available for improving the field artillery. It was obvious that the Army of the Potomac had the same thought since these same three made up most of each army's artillery force at the battle of Gettysburg.[25]

Support Equipment

Accompanying the massive number of artillery pieces to Gettysburg was an equally impressive collection of support vehicles. They transported the vital ammunition, stores, and tools needed to supply and maintain over six hundred artillery pieces and attend thousands of draft animals.

The primary vehicles that supplied the ammunition to the guns during operations were the limbers and caissons. Each artillery piece ordinarily used two limbers and a caisson. One limber pulled the gun, another pulled the cais-

The limber/caisson combination provided a four-wheeled arrangement which balanced out the load and allowed a quick turning radius. (AC)

son. In addition, there were battery wagons and portable forges to service the guns. The support vehicles were packed with an assortment of equipment, supplies, and a variety of tools needed to keep the battery operational.

Each limber and caisson was built on a two-wheeled carriage. When the limber was hitched with the gun or caisson for transport, the result was a four-wheeled combination carriage. The benefit of a four-wheeled combination allowed the distribution of the load—ammunition, stores, and tools—and balanced out the weight of the limber–cannon or the limber–caisson combination.

The four-wheeled combination was easier to operate and maneuver and was more serviceable. Horses were supposed to pull, not lift. The pole served only for guidance of the carriage. The trace harness, the side straps connecting a harnessed animal to the vehicle, pulled the load. If just a two-wheeled arrangement was used, the horses closest to the gun or carriage would have to bear part of the weight and diminish the draught power and rate of traveling. It was difficult enough just to pull the heavy load of a gun and ammunition chest across rugged terrain, up inclines or soft ground as each combination of carriages weighed close to two tons. A Napoleon and packed limber combination, for example, weighed 3,865 pounds and a limber–caisson combination weighed 3,811 pounds.[26]

Carriages for the guns, ammunition chests, and the accompanying battery wagon and forge had to be sturdy enough to endure the pounding shock of rough terrain. More important, gun carriages had to be strong enough to contain the heavy, bulky metal barrel in the carriage's grasp when it was jerked violently backward during the powerful recoil effect of the firing process. Gun carriages required the sturdiness to sustain thousands of recoil shocks and still remain in working order.

Modern-day visitors to the Gettysburg battlefield occasionally inquire why the gun carriages were not secured to the ground in some manner to prevent recoil. To do this would be catastrophic. To absorb the tremendous recoil shock of the gun, carriages had to be able to freely move backward in order to avoid self-destruction. The weight of each wheel of a Confederate gun carriage, for example, was 196 pounds. The axle, with almost four hundred pounds of wheels attached to its ends, therefore, had to be strong enough to sustain the sudden backward jolts of hundreds, or even thousands, of rounds fired. Any additional weight to the carriage increased the strain on it by causing a reduc-

Army wagons and forge at City Point, Virginia. (MCMOLL/USAMHI/WDC)

Wheel spokes were convex to the wheel rim to absorb shock, force the wheel inward on the axle, and shed water away from the carriage. (AC)

tion in the recoil when the carriage resisted being put into motion from its stationary position. If the wheels were too heavy, they strained the axletree to the breaking point. The explosion of the powder charge was so violent, in fact, the wheels skidded along the ground at first and commenced to turn only after a certain length of time.

Carriages were made of oak. Ammunition chests were mostly walnut with the lid covered with a non-sparking metal sheathing of copper or painted canvas. Without implements or barrel, a gun carriage weighed 1,128 pounds; a limber without implements weighed 860 pounds. Such carriages had no springs but they did have a suspension system subtle to the unsuspecting eye. The spokes of wheels were made convex to the wheel rim. That is, the end of the spoke near the axle was closer to the carriage body than the opposite end of the spoke at the wheel rim. This shape, called the "dish," gave elasticity to the wheel and helped absorb shock. Without this convex shape, the wheel would quickly fail. The "dish" shape also threw mud and water to the outside of the carriage and drove the wheels closer toward the carriage to prevent them from running off the axle.[27]

The ammunition carriage's subtle suspension absorbed only some of the shock of travel. Because of this, artillerymen needed to take precautions to absorb as much shock as possible to avoid the inherent dangers of gunpowder. Ammunition and friction primers, used to ignite the powder cartridges, were packed in the same chests. This combination had the potential for a deadly reaction. Ordnance and ordnance stores were not meant to be roughly handled.

Artillerymen risked their lives pulling ammunition chests packed with a quarter ton of explosives over bumpy roads at full gallop, or over stone walls or any rugged terrain they felt capable of surmounting. To protect the ammunition, any empty space in the ammunition chests was packed with filler material called "tow" to prevent projectiles from bouncing around and accidentally detonating. Tow was chopped hemp rope, carried as an inventory item in quantity, to be used as stuffing. The word "tow-head" originated in describing a child with hemp-colored or light brown hair.

Field Artillery Tactics (1861, p.14) prescribed the placing of "rounds in a proper position and then to secure them from movement by filling all void spaces closely with packing. . . . The tow should be inserted in small portions and packed down with a straight smooth stick, prepared for the purpose." Every gun limber and caisson was supplied with an iron thirteen-inch long tow hook for grabbing and pulling out that material.[28]

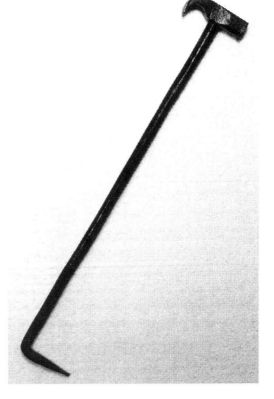

Tow-hook used to unpack ammunition and to repair sabot straps and fixed ammunition. (AC)

Even beyond the perils of hauling and handling artillery rounds under combat conditions, the transportation dangers associated with ammunition were not to be taken lightly. More than one artilleryman was accidentally injured or killed during the Gettysburg campaign when no action was taking place. On the march north, Lieutenant William D. Fuller, Battery C, Third U. S. Artillery, reported three wounded by the accidental explosion of an ammunition chest. Another example occurred shortly before the battle of Gettysburg began. Sergeant Horace K. Ide of the 1st Vermont Cavalry reported: "We moved (from Hanover, Pa.) in a northerly direction and pass[ed] a barn that had been shattered by the explosion of a caisson that belonged to the other brigade the day before and [which] arrived in Abbottstown." He was referring to Company M, 2nd U.S. Artillery. The ammunition chest of a caisson had exploded and killed Private James Moran. The explosion also killed two horses and wounded two others.[29]

Captain John Bigelow's 9th Massachusetts Battery witnessed a similar destruction in another battery as his unit raced toward the battlefield. The ground was so rugged and uneven that a jolting ammunition chest exploded killing an artilleryman. Perhaps he witnessed the mortal wounding of Private John C. Begg who died July 7th from "the accidental explosion of a caisson limber July 2" as reported by the 5th New York Independent Battery commander, Captain Elijah Taft.

Artillery ammunition posed additional hazards beyond the problems associated with storage and transportation. It was likely that the battlefield was randomly strewn with unused percussion shells ejected out of speeding ammunition chests or abandoned on the ground in a hasty retreat, awaiting the impact of any horse's hoof or the jarring collision from an unsuspecting victim.[30]

Artillery limbers contained one ammunition chest on their carriages, caissons had two chests and also carried a spare wheel. Each ammunition chest carried about five hundred pounds of ammunition or supplies. Ammunition carried in a 12-pounder Napoleon chest, for example, included thirty-two rounds: twelve shot, twelve spherical case, four canister, four shells, plus two spare cartridges, and forty-eight friction primers. The projectiles, lacquered for protection, alone weighed 484 pounds (including fuses). The smaller rifled ammunition, 3-inch Ordnance rifle and 10-pounder Parrott, carried fifty rounds per chest.[31]

Artillery caissons had two ammunition chests and a spare wheel. (AC)

This chest carried (32) 12-pounder rounds, fuses, friction primers, and accessories necessary to fire the gun. Pasted on the inside of the lid was a Table of Fire. (WDC)

In addition to ammunition, tools and spare parts were also carried in the limbers and caissons. Besides the danger of incorrectly packed ammunition, everything else had to be stored carefully for safety. As posted on the *Table of Fire* under the lid of the limber, artillerymen were instructed on the care of the ammunition chest: "Keep everything out that does not belong in them, except a bunch of cord or wire for breakage; beware of loose tacks, nails, bolts or scraps. Keep friction primers in their papers tied up. The pouch containing those for instant service must be closed, and so placed as to be secure. Take every precaution that primers do not get loose; a single one may cause an explosion. Use plenty of tow in packing." Lack of regard for the safety precautions needed in handling such a simple device as a friction primer could be catastrophic. Early in 1863, a horrible accident took place in Richmond as recounted by Josiah Gorgas:

> A fearful accident occurred at our Laboratory here on Friday, the 13th of March, by which sixty-nine were killed and wounded, of whom sixty-two were females, chiefly girls and children. Only four were killed outright from the burns they received in the burning of their clothes. The number of dead will probably reach fifty. It is terrible to think of that so much suffering would arise from causes possibly within our control. The accident was caused by the ignition of a friction primer in the hands of a grown girl by the name of Mary Ryan. She lived three or four days and gave a clear account of the circumstances. The primer stuck in the varnishing board and she struck the board three times very hard on the table to drive out the primer. She says she was immediately blown up to the ceiling and on coming down was again blown up. Cartridges were being broken up temporarily in the same room, where many operators were sent temporarily on account of repairs in the shop they usually worked in. The deaths are chiefly due to the burning of their clothes.[32]

In addition to the limbers and caissons, each Federal field battery of six guns included a battery wagon and portable forge. To keep a battery operational, artillerymen had to be furnished with a wide variety of tools and materials. Sponges, handspikes, axes, shovels, spare poles, spare wheels, tarps, buckets, and a number of other miscellaneous items were necessary to service the gun. The gun had to be maintained for instant action and also for the ordinary repairs and preservation of carriages and harness. Wood needed to be painted, leather treated, axles greased, and the animals cared for.

Limber chests of a forge carried 480 pounds of smith's supplies, including

Captured Confederate cannons, limber chests, and wagons at Richmond, Virginia.
(MCMOLL/USAMHI/WDC)

two hundred pounds of horseshoes, fifty pounds of horseshoe nails, and a supply of tow. The forge body carried almost seven hundred pounds. Supplies included tools, iron bars, rounds, and squares for repairs, 108 pounds of horseshoes, a 100-pound anvil, a vise, 250 pounds of blacksmith coal, and an additional supply of tow.[33]

The limber chest for a battery wagon carried more tow, carriage maker's and saddler's tools, and other supplies. The battery wagon body, excluding forage, carried almost 1,300 pounds. Inventory included veterinary supplies, 60 pounds of grease, 80 pounds of paint supplies, 160 pounds of felloes (wheel components), 25 pounds of tow, over 200 pounds of harness components, a 50-pound grindstone, nails, cannon spikes, lanterns, paint brushes, 75-pounds of jacks [three], bridles, feedbags, collars, whips, halters, etc.[34]

The following is a partial inventory list of selected ordnance and supplies carried by the Fifth Maine Battery on the day before the battle of Gettysburg:

six 12-pounder Napoleons	6 Pendulum Hausses [sighting implements]
288 Shot-fixed	4 Tangent scales [sighting implements]

96 Shells	113 Nose bags [for feeding horses]
288 Spherical case	22 Tow hooks
96 Canister	17 Thumbstalls
11 Revolvers	Keys for ammunition chests[35]

Animals

The total number of horses and mules involved in the Gettysburg campaign has been estimated to be about seventy-five thousand. The Army of the Potomac alone used about seven thousand horses for its artillery force. Horses were used to mount the cavalry, infantry officers, staff, and orderlies. They were also used to pull the artillery batteries, ammunition, and support vehicles. Many more were used to pull the great wagon trains and ambulances. Compared to mules, horses possessed a greater steadiness in pulling ambulances, especially important in minimizing suffering; mules were assigned almost exclusively for pulling wagons or as pack animals.

When army horses were selected for purchase, they had to have been raised to maturity, five to seven years old. However, it was found that five-year-old horses were subject to distemper and disease. The Federal quartermaster general, Montgomery Meigs, eventually ordered that no horses be purchased under six years old. The best of the horses went for cavalry mounts and then the artillery usually received its supply from those left over. Upon purchase, artillery horses were trained before being placed into service. With its full complement, each gun in a battery used two six-horse teams—one team pulled the limber that towed the gun, and one team pulled the limber that towed a caisson.

Animals were a highly consumable resource in the Civil War. The life expectancy of an artillery horse, for example, was seven and a half months. Even though the beasts could not be replaced as quickly as a musket or cannon, they were sometimes sacrificed carelessly. Without a sufficient supply of animals, an army lost its rapidity of movement, method of supply, and means of communication. Once its movements were restricted it became an army slow to react and vulnerable to exploitation.[36]

Both Lee's and Meade's armies struggled to maintain its complement of draft animals as sources for replacements were as far away as the midwestern states. The Army of Northern Virginia never did achieve a decent level of draft power for its artillery. Even before the Gettysburg campaign began, the Confederate army was desperate for artillery horses. Near the end of May 1863, Lee advised his cavalry commander, Jeb Stuart: "As to artillery horses, I fear none can be given you. The horses brought in by Gen. W. E. Jones, I understand, have to be put in condition for service before they can be used. We are unable to supply teams for the medical wagons, ambulances, and ammunition trains of the army. You have increased your artillery, when it is a question whether we shall not have to reduce the guns in the army. Four guns to a battery of horse artillery is as much as we can horse and maintain, as far as I can now see. If efficient, it is probably as much as necessary."[37]

It took time to care for a horse and, in an active campaign, time was what an army could not spare. With an army on the march, time did not allow animals to spend hours grazing on grass; for their strenuous work, grass did not have the energy value to restore them. They needed grain. Besides their food rations, animals had to be watered, groomed, and rested. Artillery horses could not be worked after eating or watered when heated; if cold well water was used, it had to be drawn and tempered to avoid injury.

Whether in an active campaign, in camp, or in winter quarters, shortages of feed caused much of the suffering for the animals. In the growing season an army on the move could subsist somewhat off the land. If an army was stationary for a period, however, all the local sources of feed quickly disappeared, and, in winter, supplying enough feed was particularly difficult. Huge amounts were needed to feed the hungry animals—four hundred tons a day for the Army of the Potomac in the winter of 1861–62. On average, each artillery horse weighed one thousand pounds. A horse's daily ration was fourteen pounds of hay and twelve pounds of oats, corn, or barley while a mule was fed three pounds less in grain and the same amount of hay.[38]

Horses were not to be mistreated. The Federal *Instruction for Field Artillery* stated: "To strike a horse whilst at the picket rope, or in the stall, is apt to make him vicious; it is strictly prohibited . . . Horses require gentle treatment. Docile, but bold horses, may be excited to retaliate upon those who abuse them, whereas persistent kindness has often reclaimed vicious ones."[39]

Although horses were instrumental in permitting an army to operate in the field, they seemed quite expendable, more so than a cannon. To have a gun captured, for example, dishonor could be attached to its battery commander depending on the circumstances surrounding its seizure. On the other hand, working the animals to death hardly drew a glance, except from the quartermaster who had to resupply them. During a campaign, thousands were rendered unfit by being subjected to harsh conditions and lack of ordinary care by the soldiers. Cast-off, crippled, and used-up animals, suffering in anguish, were often seen hobbling along the march in an attempt to join the moving column.

The hard life and weather exposure contributed to the many diseases army animals contracted. Greased heel, a disease thought to be caused by poor diet, inflamed the skin, swelled the legs, and created ulcerations with a foul-smelling discharge. They also suffered from the most dreaded equine diseases including glanders or farcy, a contagious and usually fatal disease terminated by the animal being shot. Hoof and tongue, "a most violent and destructive disease," made almost four thousand animals unserviceable during the 1862 Maryland campaign. Complete rest was needed to recover, otherwise the animals were destined for condemnation or worse. Each battery carried medical supplies for treating the ailments of its animals and the preprinted form for inventorying ordnance and ordnance stores listed a variety of veterinary supplies; included were prepared chalk, cinnamon, lard, molasses, opium, pepper, sugar of lead, tar, turpentine, and whiskey.[40]

When rested and ready to begin a campaign, artillery horses were counted upon to travel across country and were restricted, if possible, to pulling loads of seven hundred pounds each, including the carriage weight. When an army was in motion, however, the animals' proper care and attention paid to their workload limitations or proper rest and feed allowances was secondary to the necessities of the moment. They were worked until made unserviceable. Long marches, for example, habitually included moving the animals at an unnatural gait. Artillery moved at a much slower pace than other forces. An average daily march, for example, in ordinary country, for cavalry was seventeen miles in six hours; infantry marched fifteen miles in six hours; artillery horses moved sixteen miles in ten hours. Consequently, marching infantry columns interspersed with artillery batteries created a torturous combination. A moving column was only as fast as its slowest team of animals. Horses worked much better when they moved at their own speed. Constant stops and starts strained the artillery horses and wore them down. When a horse broke down more work was thrown on the rest of the team. Delays were time consuming and fatigued both men and animals. To keep the army moving, artillery horses, when in column, were not allowed to stop for water. Any delay lasting more than minutes called for the carriage to be pulled out of the column and the ones behind it to "close up."[41]

Hitched up, horse teams needed constant inspection to maximize their comfort and stretch their endurance. "It is well known that the artillery is the most destructive branch of service upon horses," wrote Lieutenant Colonel William Le Duc, Army of the Potomac's Eleventh Corps chief quartermaster. He rejected the idea that the weight of the guns and carriages alone was sufficient to cause such bad conditions of the horses. Proper harnessing of the horse teams was necessary for their well-being (A set of harnesses for one six-horse team weighed over three hundred pounds, including saddles, valises, etc.). Le Duc commented: "I believe four horses properly hitched will do the work now expected of six, and keep in good order, if hitched so as properly and fairly to divide the labor and equalize the draft upon the shoulders of the animals. In fact, I have reason to know from actual experiment that the hitching and harnessing of artillery horses has much if not most to do with the rapid deterioration of the animals."[42]

Grabbing a free ride at the expense of the horse team further aggravated the worn-down horses. It was a natural desire for tired artillerymen to hop on a carriage for relief. Federal instructions were explicit in this matter. On level, good roads, no more than "two to the piece and four to the caisson" and "no man shall be allowed to ride longer than half an hour at a time." On bad or rolling ground "no one [except artificers] shall, under any circumstances, be allowed to mount the chests." Artificers were skilled craftsmen who repaired the wood and iron parts of the battery carriages, mended saddles or harnesses, fixed chains, etc.—they were handy to have around.[43]

But grabbing a ride was never done with the horse artillery. Horse batteries had to maintain the same pace as the cavalry units they accompanied and so all members of a horse battery were mounted. Besides, it was impossible to firmly attach oneself to a carriage as it bounced into action over rough ground at full speed. The strongest grip on the handles couldn't prevent the cannoneers from being launched into the air like rag dolls.[44]

Shoeing horses. (MCMOLL/USAMHI/WDC)

The most burdensome problem in dealing with animals in a mobile operation was the need to keep them fit with shoes. From the beginning of the Gettysburg campaign, both armies were plagued with shortages of horseshoes. The oppressive march into Pennsylvania extracted a heavy toll on these animals, bloodying and lacerating their unprotected hooves. Captain E. B. Brunson, Third Corps C. S. Artillery Reserve Battalion, described the problem: ". . . the miserable condition of the horses' feet, for lack of shoes, on the limestone pikes, over which a large portion of our march was made. My ordnance officer made every effort to obtain shoes, as did the chief of artillery . . . but without avail. Consequently, we were obliged to abandon some twenty horses by the time we reached this encampment [Fayetteville, Pa.]."[45]

The Confederate ordnance manual recommended that shoes should not be allowed to remain on a horse more than five weeks. Conservatively, even if both armies had enough of them, over 200,000 shoes, weighing on average over one pound each, and supplied in different sizes, would have been needed to fill this requirement. Shoes were to be forged to fit the hooves which, like humans, came in different sizes—eight of them—four sizes for the front and four for the hind feet. It would have taken hundreds of farriers to keep up with this tremendous task. Farriers were specialists responsible for keeping all the horses and mules shod.[46]

Colonel Lindsay Walker, chief of artillery, Third Corps, C.S.A. stated in his battle report:

> The horses of the command suffered severely (although sufficiently supplied throughout the march with provender) for the want of shoes. On the first day I was placed in command of this corps, I applied to the Ordnance Department for horseshoes and nails. I repeated this application, and on leaving Fredericksburg I telegraphed, urging a supply to be sent to meet me at Culpeper. I am satisfied that most of the horses lost on the march were lost in consequence, because of their lameness in traveling over turnpikes, and especially over the road from Hagerstown to Gettysburg without shoes.
>
> The value of horses abandoned from this cause during the march was, I am persuaded, $75,000, and the injury to others amounted to the same sum.[47]

General Lee described the army's shortages and immobile condition to President Davis, two weeks after Gettysburg: "The men are in good health and spirits, but want shoes and clothing badly. I have sent back to endeavor to procure a supply of both, and also horseshoes, for want of which nearly half our cavalry is unserviceable. As soon as these necessary articles are obtained, we shall be prepared to resume operations."

Eight days later, Lee again repeated his plight to Davis: "My intention is, if practicable, to give the army a few days' rest, and refresh our weary animals, which, having been obliged to subsist chiefly on grass, are much reduced. . . . We are in great need of horseshoes, having been able to procure none on our expedition, and our constant motion preventing their manufacture from iron that fell into our possession, more than half the cavalry is dismounted, and the artillery horses and wagon teams have suffered equally."[48]

While the battle of Gettysburg distinguished many men for valor, horses performed honorably and were heroes also. Compared to mules, their temperament was perfectly suited for the artillery. When sufficiently trained, battery horses even learned to distinguish some of the different bugle calls, enough to respond before the driver initiated the command. In the cavalry, a horse that lost its rider would often get back in the line with an empty saddle, possibly to avoid being left behind.

In battle, horses were steady under fire—better than soldiers were. Soldiers could hug the ground or otherwise reduce their exposure to danger. Horses did not know the difference between a blue and a gray uniform. They did not

This engraving at the Gettysburg National Military Park depicts Cowan's 1st New York Battery, Sixth Corps. The lifespan of an artillery horse was seven and a half months. (AC)

know what to fear or where the threat was coming from. Their large size made them easy hits for flying bullets and shell fragments. But they could endure a fight with a seeming disregard for what was occurring around them. Some did not flinch even when they sustained wounds. Some exhibited only a slight uneasiness even with multiple wounds. Some fell and lay quiet for a moment and then struggled to their feet only to get wounded again.[49]

Army veteran John Billings described the sound and reaction of artillery horses being wounded at Ream's Station in 1864:

> A peculiar dull thud indicated that the bullet had penetrated some fleshy part of the animal, sounding much as a pebble does when thrown in the mud. The result of such wounds was to make the horse start for a moment or so, but finally he would settle down as if it was something to be endured without making a fuss, and thus he would remain until struck again. I [saw] one horse at the very moment when a bullet entered his neck, but the wound had no other effect upon him than make him shake his head as if pestered by a fly. . . .
>
> When a bullet struck the bone of a horse's leg in the lower part, it made a hollow snapping sound and took him off his feet. I saw one pole-horse shot thus, fracturing the bone. Down he went at once, but all encumbered as he was with harness and limber, he soon scrambled up and stood on three legs until a bullet hit him vitally. It seemed sad to see a single horse left standing, with his five companions all lying dead around him, himself the object of a concentrated fire until the fatal shot finally laid

him low. I saw one such brute struck by the seventh bullet before he fell for the last time.[50]

Captain James Hall, 2nd Maine Battery, described his retreat from McPherson's Ridge on July 1: "My own horse was shot through the rump under me, while getting the guns over the fence. There was, of course, some delay in getting over the fence, but one gun being able to pass at the same time, and the enemy got so thick it was hard to tell which outnumbered, gray or blue, and the horses on the last gun were all bayoneted, and fell dead over the fence. To stop then and hold my men to attempt to rescue was madness on my part and I moved to the rear. . . ."[51]

Union General John Gibbon recognized the steadfastness of the animals at Gettysburg in the midst of the grand cannonade on July 3:

> Over all hung a heavy pall of smoke which could be seen rapidly moving legs of the men as they rushed to and fro between the pieces and the line of limbers, carrying forward the ammunition. One thing which forcibly occurred to me was the perfect quiet with which the horses stood in their places. Even when a shell, striking in the midst of a team, would knock over one or two of them or hurl one struggling in his death agonies to the ground, the rest would make no effort to struggle or escape but would stand stolidly by as if saying to themselves, "it is fate, it is useless to try and avoid it."[52]

Besides horses, some mention must be devoted to the humble mule. Often joked about or viewed in a humorous light, mules participated in campaigns almost as much as horses, but are mentioned little. Mules numbered almost half of the total animals present in the army. In some important aspects, they were better than horses. They were not as susceptible to suffering from neglect, disease, hard usage, or bad feed. Mules were sure-footed and could travel over terrain that would lame a horse. They were not picky eaters; one mule driver had his army overcoat partially eaten by one of his teams. It was not unusual for them to eat brush or even branches when short on other feed.[53]

As horses were pulled from the wagon teams in order to replenish losses in the cavalry and artillery, mules were substituted and used to pull the supply trains. At Gettysburg, they helped pull the ammunition wagons and also had the opportunity to suffer the consequences of battle. During the July 3 cannonade, Second Lieutenant Cornelius Gillett, ordnance officer, artillery reserve, stationed at the artillery park behind the Federal line, described his experience: "Several shells passed over the train, and three or four fell among the teams, only one exploding. A mule in one of the teams was struck by a solid shot and killed, and many of the animals became so unmanageable that there was danger of a stampede." Just prior to the advance, General Gibbon's aide-de-camp, First Lieutenant Frank Haskell, noticed: "Two mules [nearby were] carrying boxes of ammunition. Another shell literally knocked them 'all to pieces.'"[54]

The proportion of mules to horses killed during an action was minuscule, however. The returns describing the animal losses for the Eleventh Corps during the Gettysburg campaign, for example, provide a breakdown for both horses and mules. The Eleventh Corps lost 187 horses from exhaustion, lameness, disease, death on the march, and included 98 lost in battle. The corps lost

A casualty of war. Estimates of the number of horses and mules killed at Gettysburg range from 3,500 to 5,000. (MCMOLL/USAMHI/WDC)

only twenty-two mules in the same period, none from battle deaths. Mules are rarely mentioned as even being included in animal burials in the aftermath and the role of a mule was largely in the background, away from the action. A mule's nervous nature could not allow it to operate with cavalry or artillery. In combat areas, they were difficult to control until removed from the danger.[55]

Perhaps mules were smarter than horses. Veteran John Billings remembered: "The explosion of a shell or two over or among them would drive the long-ears wild, and render them utterly unmanageable." Relatively few Civil War photographs of dead mules exist. Billings also recalled that "there are thousands of these [veterans] who will take a solemn oath that they never saw a dead mule during the war."[56]

After the battle of Gettysburg, harnesses were removed from the dead animals and the beasts that were badly crippled had to be killed. In the aftermath, the need to replace horses lost or temporarily disabled from the battle was urgent. The estimated losses in killed vary and have been stated to a number between 3,500 and 5,000. The day after the battle ended, Meade's chief quartermaster, Rufus Ingalls, pleaded with the War Department to send replacements: "The loss of horses in these severe battles has been great in killed, wounded, and worn down by excessive work. Gen. Meade and staff, for instance, lost 16 in killed yesterday. I think we shall require 2,000 cavalry and 1,500 artillery horses, as soon as possible, to recruit the army. Both these arms have done glorious service. I hope you have enough to make up deficiencies."

The War Department answered: "To improve the victory, you will need, doubtless, many remounts. Stand on no ceremony, but, by purchase or impressment of all serviceable horses within range of your foraging parties, refit the artillery and cavalry in the best possible manner." In desperation, the War Department sought replacement animals for the Army of the Potomac as far away as Detroit and Indianapolis. The army had to improvise and restore its mobility and it had to do it immediately. Major General Butterfield, Meade's chief of staff, ordered the wagon teams of six-mules be reduced to teams of four. This downsizing freed up the wagon horses to replace those lost in the artillery.[57]

★ ★ ★

To summarize, the battle of Gettysburg caused considerable deterioration to the animals in both armies. Most experienced their daily routine of feeding and watering disrupted or suspended; many were worn down from their participation and exposure to the battle—some were kept in their harnesses for days and many needed attention to battle wounds. As a result, a large number of the animals were in no condition to join in Lee's retreat or the Federal pursuit back to Virginia. In the wake of the chase, hundreds dropped along the way and were left where they fell. Attired in their saddles, blankets, and bridles, the expendable horses lay there unusable, unmourned, and a stench-laden nuisance to the passing men.[58]

20-pounder Parrott canister. (GNMP/WDC)

V

Artillery Ammunition

Ammunition Types and Purposes

*T*he type of artillery projectile selected depended on the nature of the terrain and the target. Each type had special characteristics with advantages over other projectiles. When artillery was used defensively, for instance, at some point in the attack the observer, whose job it was to note the effects of the cannon fire on the approaching enemy, had to decide on the type of projectile to fire. Then the observer had to decide when to shift to other types of long-range ammunition and when to switch to close-range ammunition. On July 2, for example, as the Federal troops were swept back across the wheatfield behind Captain Winslow's guns, his battery switched from firing solid shot to case shot with one-and-one-half-second fuse and then ended with canister.

Selecting the proper ammunition was usually done when there was limit-

12-pounder shot with sabot. (GNMP/WDC)

ed time to observe the effects of the artillery fire or when it was too difficult to estimate that the range was within proper limits of the specified projectile. As the enemy approached closer and closer, each battery commander, in order to choose the proper ammunition, was required to closely observe the effects produced by his guns, calculate the proximity of the enemy, and, at the same time, estimate the quantity and types of his remaining ammunition supply.

The *Table of Fire* for a 12-pounder gun instructed when to use each of the four most common projectile types:

> Use SHOT at masses of troops, and to batter, from 600 up to 2,000 yards. Use SHELL for firing buildings, at troops posted in woods, in pursuit, and to produce a moral rather than physical effect; greatest effective range 1,500 yards. Use SPHERICAL CASE SHOT at masses of troops, at not less than 500 yards; generally up to 1,500 yards. CANISTER is not effective at 600 yards; it should not be used beyond 500 yards, and but very seldom and over the most favorable ground at that distance; at short ranges, (less than 200 yards) in emergency, use double canister, with a single charge. Do not employ RICOCHET at less distance than 1,000 to 1,100 yards.[1]

Four types of ammunition were used at Gettysburg: shot, shell, case, and canister. The first type, called shot if fired from a smoothbore or bolt if fired from a rifled gun, was a solid projectile. Shot could destroy objects like no other projectile. Its solid weight resisted deflection on its flight path and made it the most suitable ammunition available for a battering effect. With its weight, shot possessed a tremendous amount of kinetic energy that was released slower than other projectiles; more than one unfortunate soldier lost a leg attempting to stop a slowly rolling round-shot that deceptively appeared as if its pent-up energy had been exhausted. Because of its density, shot was more accurate than shell, particularly at longer distances. Shot was apparently under-appreciated by Federal artillerymen. "There has been too much neglect of solid-shot fire from the smooth-bore guns, and altogether too much dependence placed upon shell," scolded the Army of the Potomac's General Order No. 2.[2]

Ideally shot was used against enemy guns, limbers, caissons, wagons, structures, live targets, or anything that needed the impact of an object with mass to break or destroy them. The penetration power of shot hurled into men or horses was horrific, especially when fired into enemy lines that had depth, such as a column of infantry or cavalry, or into flanks of troops. Shot was also used to sweep woods where other types of ammunition had little effect.

Seeking cover in wooded terrain from enemy shot had both psychological and physical consequences. When shot was fired into a wooded area that concealed enemy soldiers, there was still the possibility of it causing indirect damage to the surrounding troops from splintered wood or the crushing effect of treetops or limbs sheared off by these powerful projectiles. Exposure to such fire undoubtedly increased the anxieties of the men; on one hand they felt protected by the woods and yet were vulnerable to its presence. Federal Captain George E. Randolph, Third Corps chief of artillery, reported at Gettysburg, "The attack on the left

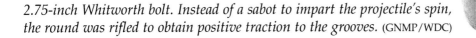

2.75-inch Whitworth bolt. Instead of a sabot to impart the projectile's spin, the round was rifled to obtain positive traction to the grooves. (GNMP/WDC)

of our line [the Wheatfield] involved Winslow's Battery. From the position of the battery and of the infantry supporting, it was deemed best for a time to fire solid shot into the woods over our troops, who were fighting in front under protection of a stone wall. This fire was very effective (as such use of solid shot always is when troops are engaged in woods, the moral effect being at least equal to the physical)."[3]

Winslow's guns, referred to above, were firing solid smoothbore projectiles. Surprisingly, the Army of the Potomac used no solid rifled projectiles at the battle of Gettysburg. In the Official Records devoted to Gettysburg, there is no positive mention of using solid rifled bolts by the Union artillery in the battle. There are frequent references to "shot and shell" but this term more than likely refers to case shot.

There is positive information elsewhere on what the Union army had or did not have in its inventory supply at the battle. Federal army regulations stated that commanders of units were required to be held accountable for all ordnance and ordnance stores issued to their men. To accomplish this, quarterly inventories were performed and, as a result, created the greatest "source of comprehensive information concerning weapons and ordnance equipment possessed by military units." After the inventory, a summary statement, verifying a unit's inventory of items and listed in great detail, was then transmitted on a prescribed form to the Ordnance Department. It is apparent, however, recordkeeping was as unpopular then as it is today. Union Brigadier General George D. Ramsay, chief of ordnance, reported:[4]

> The property accountability for these stores is a most important matter, and here the value of the system introduced is well illustrated. The number of property returns received during the year 1862 was 2,690. During the same period there were 20,000 officers who were accountable for ordnance stores, from whom 80,000 returns were due, but from whom only the above number were received; whereas the number of such returns which will be received at this office during 1863 is estimated at 60,000. In the other divisions of the office the absolute necessity of the system introduced is daily shown.[5]

Hopefully, recordkeeping had improved since 1862. The quarterly return, *Summary of Ordnance and Ordnance Stores on Hand in the Artillery Regiments*, for June 30, 1863, the day before the battle of Gettysburg began, reported no solid rifled projectiles on hand in any Federal unit that was present at Gettysburg. The belief that the Union artillery carried no rifled solid rounds is further supported by a communication sent months after Gettysburg. A memo from John Craig, assistant adjutant general to General Hunt, on November 3, 1863, to Lieutenant Colonel J. A. Monroe, chief of artillery of the Second Corps, prescribed the ratio of rifled projectiles in an ammunition chest. Solid projectiles were excluded from the inventory: "For rifled guns, 25 shells, 20 shrapnel to 5 canister is a proper proportion, the shell to be increased to 30 at the expense of the shrapnel, if the commander of the battery desires it, there is too much shrapnel used. Fifty rounds is the load to each chest."[6]

General Hunt issued a circular prescribing the ratio of rifled projectiles for the horse artillery on March 1, 1865. It did not list bolts as part of the inventory: "The proportion of ammunition for the horse artillery will be as follows: Rifled guns—thirty shell, fifteen shrapnel, five canister."[7]

Solid rifled rounds did not suddenly become obsolete. There is no doubt such projectiles were used throughout the Civil War, but not by the Federals at Gettysburg. The U.S. Army, for example, purchased almost 150,000 rounds of 10-pounder Parrott shot.

There is an explanation for the Union's avoidance of using solid rounds. As a substitute for rifled bolts, explosive projectiles, without their fuse preparation, could be used. The results would have been nearly similar to the solid round. Captain Richard Waterman, Battery C, First Rhode Island Light Artillery, in his report pertaining to the battle of Fredericksburg stated: "The ordnance ammunition with metallic packing failed in almost every instance to ignite the fuse, and I consider it worthless when explosion constitutes the chief value of a projectile. As solid shot, the ordnance shrapnel was serviceable in the cannonade of Fredericksburg." Additional flexibility could then be gained in situations calling for different types of ammunition where artillerymen could choose to use their explosive projectiles as such or as a solid shot substitute.[8]

Even smoothbore explosive projectiles were used in cases where they were deliberately fired as solid projectiles. The Army of the Potomac's General Orders Number 2, January 15, 1864, stated: "The allowance of shrapnel for the light 12-pounder gun is largely in excess of the ordinary requirements of [battle]. By reference to the table for packing ammunition chests it will be seen that for the 12-pounder gun only eight shrapnel are allowed. In determining the proportion for the light 12-pounder gun the number was increased to twelve, because circumstances might arise which would make them useful, but it was expected that habitually one-third of them, at least, would be used as solid shot."[9]

Another possible reason for not favoring solid projectiles for rifled guns by either army was probably due to the wear on the barrels. A directive from the Confederate chief of ordnance stated that "solid shot [is] forbidden in Parrott guns." This was possibly an attempt to eliminate the projectile that created the harshest stress on the burst-prone Parrott barrels and explains why few Parrott bolts, the 2.9-inch in particular, are found.[10]

With respect to the battle of Gettysburg, there are references in accounts by soldiers, authors, etc. regarding the large number of projectiles that failed to explode. At one time, an exhibit at the Gettysburg National Military Park's visitor center claimed that 55 percent of the explosive projectiles at the battle failed to detonate. One can only speculate how many explosive rounds were intentionally not armed to explode but were instead used as a substitute for solid bolts or shot.

Besides shot, there were two types of explosive ammunition: for smoothbores there were spherical case and spherical shell, but the generic names of case shot and shell included rifled guns as well. (Specific brand types of explosive rifled projectiles will be discussed later.) The purpose of explosive ammunition was to simply postpone the bursting effect until the shell was near enough to the target to inflict damage. Case shot and shell were hollow to contain the fragmenting charge. Interestingly, the body of a case shot or shell projectile had to be strong enough to withstand the tremendous explosive force to propel the rounds to their destination and yet weak enough to break at the right moment from the relatively small bursting charge they carried.

Of the two explosive projectiles, shell was designed to break into only a few pieces, hardly more than six. With so few fragments the killing power was diminished. The detonation also reduced shell's physical effects even further; some of the fragments were neutralized from its explosion. When shell burst in flight, some fragments moved forward with increased speed, some moved rearward with decreased speed. Fragments were slowed to the point where velocity was entirely overcome, and the fragment simply dropped to the ground or was forced backward.

Left: *3.5-inch Blakeley shell.* (GNMP/WDC)
Below: *24-pounder spherical shell.* (GNMP/WDC)

Although shell fragmentation did not cause significant damage and accuracy was limited, explosive projectiles had one psychological advantage over solid shot. Shells produced an unsettling effect on men and horses from the bursting noise and bright flash of energy released from their explosion. This characteristic affected morale more than the subdued visual effects of solid shot. Preferable targets for shell included cavalry, troops under cover, and wooden structures which could be broken and set on fire.[11]

The other type of explosive projectile was case shot, when used in rifled guns, or spherical case, when used in smoothbores. Referred to interchangeably as shrapnel, case shot was more destructive than shell. Case shot was loaded with lead or iron balls (a 12-pounder spherical case contained seventy-eight balls) and designed to burst above and before the enemy line. Case shot's purpose was to shower down small but destructive projectiles on the enemy.

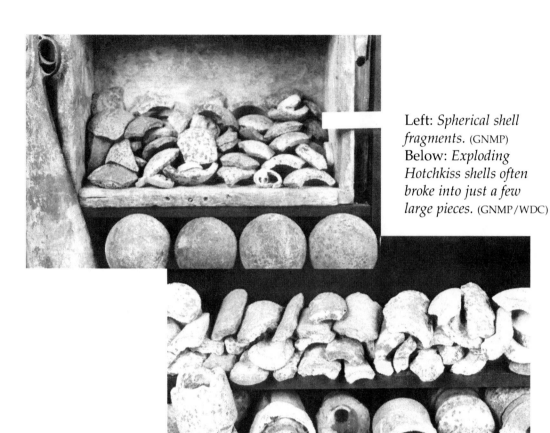

Left: *Spherical shell fragments.* (GNMP)
Below: *Exploding Hotchkiss shells often broke into just a few large pieces.* (GNMP/WDC)

In spherical case, a propellant charge smaller than that used for a solid shot was necessary to prevent the casing from rupture. In addition, with an imperfect center of gravity and lighter weight, case shot's trajectory was not as accurate and the shell's range was not as great as solid shot; but, according to the Artillerist's Manual, "when case shot burst just in front of its target, the effect was terrific."[12]

The Army of the Potomac's General Order No. 2 instructed artillerymen on when to choose case shot projectiles:

> It should be chiefly used against troops which are stationary or not moving rapidly, or directed against fixed points over which an enemy is passing. Distances must be accurately judged, the projectiles carefully prepared, the fire slow and deliberate,

and its effect well noted, with a view to the correction of errors. Shrapnel is too often wasted. Artillery officers should recollect that, although it is the most effective and powerful of projectiles if well used, it is also the most harmless and contemptible if used badly; that the elements of uncertainty in its effect are numerous, and therefore in its use nothing should be left to chance which can be made certain by care and attention. Shrapnel should never be fired rapidly, except against large and dense masses, and then solid shot would generally be better. . . . Shrapnel fire is very effective against lines of troops, columns, or batteries which are stationary upon open ground. It is not to be used against troops which are covered from view by the conformation of the ground, or by obstacles of any kind, except only when it is known that the enemy is stationed within a certain distance in the rear of a given obstacle, as in the case of field works, against the defenders of which shrapnel is effective.[13]

General Hunt was not impressed with the performance of case shot. Near the end of the war, in his assessment of its performance, Hunt said: " Solid shot is much more and shrapnel much less valuable than is generally supposed, and the large proportion of hollow shot used has been unfavorable both to the usefulness and reputation of the artillery."[14]

The fourth type of artillery ammunition was canister. Canister was a thin

12-pounder spherical case shot. (AC)

metal container loaded with layers of lead or iron balls packed in sawdust. This internal packing arrangement was done in order to maintain their symmetry during transportation and effectiveness when fired. Canister, however, could be used only at close range—effective up to four hundred yards. Beyond that the balls would disperse too much to inflict any concentrated damage.

Because of the large number of missiles that the barrels could spit out in one moment, this antipersonnel ammunition was highly destructive to men and horses. Canister was essential in the last moments of a defensive stand and could prove to be the deciding factor in breaking an attack. During the closing action of Brigadier General William Barksdale's attack on July 2, for example, Dow's 6th Maine Battery came close to annihilation had it not been for the effects of canister. First Lieutenant Edwin Dow described it: "What saved me was that I had a whole lot of canister. While those rebels were charging us we were sending 3,000 bullets a minute into them. Though everything was going to smash around us, my battery, somehow, kept in good shape. We lost only fourteen men."[15]

Canister was the deadliest kind of artillery ammunition. It did not explode when fired; when it left the barrel the balls packed within broke and disintegrated the metal wrapping. Having broken the case, canister balls struck the inside of the bore and against each other. When flung out of a barrel, the load spread the widest path of destruction of any ammunition. Adding to this ammunition's lethality, canister rounds could be loaded and fired more rapidly since aiming was almost unnecessary; and gun crews did not have to contend with fuse preparations and the problems associated with their untrustworthiness.

Canister was available for both smoothbores and rifled guns. Smoothbore canister, however, was significantly more effective than rifled canister. When the balls flew out of a smoothbore, the pattern was in the shape of a cone, with most of the balls concentrated at the center. This pattern sent a deathblow to any soldier in its path and unceremoniously rendered the human form unrecognizable. More important, smoothbores had a larger caliber bore which allowed a much larger round that contained more missiles. Conversely, when canister was fired from a rifled gun, the grooves in the bore interfered with the balls as they exited, producing a jagged non-uniform pattern. In addition, there was probably a centrifugal motion imparted on the balls when the thin

12-pounder canister with sabot.
(GNMP/WDC)

20-pounder Parrott and canister balls.
(GNMP/WDC)

walls of the canister round collapsed from the force of the explosion. This would have caused the round to expand outward, thereby imparting some rotational effect from the rifled grooves of the bore and affecting the dispersion of the canister balls. This may be the desired effect when the enemy is at close range but the dispersion effect severely reduced rifled canister's killing power at the outer range that was effective for smoothbore canister—four hundred yards. General Hunt, as mentioned earlier, said a rifled canister's effectiveness was less than half the range of a 12-pounder smoothbore.[16]

When close-up fighting occurred, double, sometimes triple, canister was fired into the advancing ranks. Firing multiple rounds from a cannon barrel, however, was hazardous. The additional weight greatly increased the stress on the rear of the barrel and the breakable gun carriage. When the charge exploded, it caused a corresponding reaction in the recoil force. Generally, the barrel of a cannon weighed roughly one hundred times more than the solid projectile that it fired. Changing the barrel to projectile weight ratio changed the performance of the reaction. Adding multiple rounds increased the projectile load weight and, as a result, significantly increased the force that repelled the gun in recoil.

On July 3, as the Confederate infantry made the final approach to the Union line, the Federal gunners switched to their final choice of ammunition—canister. This was the artilleryman's last resort in hopes that he could complete the damage and save himself from destruction. As the range faded between the two combatants, the Federal guns on Cemetery Ridge were loaded, some with multiple rounds. At three hundred yards, the lanyards were jerked; and instantaneously the barrels spit out their contents to complete the slaughter. An artilleryman from a battery just south of the clump of trees, later described the tremendous flame spurting out of the blazing cannons, grazing the dead and wounded in its fiery path, scorching and igniting their clothes and flesh in the process.[17]

Since ammunition chests contained relatively few rounds of canister and sometimes it was fired in multiple rounds, the inventory on-hand could rapidly vanish. When close-range ammunition was depleted, the resourcefulness

12-pounder canister (top) and 3-inch Hotchkiss canister (bottom). Most guns at Gettysburg used the smaller caliber and produced correspondingly less killing power.
(GNMP/WDC)

of the artillerymen switched to alternative methods of destroying the enemy. For example, when the Confederates approached the heights of Cemetery Hill on July 2, Ricketts's battery fired single, then double canister. When canister was depleted, the battery shifted to firing "rotten shot." This term refers to spherical case loaded without using fuses. Upon being fired, the shell abruptly exploded at the muzzle and reacted similarly to canister.[18]

In some cases, artillerymen would resort to more extreme measures when the ammunition was depleted. Sometimes they packed the barrel with anything to injure the attackers such as rocks, nails, parts of chain, or even bayonets. A Confederate canister dug up recently near the Savannah River in Georgia contained pieces of a wrought iron fence, iron shards, and door hinges. One hard-to-believe tale, although not pertaining to canister but regarding resourcefulness from desperation, was relayed in later years to the Pittsburgh *Commercial Gazette* by a Federal gunner stationed on Cemetery Hill. Short on ammo, General Meade, in person, ordered the hill to be held at all costs. As a resourceful expedient to replenish ammunition, they began to collect unexploded shells that had been fired at them from the Confederate batteries. The *Gazette* article described the scene:[19]

> There was a great many of those scattered over our part of the hill. [Meade, unrecognized by the artillerymen,] proceeded to supervise the collection of shells . . . finally . . . he turned his horse over to his orderly and proceeded to carry shells himself. . . .

Rusty iron balls, once lethal components of antipersonnel projectiles, lay dormant on display. (GNMP/WDC)

John Snicker was one of the best men in the battery, but was rough in speech and action. Seeing, as he supposed, a lieutenant or captain from the outside stooping to pick up a shell, he pushed the officer aside with the remark: "Get out of this, old Ginger Fingers! Your mind's willin', but your body's weak, and you are in the way." Meade surprised and amused, stood aside. [Snicker, later discovering it was Meade], insisted that what scared him was that he never came so near kicking a man in his life without doing it as he did General Meade when he stooped to pick up that shell.[20]

As if canister wasn't deadly enough, months after the battle, there was a call for improving canister's killing power. General Henry Hunt, requesting a change in the design of canister, said:

There is much complaint of the inefficiency, at close quarters, of the canister for the light 12-pounder gun, owing to the small number of balls it contains. This effect was made apparent at Gettysburg, and is complained of frequently now that the batteries of these guns in the horse artillery often come in close contact with the enemy's cavalry and infantry. The present canister shot is so large as to be effective at long ranges, so long that it would be better to use shrapnel.

I respectfully request that canister with a smaller ball, say of 2 to 3 ounces—or if of smaller diameter than that of a 2-ounce iron ball, then one of lead—may be furnished at as early a day as practicable, in sufficient quantities to furnish at least the horse artillery with one-half their canister of the new pattern. These canisters would carry from 60 to 80 shots, and would probably be much more effective within 200 yards than the present 7-ounce ball of 28 to the canister.[21]

By the end of 1863, a deadly new form of canister was ready to be battle tested. Henry Hunt's assistant adjutant general, John Craig, announced its introduction to the chiefs of artillery in the Army of the Potomac: "By a circular from these headquarters, dated December 17, 1863, paragraph I, you were notified that a supply of new canister for light 12-pounders had been ordered (seventy-two 3-ounce balls to the canister), and you were requested to make requisition for it at a rate not to exceed 10 rounds per gun. Will you please state in your report of your train if such canister has been received, and call special attention to it with a view of obtaining a report as to its efficiency in our next battles?"[22]

Besides the four primary types of ammunition described above, one other type of ammunition, grapeshot, was possibly used during the battle of Gettysburg. Grapeshot consisted of an arrangement of layered iron balls held together by iron plates and a threaded bolt at the center. Compared to a round of canister, a *stand* of grapeshot contained fewer and somewhat larger iron balls. Grapeshot used in a 12-pounder gun, for example, contained nine balls, while canister contained twenty-seven. Defending soldiers certainly must have felt more confident in holding their position against an advancing enemy line when using the deadlier canister round containing triple the number of balls.

Stand of grapeshot. (AC)

Grapeshot was the predecessor of canister and the term was frequently used interchangeably in the soldiers' accounts to mean canister. Such references should not be taken as proof of grape's usage. Citations to its employment are few but evidence does exist confirming its use—although it was no longer in use by the Union Army, the

Plates from canister found at Gettysburg on the Spangler farm. (GNMP/WDC)

Confederates apparently did use grapeshot, perhaps appropriating it from stockpiles in the federal arsenals when the war began.[23]

One such reference to grapeshot used at Gettysburg originates from a reliable source. At the Bliss farm on July 3, Colonel Theodore Ellis, 14th Connecticut, observed: "After capturing the house I went to the barn . . . and while there, a shell or projectile entered the gable toward the house and burst wide killing and wounding I think three men. The projectile was probably fired by the 'rebs' as it contained grape shot, which was not used by our artillery. One of the shot was picked up and shown me." The absence of grapeshot's iron plates in relic displays at the Gettysburg National Military Park makes the use of this ammunition at Gettysburg an open question.[24]

Projectile Technology

Smoothbore vs. Rifled

Artillery projectiles were made primarily from cast iron. It was the ideal ingredient. To deliver damage, cast iron had the essential qualities of hardness, making it prone to shattering or fragmenting. A hard substance was also needed if artillery fire was directed against inanimate targets. A projectile made from lead, for example, was too soft to be used against such objects. Besides hardness, cast iron had density or weight to penetrate battle lines or damage heavy objects, it was a plentiful commodity compared to other materials—and it was cheap.[25]

Compared to the simpler manufacturing methods used for a smoothbore gun and its accompanying ammunition, rifle technology brought forth additional burdens challenging the designers of gun barrels and the projectiles they fired. Artillery rounds had to be compatible with the gun from which they were fired. Technologic advances in rifled artillery and ammunition required access to material resources and state of the art machinery to produce these new implements of warfare.

With respect to rifled artillery projectiles, the production methods used by the Confederate manufacturers differed somewhat from the Federal suppliers of ordnance. The Federal suppliers, for example, had the production machinery to force a projectile through a die to control tolerances which resulted in the proper fit for the bore of the gun. Without such sizing equipment in the South, ingenuity found a way to overcome sizing problems and gained an added advantage in the process. Some rifled projectiles were cast with the sabot, a component used to impart the projectile's spin, and two oversize iron bands called bourrelets, encircling the body of the projectile near the top and bottom. The sabot and the two bourrelets were then machined down to the proper size to fit the bore. This method eliminated the need to machine down the entire projectile, saving on production time and tool wear. With little surface contact on the bore of the gun, bourrelets created the added advantage of having considerably less friction when the projectile was fired.[26]

Smoothbore and rifled projectiles each had their own distinct advantages. With the exception of canister, projectiles fired from smoothbores were round and those fired from rifled guns were elongated and conical or bullet-shaped. One advantage of any projectile was its shape. A smoothbore's spherical projectile, for example, allowed ricochet firing, a bouncing effect across open terrain. Ricochet firing could only be executed when firing round projectiles because rifled ammunition's conical shape tended to burrow the projectile into the ground without result.

A 3-inch Read shell, the Confederate version of the Parrott, shows two encircling bands, called bourrelets, which reduced machining to tolerance and reduced friction with the bore. (GNMP)

137

A rifled projectile's shape, however, had its own important advantages that a round projectile did not have. Its pointed shape decreased the air resistance which, in turn, maintained the projectile's speed longer than the blunt shape of round ammunition. A rifled projectile's resistance was about one-third that of a spherical-shaped ball with the same diameter. As a consequence, the sustained velocity of a rifled projectile exhibited more penetrating power, about one-fourth more, than smoothbore ammunition. A special advantage of a rifled projectile's shape allowed additional weight to be added to the projectile simply by making it longer; doing this did not increase the diameter and therefore did not increase the projectile's air resistance. As weight was added to a rifled projectile, its penetrating power was increased.[27]

The freedom to increase a rifled projectile's length thereby increasing the weight, however, was not done without a price. As the general rule-of-thumb, mentioned earlier, a cannon barrel weighed roughly one hundred times more than the projectile it fired; the 12-pounder Napoleon, for example, weighed close to twelve hundred pounds. Doubling the projectile weight of a 10-pounder Parrott to a 20-pounder, for

10-pounder Parrott shell. (AC)

instance, required an entirely new design, adding almost one thousand pounds to the barrel weight. The 20-pounder Parrott's increased projectile weight in firepower, however, was not significantly greater to a field army than the lighter 10-pounder version or the 3-inch Ordnance rifle. The additional weight of the 20-pounder approached the outer limits of what could be characterized as field artillery. Six-horse teams could not easily handle such a load and, consequently, few guns of this size accompanied an army on the move.[28]

Another primary advantage gained with rifled projectiles included the ability to design their shape to contain features that prevented most of the propellant explosive gas from escaping around the projectile. Capturing most of the propellant gas increased substantially the range of rifled guns over smoothbores. Besides added range from this enhanced efficiency, the velocity also increased thereby increasing the rifled projectiles' destructive hitting force.

There were two disadvantages, however, with rifled projectiles. First, the projectiles' high velocity and pointed shape often dug them into the ground deep enough to contain the explosive charge which fragmented the round, making them ineffective killers. Second, rifled projectiles traveled fast enough to make them invisible in flight. Higher velocity prevented them from being tracked like the slower smoothbore ammunition.

The system diversity in the design of rifled ammunition was extensive. Variations included nine different methods used to impart a spin on the projectile and will not be covered here. The diversity of artillery projectiles available for purchase was extremely troubling to the ordnance departments charged with the responsibility of supplying ammunition. In August 1862, Brigadier General James Ripley, chief of ordnance, pointed out the growing problems associated with too many choices:

> The frequent requisitions for varieties of ammunition and other ordnance supplies for guns of special patterns induce me to call the attention of the General-in-Chief to the evils, heretofore noticed and protested against by me, which have resulted from the introduction into the military service of new inventions without a previous subjection to the tests and examinations prescribed by army regulations, and essential to the ascertainment of their merits or fitness for use as military weapons.
>
> These evils have been going on and increasing until we have now not less than six hundred different kinds of cannon ammunition requisite to meet calls for supplying the various kinds of cannon in military use, notwithstanding the obvious propri-

ety of uniformity, as far as practicable, in this respect, and the efforts which this department has made to obtain and secure it.

Many of these guns are of a description requiring a special kind of ammunition and other supplies; in some cases a monopoly of manufacture, secured by patents, and in others, it is believed, purposely so made as to force a resort to certain manufacturers for such supplies. It is manifest that delay in furnishing, and confusion in using, such supplies must occur, to the serious injury of the service. . . .

Measures should be taken to rid the service of all such irregular pieces as thus embarrass the operations of the artillery, and to supply their places with, and restrict issues in future to, such only as have been or shall be regularly, and after due tests and examinations, adopted for the land service.[29]

The most common category used on rifled ammunition employed a *sabot* system as a method that allowed the efficient capture of propellant gas. The sabot moved or changed shape on the projectile and, when fired, sealed the explosive propellant gas and also grabbed the rifled grooves to impart the projectile's essential spinning motion. The spin imparted when the round left the rifled bore stabilized the projectile's flight making it significantly more accurate than smoothbore ammunition. Smoothbores also used a sabot for their round ammunition but for a different purpose than sealing the gas. The sabot, in this case, was a wooden disc with metal straps that connected the projectile to the powder bag and, if it was an explosive shell, kept the fuse pointed towards the muzzle for proper ignition.

Most of the ammunition employed by both sides at Gettysburg used the two most popular sabot systems, the expanding metal ring or band and a forcing cone. The Confederate Read projectile, or its northern version, the Parrott, was the most common round using the expanding metal ring system. The expanding metal ring sabot was attached to the base of the projectile. Upon firing, the sabot expanded into the grooves of the rifled bore.

There were shortcomings in the Parrott or Read shell's design, however. While they took the rifling 95 percent of the time, the brass rings often separated as they left the barrel, and their fragments threatened any troops forward of their guns. Another design flaw was the position of the sabot. The least efficient location for a sabot was at the projectile's base. This position was all right as long as the projectile was controlled while in the barrel by the *lands* that directed the body of the projectile out of the bore while the *grooves* imparted the spin. When the projectile was almost completely outside the barrel,

Shed metal-ring sabot. (GNMP/WDC)

10-pounder Parrott projectiles. Right example illustrates the expanding metal-ring sabot integrated into the body of the round. (GNMP/WDC)

however, the *lands* no longer controlled the body of the shell, and only the sabot at the base of the round was in contact with the bore. Some Parrott rifles had a gaining twist (variable twist rate) which often caused the projectile to fail in following the last turn of the rifling; the last rotating impulse was on the projectile's sabot, causing a wobbling effect. The unwanted motion programmed into the projectile accentuated the drift and caused it to tumble if the spin was insufficient. One method used to overcome this effect was to redesign the shape. By tapering the body of the projectile at the base of the round, like the Schenkl or Whitworth, it eliminated the last rotating impulse at this point.[30]

Another commonly used type of rifled ammunition, the Hotchkiss, improved on the efforts to eliminate the undesirable forces caused by a sabot located near the projectile's base. The Hotchkiss employed an expanding soft lead band or ring encircling the middle. When forced forward, the sabot sealed most of the gases and caught the rifled grooves. In this design, the sabot was closer to the projectile's center of gravity, transmitting the spinning motion at a more appropriate point, and greatly improved the projectile's stability in flight. Comparing the effect of propelling an object from its base and then from its center of gravity can be illustrated by holding a football at its widest point and throwing it to impart a spin and then throwing it from its narrowest point.

To diverge for a moment, Hotchkiss case shot rounds had an improved bursting ability over most of the other commonly used versions. The bursting charge, separated by an iron plate, was behind the case shot balls. Upon detonation, the powder's location forced the balls forward with increased velocity. In comparison, case shot balls, such as in Parrott and Schenkl rounds, encircled or were to the rear of the powder charge. The explosion forced most of the balls outward and some to the rear of the projectile, suppressing their forward velocity.[31]

Like Parrott or Read projectiles, Hotchkiss shells had the same problem shedding the expansion components on friendly troops. Henry Hunt discouraged their use and stated: "Hotchkiss is objected to by other troops, on account of the stripping of the lead band, which endangers skirmishers and other troops in front of the artillery . . . Schenkl ammunition is recommended."[32]

The concern over being injured from friendly fire by such debris was very real to the soldiers in front of the artillery. This anxiety was illustrated during the July 3 cannonade. Union General Oliver Howard, his safety threatened,

3-inch Hotchkiss shell showing groove necessary to transmit flame to the time fuse. (GNMP/WDC)

3-inch Hotchkiss case. (GNMP/WDC)

Three components of a Hotchkiss shell.
(AC)

143

Above and below: *Shed Hotchkiss sabots. Hotchkiss sabots frequently detached in flight endangering friendly troops forward of the gun.* (AC)

Artillery shell sabots (lead)

(WDC)

wrote: "During this artillery duel I had been watching the events, sitting in front of my batteries on the slope of Cemetery Hill. Feeling that my greatest danger came from the strippings of the shells as they flew over my head, I had cracker boxes piled behind us-affording protection from our own cannon."[33]

If the Hotchkiss's lead bands did not detach from the body of the projectile, they deformed to create a sound frightening enough to disturb the brave men awaiting the projectiles' fury. Confederate Private Alexander Hunter graphically described the impression of the Hotchkiss shell on the soldiers' minds at Sharpsburg:

> The shells begin to sail over us as we lay close behind the fence, shrieking its wild song, a canzonet of carnage and death. These missiles howled like demons, and made us cower in the smallest possible space, and wish we had each a little red cap in the fairy tale, which, by putting on our heads, would make us invisible. But what is that infernal noise that makes the bravest duck their heads? That is a "Hotchkiss" shell. Thank goodness, it busted far in the rear. It is no more destructive than some other projectile, but there is a great deal in mere sound to work on men's fears, and the moral effect of the Hotchkiss is powerful.
>
> The tremendous scream of this shell is caused by a ragged edge of lead which is left on the missile as it leaves the gun. In favorable position of light the phenomenon can sometimes be seen as you stand directly behind the gun of the clinging of the air to the ball. The missile seems to gather up the atmosphere and carry it along, as our globe carries its air through space. Men are frequently killed by the wind of a cannon ball.[34]

The James projectile, although little used at Gettysburg, also shed its sabot in leaving the gun. James ammunition looked quite different than conventional projectiles. Nicknamed the "wagon wheel" because of the unique shape of its base, James projectiles had a sheet of tin-lead composition covering the slots on its base. Upon firing, the propellant gas was forced through the hole in the base and through the slots on the sides, causing the sheet to expand into the rifled grooves to impart the spin. The sheet usually blew off in exiting the barrel and was not supposed to be fired over friendly troops. In flight, the James shell reportedly broadcast an identifiable screaming noise, caused by the rushing air through the slots exposed by the sheet blown off, and must have also unnerved those on the receiving end of it.[35]

Another common type of projectile was the Schenkl which used the forced cone system. Schenkl projectiles were designed with a papier-mâché sabot on

3.8-inch James shell with sabot. (GNMP/WDC)

3.8-inch James shell without sabot. (GNMP/WDC)

a conical base. Stability was improved with the design of their tapered base. In addition, the spin was imparted near their center of gravity and used a sabot that was safe. This projectile's design characteristics are described in Dickey and George's informative book, *Field Artillery Projectiles*:

> Upon firing, the sabot rode up the cone-shaped base and was crowded into the rifling, and on leaving the gun, was blown to bits. This was a great advantage when firing over the heads of friendly troops. Many accidents occurred when lead, brass, and copper sabots were torn off projectiles and fell in the midst of forward friendly troops. Its flight was true and silent with a center-of-gravity well ahead of the center of resistance. It flew like a well-feathered arrow and had the added aid of stability of rotation.
>
> The disadvantages were that the long taper of the lower half restricted the capacity of the bursting chamber. Also some sabots swelled in damp weather and the projectile refused to enter the bore . . . The contemporary ordnance experts were all of the same opinion as to the merits of the Schenkl—when it had a good sabot it was the best, but if the sabot was defective, it was terrible.[36]

Smoothbore technology was making way for rifle technology. Improved stability of the projectile's flight was fundamental if accuracy was to be achieved. When firing a projectile from a smoothbore barrel, the gunner's control over hitting the target was essentially limited to pointing the gun and firing it. Rifled barrels, on the other hand, stabilized the projectile. When the rifled grooves in the gun bore spun the projectile, a rotational force was imparted to keep the flight path straighter than smoothbore ammunition. This rotation caused the projectile to move in the direction of least resistance and corrected the cause of deviation by distibuting it unifomly aound the line of flight. The result was increased range and accuracy over smoothbore ammunition.

Rifled guns were made with a variety of rifled designs or twist rates. Each rifle design communicated its own characteristics into the projectile and affected the motion of its trajectory. The twist of the rifling needed to spin the projectile at sufficient rotational speed to stabilize its flight long enough to hit targets within the range for which the artillery piece was supposed to operate. The Whitworth's range, for example, exceeded five miles. This long range demanded an exceptionally faster spin rate than artillery pieces with lesser ranges. In order to hit targets that distant, a rapid rate of twist was needed to impart enough energy in the projectile's spin that would last during the projectile's lengthy flight. Otherwise, the round would tumble uncontrollably out of its intended path.

3-inch Schenkl case. (AC)

An exploded 3-inch Schenkl shell and fuse dug, almost in its entirety, from Cemetery Ridge. (GNMP/WDC)

With different degrees of twist among different models of cannons, the spin frequency of artillery projectiles varied. The twist rate of a 3-inch Ordnance rifle, for example, was one turn in eleven feet and the twist rate of a Federal Parrott was one turn in sixteen feet. In extreme contrast to these two examples, the spin rate of a Confederate 10-pounder Parrott barrel turned the projectile once in twenty-four feet, while the rifled grooves of a Whitworth barrel turned the projectile once every four and one-half feet—a marked difference. The Whitworth's remarkably rapid twist rate caused the round to spin over five times faster than that fired from the Parrott. Unlike most artillery projectiles, the Whitworth round itself contained rifled lands and grooves. This created positive traction by linking the projectile with the rifling of the bore and eliminated the necessity of a sabot. Consequently, Whitworth barrels could be made with a substantially greater twist than other rifled cannons whose sabots could not withstand the shock. Sir Joseph Whitworth conducted tests that spun his projectiles up to 60,000 rpm's.[37]

Consider the jolt on this projectile when it was suddenly transferred from the "at rest" state to its spinning motion. A Whitworth's muzzle velocity was 1,600 feet per second. This acceleration means that from the time the projectile moved from the rear to the front of the barrel it was traveling at 1,090 miles per hour. In order to move from its inert state to an instantaneous and rapid spin, the Whitworth projectile needed to grab the rifled bore to insure that it "took the grooves." Because of its rapid turning in flight, the Whitworth shell broadcast an easily identifiable sound signature, an unmistakable and chilling scream-like resonance. Major Osborn described the sound as a "sharp whistle" and "the sound of the long steel bolt used for a solid shot, as it passes through the air, is readily recognizable and distinguished from the reports of all other guns."[38]

Complicating matters for artillerymen was the fact that barrels were made with different directions of rifled twists. Most bores were made with a right-hand twist, but there were at least a few Confederate 3-inch Parrott rifles with a left-hand twist. The 2.6-inch Wiard rifle, not used at Gettysburg, had a left-hand twist. In addition, some barrels were made with a uniform twist rate, while others might have the variable gaining twist as mentioned above. A gaining twist started from its slowest rate at the rear of the bore and increased towards the muzzle. (Federal Parrot rifles used a gaining twist while the Confederate version of the Parrott probably did not.) This variability signifi-

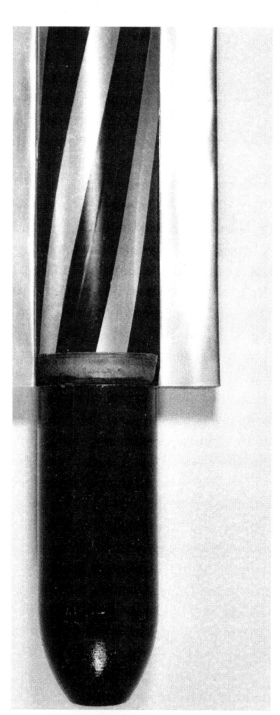 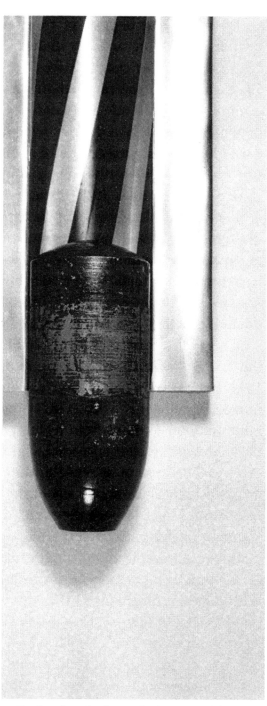

On leaving the bore, the last impulse on a Parrott projectile was at its base, causing a wobbling effect. (AC)

On leaving the bore, the last impulse on a Hotchkiss projectile was near the round's center-of-gravity, improving stability. (AC)

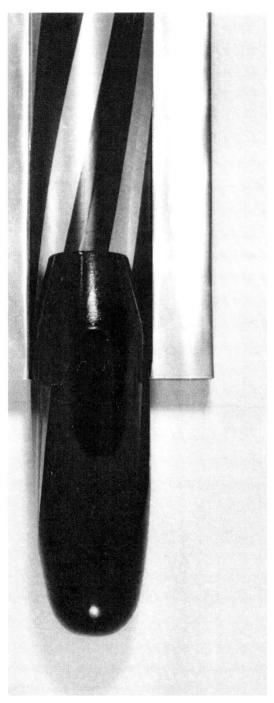

The tapered base of the Whitworth moved the projectile's last impulse closer to the round's center of gravity. (AC)

The tapered base of the Schenkl, combined with its papier-mâché sabot (not shown) crowding near its center of gravity, caused the projectile to fly "like a well-feathered arrow." (AC)

151

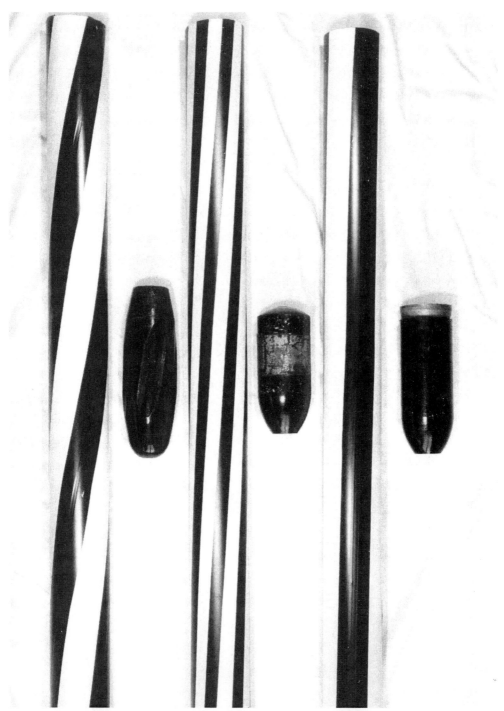

Variations in rifled twists: **Left:** *Twist rate of a Whitworth; one turn in 4½ feet.*
Center: *Twist rate of a 3-inch Ordnance gun; one turn in 11 feet.*
Right: *Twist rate of a Confederate Parrott; one turn in 24 feet.* (AC)

cantly complicated a gunner's skill in aiming when switching operations to different gun models. By 1863 the ideal design for the twist rate used in rifled cannon had not yet been determined.[39]

Incompatibility of ammunition between artillery pieces of different models and of the same caliber was another problem. Even though there were instances where various projectiles' diameters were the same, through experience it was soon learned that certain projectiles of a specific design performed best when fired from specific models of artillery pieces. The 3-inch bore models of the 10-pounder Parrott and the 10-pounder Ordnance rifle, for example, were of the same caliber. Although their different projectiles were, in a pinch, interchangeable, experience proved that Parrott ammunition was more suitable for the Parrott gun, and the Schenkl and Hotchkiss ammunition was more effective in the 3-inch Ordnance rifle. Eventually a directive was issued by Brigadier General George Ramsay, U. S. chief of ordnance, forbidding the use of Schenkl projectiles altogether in Parrotts. They could use only Parrott or Hotchkiss projectiles. Conversely, Parrott projectiles were forbidden to be used with 3-inch Ordnance rifles. This directive may have been due to the fact that many Federal Parrott projectiles had three prestamped projections in their wrought iron base cup which helped prevent breakage when expanded. Such projectiles were incompatible with the seven lands and grooves of the 3-inch Ordnance rifle.[40]

With improved projectile systems came additional problems interfering with the ones just solved. After Gettysburg, for example, the 2.9-inch Parrott rifle was discontinued for the 3-inch Parrott version. Ironically this change then matched the caliber of the 3-inch Ordnance rifle, but it did not solve the compatability problems and allow the interchange of ammunition between the two models. The rifling design of the bore determined if the projectile could withstand the propellant shock. The Federal 3-inch Parrott, for example, had only three lands and grooves (some Confederate Parrotts had twelve lands and grooves), but, as just mentioned, the Federal 3-inch Ordnance rifle had seven of each. More lands and grooves distributed the stress more evenly on the round, thereby reducing the shock upon it. The Hotchkiss projectile was unsuitable for firing from Federal Parrott rifles because of the bore's increased rate of twist. This gaining twist design imparted an extreme shock on the Hotchkiss's soft lead sabot. Sabots were often torn off the projectile because of the shock in transferring the spin to the body. Consequently, this projectile was used mainly with the 3-inch Ordnance rifle.[41]

Throughout the war, Parrott, Schenkl, and Hotchkiss ammunition established a somewhat mixed reputation in their performance—depending, of course, on the varied experiences of the artillery officers.

> Our ammunition, Parrott's (the percussion shell with Schenkl plungers), was all that could be desired. Of an average of 30 rounds to a gun I remember but two that did not explode.

> The Schenkl percussion and the Hotchkiss fuse shells worked to entire satisfaction.

> The Hotchkiss shell and case shot is the only variety of ammunition upon which I can rely.

> Many of the [Hotchkiss's percussion shell] failed to explode; from what cause, I am unable to say, as the fuses seemed to be perfect. The Schenkl ammunition, as far as I am able to judge, worked admirably.

> In accuracy, range, and certainty of flight and explosion, this gun (the 4½-inch rifled gun), when served with Schenkl projectiles (especially his percussion-shell) really leaves nothing to be desired. The [Schenkl] percussion shell was in this case, as I have always found it, true to its reputation. I want no better projectile in my chests.

> The wretched Schenkl stuff is throwing discredit on my gunners, and the Hotchkiss I will not use except as a last resort.

> The Dyer projectile [a shell employing a lead cup sabot designed for the 3-inch Ordnance rifle] has proved a failure whenever used, and the Hotchkiss projectile a complete success in every engagement, especially with the percussion-shells.[42]

In Union battle reports, the majority of observations favored the Schenkl percussion shell. Major General McClellan reported: "The Parrott ammunition heretofore furnished the 20-pounder Parrott guns sent to this army has proved unsatisfactory. The enemy thus far fire better than we can. The Schenkl ammunition we have had has, however, done well, and I consider it of the highest importance that a large quantity of that kind be sent here immediately."[43]

A great challenge to the ordnance department was standardizing its ammunition from the variety of projectiles available. Federal buyers for ammunition apparently favored the Hotchkiss over the Schenkl. Purchases made by the U.S. Ordnance department for 1862 showed the ratio of the projectiles:

Smoothbore ordnance	541,214
Parrott projectiles	270,699
Hotchkiss	203,888
Schenkl	108,115
All others	242,297[44]

For the Confederate side, E. P. Alexander evaluated the performance of Southern ammunition:

> [The projectile for the 3-inch Ordnance rifle] considerably resembled the heavy Parrot [sic] projectiles, and was the best field rifle shell the Confederates ever made, but was always liable to explode in the gun, to "tumble," or not to explode at all. The last defect was partially corrected by the use of "McAvoy's Fuse Igniter," a very simple and ingenious little contrivance attached to the fuse when loading, and later by fuses with strands of quickmatch for "priming." The first two defects were very serious and of very frequent occurrence, not only with the three inch rifles, but still more so with the Parrott guns. The "tumbling" was due to imperfect connection between the copper ring and the shell, which in its turn was due to the inferior quality of iron necessarily used (the best iron was saved for gun metal), to unskilled workmen, and to the fact that the demand greatly exceeded the supply, and even those which a careful inspection would have condemned were better than none.[45]

Even though recommendations allowed Parrott guns to use either Parrott or Hotchkiss ammunition and 3-inch Ordnance rifles were allowed to use either the Schenkl or Hotchkiss, artillery commanders still had to use caution to avoid mixing more than one approved brand type of ammunition within the unit. Gun crews had enough technical obstacles to overcome during operations, and firing ammunition of mixed brands would render a gun crews aiming ability worthless. Each type exhibited its own flight characteristics from the method used to impart the spin, each reacted differently to the rifling design of the bore, each had its unique aerodynamic shape and flight performance, and each had a different weight that affected its trajectory. John Craig, assistant adjutant general, Army of the Potomac, issued instructions which stated:

As both the Hotchkiss and Schenkl ammunition are provided, commanders of batteries can use either system, but in no case must two projectiles of the same kind be used in a battery. That is, no battery must have both Hotchkiss and Schenkl shell or both 'Hutch-kiss' and Schenkl shrapnel. They may have Hotchkiss shell and Schenkl shrapnel, or *vice versa*, but he recommends strongly that, unless they have a marked preference for special projectiles, all should be of one system, either Hotchkiss or Schenkl. He believes Schenkl to be best and safest in every respect.

The object of the latitude given to battery commanders is to make them responsible for the efficiency of their batteries. Ammunition to which men and officers are most accustomed is the best to supply them. There is an evil, however, in using two kinds of the same description in the same battery or in the same army corps, or even in the same army, but with two systems which have such strong supporters as the Schenkl and Hotchkiss, it can hardly be avoided without a worse evil.[46]

Because of a rifled barrel's impact on aiming accuracy, an additional physical force caused from the rotational motion of the projectile must also be mentioned. Inherent in this rotary motion was the unavoidable turning or twisting force on the object—torque. The projectiles of all rifled cannons were especially subjected to it. Torque caused the projectile to drift off course. The round would deviate in the direction in which it revolved which depended upon whether the cannon bore was rifled with a left-hand or right-hand twist. Artillerists, aware of drift, overcame this deviation by pointing to the left or right of the target. While the torque effect interfered with accuracy, the drift caused by it was predictable. The increased precision and range gained from spinning the rifled projectile far outweighed any side effects.[47]

Overall, the new technology of rifled guns and ammunition that was gradually replacing that of the smoothbore was underwhelming to some experts. E. P. Alexander later wrote: "The difficulties which beset the rifled guns and their ammunition were, however, even greater than those under which the smoothbores suffered so long, and they were never so nearly solved."[48]

Gunpowder

Gunpowder was produced in a variety of types according to its end use. Artillery gunpowder, used as a propellant, was different than the gunpowder used to explode the projectile and different than small-arms gunpowder. The power of the explosion was determined by grain size. Artillery gunpowder was large-grained and coarse, like cake. Large-grained powder provided less surface area than small-grained powder for exposure to oxygen and burning. Compared to small-arms powder then, the coarser powder burned slowly and in successive layers. Cannon barrels could not withstand the shock from an explosion that used small-grained powder. Artillery propellant needed a more gradual discharge of explosive energy than the finer-grained powder used in small-arms. Although artillery propellant was packed in large cartridges, its explosive power was substantially diminished. The powder itself inhibited the burning rate as it exploded. Slowing the burn rate reduced the instant conversion into gas that otherwise would rupture the barrel. Nevertheless, ignited powder expanded at a velocity of about 5,000 feet per second and a pressure of about 2,000 atmospheres.

Conversely, small-grained powder provided more surface area for exposure to oxygen and burning. Consequently, the smaller the grain, the more instantaneously it was converted to a gas and resulted in more explosive power. Small-arms ammunition needed this reaction. Soldiers firing shoulder-held or hand-held weapons had to be able to sustain the recoil effects of the powder charge and yet deliver a bullet to its intended target. In addition, small arms were made with light, thin-walled barrels and needed only a small powder charge to produce a sufficient explosion to propel the bullet and yet not injure the weapon.[49]

The size of an artillery propellant charge was dependent on the specific type of projectile and the barrel it was designed to be fired from. The *Artillerist's Manual* stated:

> With a given length of gun, and particular projectile, there is a maximum charge beyond which no increased velocity is obtained. This charge must be determined by experiment; though the charges used are generally less than the maximum, the rule generally laid down being, that as the velocity increases very slowly from a third of the weight of the shot up to the maximum, it is not advisable to use a greater charge than one-third, on account of the effect on the piece, the waste of powder, and the recoil. . . .
>
> The longer a gun is, the greater length of time is the projectile submitted to the accelerating action of the gases; but past a certain length, the shocks and friction experienced by the ball overcome its increase in velocity.[50]

Propellant charges for most guns at Gettysburg were as follows:

Gun	Weight of charge (in pounds)
12-pounder howitzer	1.00
24-pounder howitzer	2.00
12-pounder Napoleon	2.50
10-pounder Parrott	1.00
3-inch Ordnance rifle	1.00
20-pounder Parrott	2.00
12-pounder James	0.75
12-pounder Blakely	1.00
12-pounder Whitworth breechloader	1.75[51]

Projectile Fuses & Evaluation

Besides the accuracy needed in aiming artillery pieces, the effects of explosive ammunition upon enemy targets was most dependent on the reliability of the fuses. The state of the art for fuse technology was woefully short in applying it to the new projectiles being introduced. Little information existed on the subject of fuses. When the war began almost nothing had been done to improve on these seemingly uncomplicated components of a projectile. But any fuse not working as it was intended would nullify all the efforts made to transport and deliver the ammunition safely to the battery for use. Unreliable fuses negated all the careful preparations of artillerymen in loading the gun, aiming it, judging the ranges, and estimating the precise burn times for fuses to detonate the projectile. If fuse failure was a common occurrence, it could frustrate a gun crew's effort to take the necessary care to achieve accuracy, convey a sense of confidence upon the undamaged enemy, and as a result, inject important influences upon the outcome of a battle.

Most explosive ammunition was designed to use one of three common types of fuses: a time fuse to detonate the projectile and achieve an aerial burst, a percussion fuse to ignite on contact, or a combination of the two to insure detonation. Aerial bursts had the advantage of spreading fragments over a broader area with velocity. Explosive projectiles had comparatively small powder charges. In a 12-pounder case shot, for example, its bursting charge of 4.5 ounces was enough to break the casing and not, by itself, designed as a powerful discharge to kill soldiers. Velocity at the time of detonation therefore was an important part of inflicting damage. In contrast, projectiles exploding on contact could burrow into the ground and muffle the explosive force. The great advantage of contact detonation, however, was eliminating the problems associated with time fuses attaining proper aerial bursts.

Aerial bursts at the right place were difficult to accomplish. For one thing, the skills of the gunner in estimating the projectile's flight time to the optimum point of detonation had to be accurate. Furthermore, the time set for the fuse to ignite the bursting charge according to the burn time marked on the fuse and its actual burn time had to be precise. As an example, a gunner overestimating the flight time of a 12-pounder spherical case shot towards a target at a range of 1,100 yards by just a quarter of a second and a fuse that burned just a quarter of a second longer than its set time would have a half second error. The projectile, in this case, would fly more than one hundred yards past the intended detonation point before exploding.[52]

For time fuses in rifled projectiles, it was increasingly more difficult to estimate the correct fuse length in comparison to those used in smoothbore

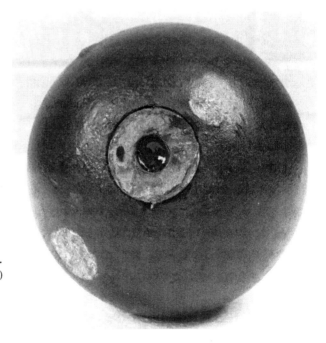

Confederate 12-pounder case.
(GNMP/WDC)

159

A 3-inch Hotchkiss shell (museum display) showing flame grooves which communicated fire to ignite the time fuse. (GNMP/WDC)

ammunition. Because of the increased velocity at which the rifled projectile reached its target, the margin for error was correspondingly increased. Judging and applying the correct time for a fuse in a rifled explosive projectile, therefore, demanded much greater precision.

For smoothbore guns, the explosive ammunition used was spherical case shot and spherical shell. Both types had a bursting charge to scatter the shell casing or, in case shot, its contents of lead or iron balls. Time fuses were the primary means for detonation of smoothbore projectiles. Rifled guns fired explosive shot and shell also. The majority of rifled explosive ammunition, discussed earlier, consisted of Parrott or Read projectiles, Hotchkiss, and Schenkl. This rifled ammunition could use either time fuses, percussion fuses, or combination fuses.

Time fuses were ignited from the flame of the propellant that passed through the windage gap that in most field pieces was about one-tenth of an inch; or, if a rifled projectile, the body of the round contained channels to transmit the flame forward to the tip. For smoothbore ammunition, the Bormann time fuse was the most common type used. It consisted of a soft metal disk on a threaded cylinder screwed into the shell. Most were marked with time graduated in quarter seconds up to a maximum of five and a quarter seconds. The fuse burn time was determined by cutting the thin metal at

12-pounder shell with Bormann time fuse.
(GNMP/WDC)

the appropriate mark and exposing the fuse powder which was ignited when the gun was fired. The Bormann fuse had an advantage over the cut-to-length paper time fuse. It could be inserted in the shell, ready for use, and remain there indefinitely and safe from detonation until the metal was cut to expose the powder train.

Ironically, 12-pounder Napoleons often fired at ranges beyond the maximum burning time of the Bormann fuse. When the Wright 12-second time fuse was introduced to the Federal army in 1864, First Lieutenant Edward Williston, 2nd U. S. Artillery, wrote to the ordnance department praising the dramatic results of the Napoleons when using the longer burning fuses:[53]

I find no difficulty in throwing these shells over 2,000 yards, which distance I consider to be nearly the limit of effective field fire. The superior effort of the light 12-pounder shell has always been noticed when compared with those of the 3-inch ordnance, 10-pounder Parrott, or any rifles of similar caliber. Consequently, by use of these fuzes we are enabled to demoralize troops hitherto outside our range and there-

Fuse punch for breaking into the Bormann fuse; Bormann fuse; Schenkl fuse wrench for setting metallic fuses into projectiles. (GNMP/WDC)

fore only exposed to a fire from rifles. Many instances could be cited wherein the use of these shells have produced a very unfortunate result and one which could not have been obtained with the 5-second Bormann now in service.[54]

Confederate artillerymen experienced continual difficulty with the Bormann fuse. E. P. Alexander described the problems:

When the war commenced a small amount of smoothbore ammunition was on hand in the Southern arsenals, which was of good quality and was used in the early affairs and issued to the batteries first put in the field. This ammunition was all put up with the Bormann fuse, and this fuse being adopted by the Confederate Ordnance Department, a factory was established for its manufacture. Large quantities of ammunition fitted with these fuses were sent to the field in the summer of 1861, and complaints of its bad quality were immediately made. Careful test being made of it, it was found that fully four fifths of the shell exploded prematurely, and very many of them in the gun. The machinery for their manufacture was overhauled, and a fresh supply made and sent to the field, where the old ones were removed and the new were substituted, but no improvements was discernible. The trouble was found to be in the hermetical sealing of the underside of the horse shoe channel containing the fuse composition. Although this was seemingly accomplished at the factory, the shock of the discharge would unseat the horse shoe shaped plug which closed this channel, and allow the flame from the composition to reach the charge of the shell without burning around to the magazine of the fuse. Attempts were made to correct the evil by the use of white lead, putty and leather under the fuse, and in the winter of 1861 these correctives were applied to every shell in the army with partial but not universal success. Repeated attempts were made to improve the manufacture, but they accomplished nothing, and until after the battle of Chancellorsville the Bormann fuse continued in use, and premature explosions of shell were so frequent that the artillery could only be used over the heads of the infantry with such danger and demoralization to the latter that it was seldom attempted. Earnest requests were made of the Ordnance Department to substitute for the Bormann fuse, the common paper fuses, to be cut to the required length and fixed on the field, as being not only more economical and more certain, but as allowing, what is often very desirable, a greater range than five seconds, which is the limit of the Bormann fuse. These requests, occurring from our own guns among the infantry in front during the battle of Fredericksburg were at length successful in accomplishing the substitution. The ammunition already on hand, however, had to be used up, and its imperfections affected the fire even as late as Gettysburg. The paper fuse was found to answer much better, and no further complaints of ammunition came from the smoothbores.[55]

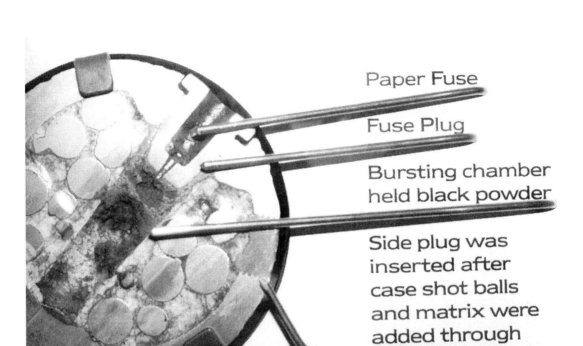

Paper Fuse

Fuse Plug

Bursting chamber
held black powder

Side plug was
inserted after
case shot balls
and matrix were
added through
this hole

Cross-section of a spherical case shot. (AC)

Left: *Fuse measure used to gauge fuse lengths.* Right: *Gunner's calipers measured time fuses, fuse plugs, diameter of rounds, and caliber of guns.* (GNMP/WDC)

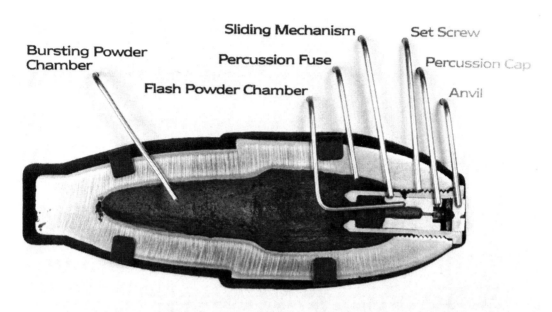

Bursting Powder Chamber

Flash Powder Chamber

Sliding Mechanism

Percussion Fuse

Set Screw

Percussion Cap

Anvil

3-inch Schenkl Shell with Percussion Fuse. Note that fuse is positioned for safe transporting of the shell. The anvil is turned away from the percussion cap and the set screw is in place.

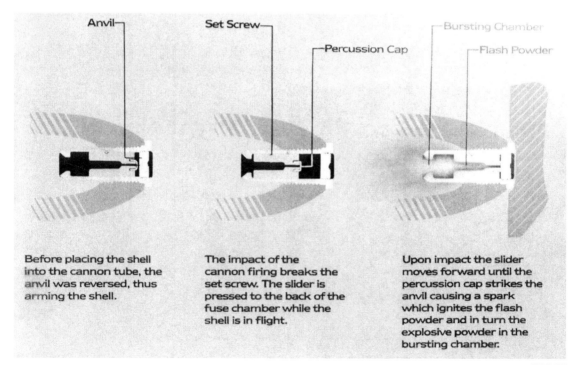

Anvil

Set Screw

Percussion Cap

Bursting Chamber

Flash Powder

Before placing the shell into the cannon tube, the anvil was reversed, thus arming the shell.

The impact of the cannon firing breaks the set screw. The slider is pressed to the back of the fuse chamber while the shell is in flight.

Upon impact the slider moves forward until the percussion cap strikes the anvil causing a spark which ignites the flash powder and in turn the explosive powder in the bursting chamber.

(GNMP)

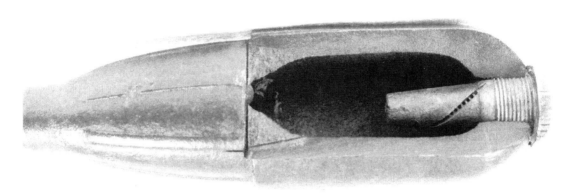

Cutaway Schenkl case with time fuse plug. (GNMP/WDC)

Besides the Bormann fuse, the above mentioned unsophisticated paper time fuses were used. The projectiles using paper time fuses held a threaded plug in which a cone-shaped paper fuse was inserted. This type was supplied with different burning times and could be modified to suit the range.

Another type of fuse, the percussion fuse, was designed with a plunger mechanism inside a fuse plug. On impact, the plunger detonated the musket cap and exploded the bursting charge. Percussion fuses worked better than time fuses in projectiles fired from rifled guns. With rifled projectiles the windage was restricted when the gun was fired and made it difficult for the transmission of the flame to the time fuse in the front of the projectile. Because the rotating rifled projectile was stable in flight, its tip remained aligned towards its target, allowing it to detonate on contact. In contrast, a round projectile's fuse alignment could not be controlled to face the enemy because of the projectile's random spin. One of the most successful impact fuses in the Federal army was the Schenkl percussion fuse, measuring an average effectiveness of 82 percent.[56]

The third type, the combination fuse, contained both an adjustable time fuse and plunger device. The combination fuse was self-igniting. This feature was essential if Schenkl shells or Schenkl case shot projectiles were used. The Schenkl's papier-mâché sabot was so effective in cutting off the propellant gas, no flame could communicate and ignite a time fuse in the nose. The combination fuse armed itself when the gun was fired. The backward force of the plunger ignited the preset time fuse. If the projectile landed before the fuse finished burning, the impact of the projectile smashed the burning fuse compound that transmitted its flame to the explosive powder charge. The Schenkl combination fuse, however, was considered undependable under combat conditions.

One other type of fuse, the concussion fuse, would be introduced after Gettysburg. It was designed to be used primarily for smoothbore ammunition and explode from the shock of it hitting an object. Since smoothbore projectiles could not be controlled to hit targets with their fuses being the point of contact, the concussion fuse was an alternative to the percussion fuse.[57]

The technology of newly introduced ammunition in the Civil War could have produced wondrous effects had it performed according to design. The flawed performance of ammunition, however, injected a considerable amount of uncertainty involving artillery operations. Defective fuses were reported to be a constant problem. Explosive projectiles detonated before they left the gun and burst the barrel. Some caused injury as they passed over friendly troops. Because of this problem, many Southern batteries were reduced to only using solid projectiles during the infantry advance on July 3, 1863.

Colonel E. P. Alexander compared the performance of Southern and Northern artillery and ammunition at Gettysburg: "The Confederacy did not have the facilities for much nice work of that sort, and we had to take what we could get without rigid inspection. How our rifled batteries always envied our friends in the opposition, their abundant supply of splendid ammunition! For an unreliable fuse or a rifle-shell which 'tumbles', sickens not only the gunner but the whole battery; more than 'misfires' at large game dishearten a sportsman. There is no encouragement to careful aiming when the ammunition fails, and the men feel handicapped."[58]

Bormann time fuse; Hotchkiss fuse plug; paper time fuse; and Parrott fuse plug. Paper time fuses were held in a variety of fuse plugs. (GNMP/WDC)

While Southern soldiers marveled at the splendid performance of Yankee ammunition, being on the receiving end of Northern missiles did not always divulge some of their shortcomings. Unreliable ammunition was not a problem exclusive to the Confederate army at Gettysburg. Federal cavalry brigade commander Colonel William Gamble mentioned: "I think it proper to state that our battery, under Lieutenant Heaton, Second U. S. Artillery, had the very worst kind of ammunition, and consequently could do but comparatively little execution. About one shell in twelve would explode, and then it would be prematurely, over the heads of our own men."[59]

The reliability of artillery fuses was a perpetual problem. Although the projectile might perform flawlessly towards its target, it needed to explode at a specific point to be effective. In fact, it was the fuse component of the explosive projectile that received most of the blame for bad ammunition and plagued both armies with unending frustration. A properly working fuse seemed to present the most difficulty in either perfecting or maintaining uniform quality among the arsenals that produced them.

The chief problems concerning time fuses were that they either did not ignite or their composition was so non-uniform that it was impossible to predict when they would burst the charge over a target. Federal Brigadier General Barry complained to the chief of ordnance: "The fuses most complained of are the paper-case time-fuse, though in many instances the Bormann fuse does not give the satisfaction we ought to expect. The paper-case fuses of short time-say up to seven or eight seconds-burn with proper regularity, but those of longer time are very uncertain; twelve seconds often burning no longer than five or six seconds, and fifteen or sixteen seconds frequently proving of shorter time than either. This happens so often that it has occurred to me that careless mistakes have been made in marking the time on the outside of the cases."[60]

At Gettysburg, Captain Hubert Dilger, 1st Ohio Light Artillery, reported:

In regard to the ammunition, I must say that I was completely dissatisfied with the results observed of the fuses for 12-pounder shells and spherical case, on the explosion of which, by the most careful preparation, you cannot depend. The shell fuses again, were remarkably less reliable than those of spherical case. The fuses for 3-inch ammunition caused a great many [premature] explosions [on] our right before the mouth of [nearby] guns, and it becomes very dangerous for another battery to advance [forward of them], which [the necessity] of advancing of smooth-bore batteries is of very great importance on the battlefield, and should be done without danger. I would, therefore, most respectfully recommend the use of percussion shells only.[61]

No type of fuse seemed to be free from defects. Lieutenant Elbert W. Fowler, 10th Wisconsin Battery, reported: "The fuses provided for 3-inch rifled guns I have found very defective, not over half of the shells exploding."

After the battle of Fredericksburg, Lieutenant Samuel Benjamin, 2nd U.S. Artillery, reported: "We threw 53 rounds of shell and shrapnel into a brook, they being unfit for use, having large flaws in their butts. I would respectfully call attention to the miserable quality of the ammunition I was supplied with. The time fuses (paper fuses) in the majority of cases did not ignite. Many of the Schenkl percussion shell upset, and some broke in the gun, while many of them failed to burst in striking. Many of the Parrott shells and shrapnel broke in the guns or exploded near the muzzles."[62]

Also at Fredericksburg, Captain James Smith, Fourth New York Battery, reported: "The ammunition furnished me by Captain Young, ordnance officer of Sickles' division, was of an inferior quality. The concussion projectiles (Parrott) were used as solid shot; the case shot worked poorly. About one in twelve exploded, although care was taken to prepare and fit the fuses. The cartridges were composed of different kinds of powder or of various quantities, which made accuracy almost impossible."[63]

Although fuses were blamed for many premature explosions in shells, they were not necessarily the cause. Gunpowder exploded at about six hundred degrees and when it was struck a violent blow with a hard substance. General Gibbon observed, "It is more than probable that many premature explosions of shells, and more especially of spherical-case shot, in the bore of guns, are due to this fact [of explosive shock], instead of to the driving in of the fuze, as has been sometimes supposed."[64]

E. P. Alexander later evaluated the unpredictable results of Southern explosive ammunition and also looked beyond the fuse as the main cause of premature explosions:

The causes of the premature exposition [sic] were never fully understood. They were generally attributed to defects in the casting, which either allowed the flame of the discharge to enter the shell, or by weakening the shell caused it to crush under the shock of the discharge and the "twist" given by the grooves of the gun.

As a single illustration of the extent to which these defects of the Parrott projectiles sometimes went: at the siege of Knoxville, Captain Parker's battery of four captured Parrott rifles fired one hundred and twenty shell at the enemy's batteries and pontoon bridge, of which only two failed to "tumble," or to burst prematurely.[65]

Whatever the reason for frequent premature explosions, it was too risky for batteries to fire their cannons over their own infantrymen as they moved forward. Infantry knew that hazard all too well and, on occasion, threatened to fire at their own artillerymen if they opened up over their heads. Firing solid shot was safe, but it could rile the troops in front of their artillery just as easily as other projectiles. E. P. Alexander knew that "solid shot could be safely so used, but that is the least effective ammunition, & the infantry would not know the difference [between shot, shell and shrapnel] & would be demoralized & angry all the same."[66]

Some of the difficulty with fuses originated from sources other than the manufacturers. Care in handling during transportation, fuse preparation in battle, and even weather conditions would cause different reactions. Union Colonel Charles Wainwright, chief of artillery, First Corps, reported:

> I would submit the following observations in regard to the 3-inch projectiles. The Schenkl common fuse worked well, but can only be used within 2,500 yards. The head of the fuse was found in some cases to stick in the hollow at the end of the rammer, and the shot displaced after being sent home, causing it to fail in taking the grooves. The Hotchkiss shell and shrapnel did well, but the paper fuses were far from certain. This was doubtless partly owing to the dampness of the atmosphere and the powder in the fuse-head having got more or less rubbed off by abrasion in the chests. Both these difficulties are removed by the new mode of putting up fuses, I notice, in some of these issued since our return.[67]

The use of time fuses was discouraged in a circular issued by the Army of the Potomac in March 1864: "There is scarcely any occasion on which the percussion-fuse is not superior to the time-fuse shell. It would be a good rule to use only the percussion. Every effort is now being made to provide a concussion shell for the light 12-pounder to supersede the time-fuse."[68]

Attempts made with suppliers to improve the performance of ammunition were ongoing but finding solutions proved difficult. Richmond, for example, was getting mixed signals in the level of quality encountered in the field and the frustration was apparent. Colonel Josiah Gorgas, C.S.A. chief of ordnance, grumbled:

> Officers are always ready to praise when they succeed and to blame when they fail. Colonel Cabell, of the artillery, at Fredericksburg, complimented our ammunition yesterday. Every effort is constantly made to overcome the many obstacles we have had to contend with in the production of the laboratory, and I am quite as much inclined to blame General Jones' artillerists, as he is to blame my ammunition. Without wishing to detract from his skill as an officer, I may be allowed to state that he is known to be very apt to find fault. His depreciation of the ammunition is, however, taken in good part, and will only stimulate the endeavor to improve where there is still much room for improvement.[69]

During the war, efforts were made to record the performance of ammunition, but an army on the move, such as in the Gettysburg campaign, made it difficult to collect such information. If time permitted, detailed observations were made and lengthy reports prepared. Artillery officers described their battery's participation, its effectiveness, the numbers of specific projectiles fired, angles of elevation used, and other details related to its performance. Records were maintained on the number of rounds fired by each piece and a critique made on the performance of various projectiles and fuses. In the Richmond campaign of 1864, for example, Colonel Henry Abbot, commanding the Federal siege train noted:

> The great problem, what is practically the best projectile for rifled artillery, has been carefully investigated during this campaign, both by requiring full reports of our own firing and by carefully collecting all varieties of projectiles fired by the rebels in return. Drawings of this collection and of our own projectiles have been kindly photographed for me by Major Michler, chief engineer, Army of the Potomac . . . The collection itself has been sent to the military museum at West Point. The following facts as to the rebel projectiles are worthy of notice. Their variety is very great, forty-five kinds being shown in the photograph, while three more have been since secured. They may, however, be classified into eight systems, according to the devices for making them take the grooves. . . . The specimen (No. 33, Plate II) is one of Mr. Schenkl's old model 30-pounder projectiles, which may possibly have been received from our batteries and fired back. It, however, has the characteristic copper fuse plug of the

rebels, and they evidently must have made a sabot for it, of what material is not known.[70]

Correcting any imperfections of unreliable ammunition was aggravated by vague feedback from the field. Lack of detail slowed the ability to correct problems and focus on what caused them. Brigadier General J. J. Pettigrew, C.S.A., evidenced this problem in a report to the inspector general:

> . . . The subject of fuses has constantly received the anxious attention of the Ordnance Department . . . All representations from the field receive prompt notice, and when any imperfection is suggested it is remedied as soon as possible. Whenever any imperfection is discovered, intelligent information is required, in order to correct the defect. This has not been furnished from Charleston, although repeatedly applied for. Not even the remote cause of imperfection has been indicated.
>
> A competent officer, on special service at Charleston, writes: "I have already examined the subject of fuses, and have reported to General Beauregard all that I could ascertain. The complaints of officers are so indefinite-merely saying that the fuses were 'bad,' without any specification-that little could be learned from them. My own opinion, after careful examination and testing of various fuses, is that the fault is with the officer and not with the fuse."
>
> What is really wanted is a more intelligent use by artillery officers of the best resources at present commanded by the Ordnance Department, and a hearty cooperation in pointing out and correcting defects in ammunition or arms.[71]

Weeks before Gettysburg, Colonel Josiah Gorgas reflected on the progress made regarding poor ammunition. Included in his report to Secretary of War James Seddon was an officer's excerpt from the field which stated: "I remark generally that everything connected with ordnance operations have as far as I can learn gone off admirably; artillery officers speak of great improvement in our projectiles and ammunition. Complaints are made of the 20-pounder Parrott shells; many of them, from defects in the castings, burst near the muzzle of the gun. The Whitworth shells, fabricated at Richmond, are a decided success; they did admirable execution."[72]

Complaints were made on just about anything pertaining to operating a gun. Lieutenant Fontaine, C.S.A., reported that "the friction primers were very defective from improper filling, and also from the top part not being properly closed." Reports were made stating that Confederate fuses could not be used with "Yankee ammunition." Another complained: "The artillery ammunition lately received from Richmond is packed in such miserably weak boxes that they are always bursting and, in consequence, several boxes have been so much damaged as to render the ammunition entirely unserviceable. Besides, there is great danger of explosion in the wagons from the loose powder."[73]

Every component necessary to fire an artillery piece seemed to interfere with the conscientious gun crews operating their pieces. It is surprising artillerymen did not abandon their unit to join the infantry.

Ammunition Supply at Gettysburg

The inventory that made up the huge supply of ammunition in both armies consisted of an enormous variety of projectiles to match the different caliber and model of artillery pieces. The Army of Northern Virginia's mixed gun batteries were, as mentioned earlier, complicated enough, but in addition Confederate artillerymen also had to contend with calibers which were only slightly different. Their Parrott rifles at Gettysburg, for example, had either a 2.9-inch bore or the newer 3-inch caliber. Unless care was taken, similar projectiles were mixed in the same battery and caused some guns to be put out of action.

Several Confederate batteries experienced problems at Gettysburg associated with ammunition incompatible with the gun. Lieutenant Osborne, Carter's battalion, reported that "some of the 3-inch Parrott ammunition was issued to him for the 2.9-inch Parrott ammunition." Lieutenant Selden, Dance's battalion, reported the same. Lieutenant Fontaine, Jones's battalion, complained that "the ammunition of the 3-inch (banded) gun, or Navy Parrott, is mixed up with the 2.9-inch 10-pounder Parrott in such a way as to cause great inconvenience. Two guns were rendered unserviceable after firing 12 rounds from the shell lodging in the bore." The shell, being too large and impossible to force home, lodged halfway down the barrel rendering the gun useless; artillery projectiles made of rigid cast iron could not be forced into the grooves of a gun barrel like the soft leaden ball used with small-arms.[74]

In addition, there was an assortment of projectiles available to choose for each artillery piece—shot, shell, case shot, and canister. When resupplying their limbers and caissons, artillerymen had to seek out the ordnance wagons that contained the specific kind and caliber of ammunition. To ease the complex chore of resupplying batteries, visual aids were used to quickly identify where specific ammunition could be retrieved. In August 1862, the Army of the Potomac's General Order No. 152 described the method to locate ammunition stored in the reserve trains: "Ammunition wagons will be distinguished by a horizontal stripe, 6 inches wide, painted on each side of the cover—for artillery ammunition, red; for cavalry, yellow; for infantry, light blue. The wagons will also be distinctly marked with the number of the corps and division to which they belong and the kind and caliber of ammunition contained."[75]

A problem, borne from using different types of ammunition, was the complicated task of keeping track of inventory levels to replace specific projectiles for the ordnance wagons in battle and the supply depots.

The total estimated consumption of ammunition at the battle of Gettysburg was 569 tons—all of it, plus an even greater amount that was not fired, was carted in by wagon or in the ammunition chests of the batteries. The planned ammunition inventory accompanying the Army of the Potomac averaged 250 rounds per gun. In addition to this amount, General Hunt had organized another special ammunition train containing an extra twenty rounds per gun above and beyond the authorized amount. The train's purpose was to cover any contingencies that Hunt expected to encounter. Although carrying close to 100,000 rounds of artillery ammunition for one army seemed extravagant, this amount was significantly less than previously recommended. At the beginning of the war it was proposed that "the amount of ammunition to accompany the field batteries was not to be less than 400 rounds per gun." Just after Gettysburg, the Army of the Potomac arrived at a seemingly scientific formula for its reserve ammunition supply. General Order No. 100 written in November 1863 stated:[76]

> For artillery ammunition trains, the number of wagons will be determined and assigned upon the following rules: Multiply the number of 12-pounder guns by 122 and divide by 112; multiply the number of rifled guns by 50 and divide by 140; multiply the number of 20-pounder guns by 2; multiply the number of 4½-inch guns by 2½; multiply the number of rifled guns in horse batteries by 100 and divide by 140. For the general supply train of reserve ammunition of 20 rounds to each gun in the army, to be kept habitually with Artillery Reserve, the following formula will apply: Multiply the number of 12-pounder guns by 20, divide by 112=number of wagons; multiply the number of rifled guns by 20, divide by 140=number of wagons. To every 1,000 men, cavalry and infantry, for small-arm ammunition, 5 wagons; for Artillery Reserve, for carrying fuses, primers, and powder, 2 wagons.[77]

Ammunition, transported in the wagon train, was packed in wooden boxes marked for easy identification. (GNMP/WDC)

General Hunt's inventory planning turned out to be more than adequate for the battle of Gettysburg. Excluding the horse artillery's forty-four 3-inch rifles, his 320 guns used 32,781 rounds. On average then, only 102 Federal rounds per gun were either fired or lost in exploding caissons and limbers. A number of Federal batteries expended ammunition far beyond the average consumption of 102 rounds each; Cooper's battery, for example, averaged 175 rounds, Ricketts's battery, 200 rounds, and Reynolds's battery used an impressive 215 rounds. At Gettysburg, some Southern batteries were worked as hard as Federal batteries. Captain C. W. Fry's battery, Carter's battalion, used an average of 220 rounds per gun; Major Pegram's battalion of twenty guns averaged 190 rounds, 2,500 rounds more than any other battalion in the Third Corps. Considering ammunition expended, the Army of the Potomac could have re-fought the battle of Gettysburg almost two more times with the unfired ammunition still on hand. Meade used only about one-third of his total inventory available, leaving more than 60,000 projectiles for future use.[78]

Although General Meade's overabundance of artillery ammunition was scattered at different places with his army, most of it was not instantly available. The immediate ammunition needs of the batteries were packed in the limbers and caissons that accompanied the artillery pieces or in supply wagons attending them. The bulk of the Army of the Potomac's reserve ammunition supply was located twenty-five miles away in Westminster, Maryland. This supply's remoteness from the main body of the Federal army provided safety from the enemy and prevented this massive collection of slow-moving vehicles from interfering with its own troop movements, hurrying to the front on the already jammed and narrow roads.

When ammunition trains did move with the army, they usually moved slower than infantry and arrived after the battle was underway. When artillery units exhausted their immediate supply and could not draw ammunition from their trains, they typically borrowed from others. At Gettysburg, for example, the Third Corps left its entire ammunition train behind as it raced onto the battlefield. To make do, it was supplied by the artillery reserve. The First Corps batteries replenished from the Eleventh Corps; when the Eleventh ran out, it replenished from the train of the artillery reserve. The Second Corps used the reserve as well. Brigadier General Tyler spoke of its importance at

Ammunition box loaded with fragmented Schenkl shells. (GNMP/WDC)

Ammunition box for ten rounds.
(GNMP/WDC)

Gettysburg: "Lieutenant Gillette, First Connecticut Artillery, ordnance officer of this command, was engaged the entire night [July 2nd] in issuing ammunition to the batteries of the several corps, as well as those of the Artillery Reserve. Seventy wagons were unloaded, which were sent to the rear on the morning of the 3d . . . 10,090 rounds were issued to batteries outside of the reserve during the battle. [A total of 19,189 rounds were issued from the Reserve at Gettysburg which left only 4,694 more projectiles remaining in its inventory.]" Almost 30 percent of Federal ammunition expended at Gettysburg was issued from the artillery reserve. This valuable organization covered shortages while additional ammunition from Westminster was moved to the front.[79]

The supply of ammunition for the Army of Northern Virginia at Gettysburg was significantly less than the Federals. Each gun carried into Pennsylvania about 125 rounds in their limbers and caisson. With the additional amount carried in the ordnance reserve wagons, Colonel E. P. Alexander estimated the total amount to be "about 200 rounds per gun."

Lee had to bring enough ammunition to carry out his plans. His blueprint for the invasion did not include participating in a major battle so far from his base of supply, nor could he anticipate fighting one with such intensity. Once the battle began and Lee chose to operate as an offensive force, the inventory level of his artillery ammunition dwindled rapidly. Offensive tactics called for artillery bombardments as a prelude to an infantry assault. Such activity habitually used more ammunition than the defenders who had the option to observe and choose the right moment to reply. For artillery to do its job in an offensive, however, it had to prepare the way for the infantry. It had to damage the enemy by throwing iron at it, and lots of it. Ammunition could not be squandered in such situations.

As both armies' inventory levels of ammunition were reduced, this diminished condition played an increasingly greater role in influencing commanders' decisions in how to fight. Ammunition shortages forcibly restrained the artillery's participation in battle. Generals imposed conservation measures including the duration of bombardments, what targets to aim for and which to ignore, and when to disengage from the fight.

Resupplying ammunition for Lee's army during the battle of Gettysburg was difficult due to the fact it was operating in enemy territory. Protecting ammunition trains from roving enemy cavalry or militia units, or even citizens, required a heavy escort. The Army of Northern Virginia was without access to railroad transportation in the North, and Lee was a great distance from his ammunition source—Staunton, Virginia, one hundred fifty miles south. Unless the Army of Northern Virginia could boost its supply with captured ammunition, Lee would not only have to win the battle with what was carried with him but he also needed to protect the army during the withdrawal into Virginia with what remained.

Also, some ammunition Lee brought along was of little use at Gettysburg. Canister, for example, was used by the Army of Northern Virginia very little during the battle. Short-range canister was used mostly on the defensive and the Confederate army's moves were almost entirely offensive. While records on the Confederate expenditures of ammunition are incomplete, A.P. Hill's Third Corps, for example, reported using 7,112 rounds—none of it canister.

As the Confederate army retired from Gettysburg, its reserve wagons were almost empty except for canister. The supply of ammunition they carried back was estimated to be enough for only one more day's good fight.[80]

Federal gun drill. (MCMOLL/USAMHI/WDC)

VI

Artillery Operations

Tactics

Overview

Assessing the role that artillery played at Gettysburg, requires a brief review of the guidelines in which it was to be employed. Artillery tactics consisted of three main principles: surprise or concealment, economy of force, and concentration of strength.[1]

Instruction for Field Artillery stated artillery's principle objectives thus: "Field artillery is used to attack and defend the works of temporary fortification; to destroy or demolish material obstacles and means of cover, and thus prepare the way for the success of other arms; to act upon the field of battle; to break an enemy's line to prevent him from forming; to crush his masses; to dismount his batteries; to follow and support in a pursuit, and to cover and protect a retreat."[2]

For artillery to be used properly in achieving its objectives, infantry commanders controlling artillery batteries scattered throughout their assigned infantry front, either had to be familiar with its principles and capabilities or rely on their designated artillery officers to employ the guns to gain the best advantage. Commanders unversed in artillery's applications, wielding the brute force of artillery's firepower without purpose, could waste this important resource.

Overall, artillery's role was most effective on a much smaller scale than the grand cannonade on July 3, 1863. Participating in lesser gun duels was easier to set up and manage and simpler to coordinate firepower. Smaller cannonades also created less smoke to interfere with aiming and, consequently, this reduced level of activity produced more conclusive results. Grand cannonades were certainly a spectacle but they were often a waste of ammunition. Massive gunfire produced not only the problem of too much smoke, but complicated "reading the battle" because of the great noise generated from the reports of the artillery fire and the detonations of the explosive ammunition. The intense sound was not only deafening but deceptive. Noise measured the intensity of a battle, but it was not indicative of the damage sustained. And usually the damaging physical effects of grand cannonades, firing at long ranges, were not a determining element in the outcome of the action.

Artillery tactics were employed to accomplish objectives beyond the obvious desire of commanders to cause physical damage to the enemy. Artillery fire, in fact, was not always physically effective, and compared to twentieth century warfare it was disappointing. Estimated casualty rates from artillery fire during the Civil War vary but most do not exceed 10 percent of total battle casualties. World Wars I and II, and Korea, however, saw casualty rates soar close to 75 percent from artillery or mortar fire.

Despite the comparatively modest physical effects of firepower in the Civil War, artillery possessed a powerful intangible quality that could not be quantified. Ever since the introduction of massed guns to conduct grand cannonades, the use of artillery firepower was one of the best means of eroding the enemy's strength, lowering morale, and disuniting enemy troops.[3]

Commanders knew the psychological value of artillery and used it to create or intensify the enemy's lack of confidence and sap its will to fight. This fear-producing value caused by artillery fire was important enough to be included in the instructions on the *Table of Fire*, as mentioned earlier, in the use of shell "to produce a moral rather than a physical effect." Artillery fire could also destroy the invincible feeling held by an overconfident enemy readying itself for an attack. A sense of arrogance or superiority, for example, felt by soldiers and their leaders that originated from a string of victories could, on one hand, cause commanders to take chances not ordinarily feasible. An enemy, flushed with overconfidence, could attempt to overcome enormous odds, forgetful that it was taking careless risks in the process, which could cause the deaths of more soldiers than necessary on both sides and without any positive results. It was best to remind aggressive enemy troops of their mortality by subjecting them to a damaging artillery barrage lest they make any foolish moves that helped neither side. It was safer to avert the enemy's attempt against enormous odds, which sometimes proved successful. A well-planned, prolonged, and mentally damaging cannonade could easily deflate the enemy's mental toughness and fighting spirit. With little or no damage inflicted, artillery fire could, on occasion, break an attack even before it began, just from its psychological effects.[4]

Cannonades then, besides any physical advantages, were an important psychological force in rearranging the odds of winning a battle. Heavy bombardments forced the enemy to take cover or stopped its aggressive action altogether. On the other hand, a cannonade could also cause the undesirable effect of preventing the enemy from fleeing the attack point. During the cannonade at Gettysburg on July 3, for example, the overshots from Confederate guns ironically kept more men on the front than usual. Any smart soldier with a strong sense of survival could easily see it was safer to stay put near the front, thereby discouraging any weak-willed soldier from going to the deadly zone behind the ridge in an attempt to seek relief.

The psychological suffering created from cannonades stemmed from the limited options enemy troops could take to remedy their situation. An infantry force made immovable by artillery fire was deprived of coping with its situation in a direct manner. The most difficult thing in combat was "to be afraid and sit still." Many World War II veterans testified that the harshest, fear-producing experience they endured in combat was their immobilization for hours or days from artillery or mortar fire. A passage in *The American Soldier, Combat and its Aftermath* succinctly described experiencing the whirlpool of combat: "War is a special province of chance, and the gods of luck rise to full stature on the field of battle. Uncertainty and confusion are inseparable from combat: 'Every action . . . only produces a counteraction on the enemy's part, and the thousands of interlocking actions throw up millions of little frictions, accidents and chances, from which there emanates an all-embracing fog of uncertainty . . . the unknown is the first-born son of combat and uncertainty is its other self.'"[5]

First Lieutenant Smith, 136th New York Infantry, recollected his men's discomfort during the July 3 cannonade: "All this time our nerves were strung to the highest pitch; water ran from every pore in the skin like squeezing a wet sponge, and our clothes were wringing wet. It was nature's provision for our safety, as it prevented total collapse of the nervous system, and the mind from going out in darkness."[6]

Methods were tried in order to cope with this terrorizing predicament. Under artillery fire at Fredericksburg, for example, Colonel Henry Morrow, 24th Michigan Infantry, realized his men were suffering under an intolerable situation. In their first battle, their movements were restricted and they were unable to fight back. Morrow sought to relieve the tension by bringing his regiment to attention and drilling them in the manual of arms. At Gettysburg, during the cannonade of July 3, to divert the minds of his troops' helpless predicament, Union Brigadier General Alexander Hays, Second Corps, suddenly appeared and ordered his men to gather all the abandoned muskets, clean them, and load them for use. When the Confederate infantrymen were approaching the Emmitsburg Road, Hays drilled some of his troops, in the manual of arms to subdue their natural instincts of survival which would soon react to the imminent realities they were about to experience.[7]

Infantrymen, under sustained artillery fire, felt helpless to respond; they became particularly uneasy if artillery fire was landing in their flanks or rear, even though the damage was insignificant. Colonel Archibald L. McDougall, 123rd New York Infantry, commanding the 1st Brigade, described the pounding his men endured on July 3: "My command for several hours was under the range of the artillery of the enemy, covering us with an enfilading fire, shells and solid shot passing through and crushing the tops of trees over our heads and falling within and on both sides of our works. The command bore this dangerous fire with commendable coolness."[8]

Cannonades sapped the resolve that kept the troops manning the front line, responsive to their officers, and it shook their confidence in winning. The constant pounding of the line and viewing the mounting casualties in the ranks from enemy artillery wore away soldiers' collective spirit and determination.[9]

Any soldier who was on the receiving end of an artillery projectile and witnessed its shocking effects recognized artillery's deterrent potential. At Fort Harrison near Richmond, for example, Federal Brigadier General Edward H. Ripley was observing immediately behind an artilleryman when he was unexpectedly "dashed in the face with a hot steaming mass of something horrible" that covered his eyes and filled his nose and mouth. "I thought my head had gone certainly this time," Ripley later stated. "A staff officer happened to have a towel with which he cleaned away the disgusting mass from my face and opened my eyes; unbuttoning my sabre belt and throwing open my blouse, I threw out a mass of brains, skull, hair and blood. As I opened my eyes the headless trunk of the artilleryman lay between my feet with the blood gurgling out."[10]

While artillery could instill fear in enemy soldiers, it also inspired confidence in the men that the cannons were defending. Batteries interspersed down a battle line maintained a protective feeling for infantry soldiers, particularly inexperienced ones. The presence of large numbers of artillery pieces in a battle line was a welcome psychological relief for soldiers, and they gained enormous encouragement from it. At the beginning of the war, for example, Union General Irvin McDowell wanted more artillery in his unskilled army to instill confidence in his troops. General Sherman said later: "In the early stages of the war the field guns often bore the proportion of six to a thousand men; but toward the close of the war, one gun, or at most two, to a thousand men was deemed enough."[11]

Soldiers liked the sound of their artillery. The confidence-building intangible value produced by their own guns was called upon on more than one occasion at Gettysburg. From Little Round Top on July 2, Lieutenant Charles Hazlett's Federal guns opened on the Confederates even though he knew the barrels could not be depressed enough on the steep slope to damage the enemy troops approaching its heights.

Another instance, mentioned earlier, was General Hancock's depletion of his long-range artillery ammunition during the cannonade on July 3 to reassure his waiting infantry. He was willing to trade his firepower and cause a temporary loss of it later, for the immediate benefit of boosting the confidence and steadfastness of his men. Artillery then, did not have to inflict damage or win battles to perform its duty, but rather could keep the enemy away, inspire troops, and provide a counterbalance to the enemy's guns.[12]

Combat did, however, occasionally create ambivalent feelings between infantrymen and their own artillery. During cannonades, infantry troops on one hand depended on the return fire of their guns to destroy the enemy or at least create the illusion that something was being done to counter the situation. But on the other hand, when positioned near their guns, this arrangement created a jarring uneasiness—and for good reasons. Working in front of or near friendly guns was a dangerous proposition. At Gettysburg on July 3, for example, Federal guns blasted into the backs of their own infantry near Culp's Hill, killing and wounding a number of them. Colonel James L. Selfridge, 46th Pennsylvania Infantry, threatened to shoot a battery commander with his pistol if their artillery rounds continued to fall short.

First Lieutenant L. A. Smith, 136th New York Infantry, also recollected the discomfort created in his unit from nearby friendly batteries during the cannonade of July 3:

> It is a terrible experience to support batteries when located in their front . . . I don't believe men ever suffered more in the same time than those who lay along the [Taneytown] road in front of the cemetery on that memorable day . . . In spite of all a soldier's ingenuity in adjusting himself to the situation there was no relief; the last condition was always worse than the preceding. If you laid down on the ground and put your fingers in your ears you got, in addition to the crash in the air, the full effect of the earth's tremor and its additional force as a conductor.
>
> One of our men found afterwards that his teeth were loose and within a few days nearly all of them dropped out. If you rolled over on your back and looked up into the heavens fairly black with missiles exploding continually and sending their broken fragments in every direction, the situation was not more assuring.
>
> If you sat down with your back to the stone wall and looked over into the cemetery, you saw long fiery tongues leading toward you, thick clouds of sulphurous smoke settle down around you, blackening the countenance almost beyond recognition.
>
> If you turned around and looked over the wall toward the enemy each cannon ball seemed directed toward that particular spot.[13]

Premature explosions of ammunition and shed metal sabots also added to infantrymen's discomfort and endangered any troops in front of the cannons. Even more of a concern to soldiers was that their own artillery attracted the fury of enemy fire, threatening anyone nearby. Poor aiming from an enemy battery could easily land a round unintentionally into a crowd of infantrymen.

★ ★ ★

To summarize, some of artillery's greatest tasks in battle resulted in the least notice or glory. Artillery inspired confidence in soldiers to withstand the onslaught of the enemy, promoted inaction by creating reluctance upon the enemy to move against it, and it delayed enemy action or prevented it from taking place altogether. By artillery's very presence, it kept the enemy at bay. Even if no shots were fired, artillery was a great psychological comfort for the defenders and it instilled terror in the attackers. Battle plans were not made without considering the effects of artillery.

Offensive Tactics

Tactically, artillery was called on to be used both offensively and defensively. Used offensively, and prior to an infantry attack, the artillery would typically bombard the enemy lines to disable their guns, cause the defending artillery to use up its ammunition supply, and hopefully instill fear in the troops waiting to receive the assailants. Much of the success of the infantry phase of Pickett's Charge on July 3, for example, depended on an artillery cannonade to soften up the enemy's defenses by reducing the Union's killing power, terrorize the defenders, and hopefully pave the way before the Confederate infantry went forward. The responsibility for unleashing this massive firepower fell upon Colonel E. P. Alexander. He stated in no uncertain terms what his objectives were: "My orders were as follows. First, to give the enemy the most effective cannonade possible. It was not meant simply to make noise, but to try & cripple him—to tear him limbless, as it were, if possible. Note [sic] Gen. Longstreet's expression in a note, . . . [was to] 'drive off the enemy or greatly demoralize him.' When the artillery had accomplished that, the column of infantry was to charge. And then, further, I was to 'advance such artillery as you can use in aiding the attack.'"[14]

Offensively, artillery was an important force in securing success when combined with infantry operations. When the infantry troops began an assault, for example, the offensive artillerymen then attempted to entice the defensive artillery fire away from the attacking infantrymen so they could pass unharmed. Such was the case on July 3 when Lieutenant Colonel Thomas Carter's Confederate artillery tried to divert the fire away from its advancing infantry when his ten rifled guns and three additional batteries were placed by the railroad cut and on Seminary Ridge. Colonel William Nelson, Reserve Artillery, was assigned the same task on the Confederate left.[15]

Offensive artillery was also used effectively in close conjunction with its infantry in other ways. On the first day at Gettysburg, for example, Confederate artillery was instrumental in assisting its troops to a sound victory. As Major D. G. McIntosh's and Major W. J. Pegram's Confederate guns pounded the Federal forces west of town, Lieutenant Colonel Thomas Carter's battalion swung into action on Oak Hill from the north and poured a heavy fire into the Federals's vulnerable right flank. Defending troops of General Reynolds's Union First Corps could not ignore the flanking enemy artillery fire if they wanted to survive. In receiving artillery fire from two directions and under attack by Confederate infantry, the Union infantry had to jockey their lines back and forth to face the greatest danger. In the process, McIntosh reported that "the enemy, entirely discomforted, disappeared from the field."

This cooperative success was repeated the same day in the attack on the Federal right of Major General Howard's Eleventh Corps. Lieutenant Colonel H. P. Jones's artillery supported Major General Jubal Early's infantry assault, and pushed back the Federal line to begin the ripple effect and the eventual retreat through Gettysburg.[16]

Artillery though, when on the attack, had a greater potential for disadvantages than when operating defensively. Offensive firepower used in a cannonade divulged to the enemy what all commanders held closely—their intentions. Commanders choosing to use offensive firepower prior to an infantry assault had to weigh the beneficial effects of the cannonade against the detrimental effects that it produced by announcing the attack. Offensive firepower preceding an assault also, most likely, pinpointed the objective of the infantry attack.

Detrimental effects of a cannonade also included the possibility of failure to "rattle" the defending enemy troops by missing them as targets, thereby encouraging the men's confidence on the receiving end of the shellfire. On July 3, for example, when considering the magnitude of involvement, the dispersed Confederate artillery fire caused relatively little damage. With the Union line suffering only slight casualties, the cannonade failed to terrorize and demoralize the infantry lying in wait.

A preliminary offensive cannonade also gave the defending artillery batteries the opportunity of choosing to respond in kind or simply waiting until the right moment to unleash their firepower. The defending infantry force also could seek safer cover. With the offensive fire usually divulging the intended point of attack, it allowed commanders to transfer reinforcements accordingly. Overall, offensive fire helped little when compared to what it provided to the defenders. Any benefit gained from the damage inflicted in a preliminary cannonade could be canceled out by advertising the offensive intentions.[17]

Defensive Tactics

When used defensively, artillery tactics were to focus on stopping the attackers. Infantry was to be the primary target for defending artillery rather than enemy works or batteries. One of the most effective ways in which artillery was used in the Civil War was to hold its defensive fire until the massed columns of the enemy presented themselves within the effective range of the defending cannons. During the Confederate cannonade before Pickett's Charge, for example and as discussed previously, many, but not all, of the Federal guns on Cemetery Ridge responded by waiting to return the fire, or at least fired conservatively, in order to have enough ammunition for the anticipated assault.

Those guns that opened up early and fired without restraint before the infantry assault, however, were also using a defensive tactic. This artillery fire was not a tactic used to stop infantry but, instead, to help counter the punishing and terrorizing effects of an offensive cannonade and sustain the morale of the defenders.

Used defensively though, artillery's protective ability had limitations. When hardpressed, artillery could not usually produce enough firepower to stop an enemy advance. The battles of Malvern Hill and Gettysburg, where guns were able to concentrate massed firepower, provide exceptions, but in general artillery needed infantry or cavalry nearby to support and protect it when the enemy was near. Attacking infantry, for example, marching at the double-quick, could cover a distance of two hundred yards in two minutes. Attacking cavalry, at a gallop, over the same ground could do it in a half minute. Because of this, defending infantrymen, in support of their artillery, needed to be placed in positions that could intercept offensive threats before the attackers reached the line of cannons, otherwise the greatest disorder occurred if the enemy passed through the batteries.

Several of the principle objectives related to defense in *Instruction for Field Artillery* stated the field guns were "to act upon the field of battle; to break an enemy's line to prevent him from forming; to crush his masses; to dismount his batteries." These principle objectives had an excellent opportunity to be fulfilled by the Federal artillery at Gettysburg beginning in the early light of July 3 when the Union commanders started to witness Lee's preliminary artillery preparations for that day's battle. Arguably, the most momentous decision in choosing the correct defensive artillery tactics to be employed at the battle of Gettysburg occurred on the third day. From 3:00 A.M. the Confederate artillery units that would participate in the great cannonade were positioning for the event. Battery movements were done slowly and deliberately to avoid arousing the wrath of the observant enemy lines. Bringing on a premature gun duel could easily disrupt the Southern gun crews, prevent them from setting up, and, in turn, foil any grand plan of General Lee's.

Colonel Alexander did not like the vulnerable ground that his Southern guns were to occupy in the vicinity of the Peach Orchard: "[It was] generally sloping toward the enemy. This exposed all our movements to his view, & our horses, limbers, & caissons to his fire. . . . I studied the ground carefully for every gun, to get the best cover that the gentle slopes, here & there, would permit, but it was generally poor at the best & what there was often gotten only by scattering commands to some extent. And from the enemy's position we could absolutely hide nothing."[18]

At daybreak, some of the Federal guns took "pot shots" and wounded some in the Washington Artillery, but according to Alexander: "It was our policy to save every possible round for the infantry fight, & I would never allow more than one or two shots in reply, if any; leaving the honor of the last to them, & trying to beguile them into a little artillery truce. It worked excellently, &

View from Peach Orchard. Alexander's guns on his right flank were threatened by Federal artillery on Little Round Top [in center background]. (AC)

View from Peach Orchard overlooking Alexander's forward Confederate artillery positions and Seminary Ridge in the distance. (AC)

though, occasionally, during the morning, when we exhibited a particularly tempting mark [,] we would get a few shots [and] we got along very nicely."[19]

The growing disposition of the Confederate artillery line for the planned attack was a most impressive sight. Practically the entire Army of the Potomac could witness it. Major Osborn, Eleventh Corps artillery, reported: "Before the afternoon battle opened, with our glasses we could see Lee's batteries in position on Seminary Ridge, standing at regulation intervals covering a line of two miles. It was the longest and finest of light batteries ever planted on a battlefield. We were fully aware that this line of batteries meant mischief to us and that immediately behind it was a corresponding body of infantry."[20]

General Henry Hunt saw it thus:

[Their guns] were on an open crest plainly visible. Between 10 and 11 a.m . . . [on Cemetery Ridge], a magnificent display greeted my eyes. Our whole front for two miles was covered by [Confederate] batteries already in line or going into position. They stretched—apparently in one unbroken mass—from opposite the town to the Peach Orchard, which bounded the view to the left, the ridges of which were planted thick with cannon. Never before had such a sight been witnessed on this continent, and rarely, if ever, abroad. What did it mean? It might possibly be to hold that line while its infantry was sent to aid Ewell, or to guard against a counter-stroke from us, but it most probably meant an assault on our center, to be preceded by a cannonade in order to crush our batteries and shake our infantry; at least to cause us to exhaust our ammunition in reply, so that the assaulting troops might pass in good condition over the half mile of open ground which was beyond the effective musketry fire. . . . [21]

General Hunt's mind must have been racing in deliberation as he surveyed the large buildup of enemy artillery facing the Union line. Even before the firing opened, Hunt instinctively predicted what was about to take place and planned how the Union artillery could best respond to this grave situation. If what he was seeing on his front were Confederate preparations for a cannonade, he decided that the duty of his batteries was not to fritter away precious ammunition in hopes of knocking out enemy guns. It would be best to wait for the enemy to open fire and then reply slowly and deliberately. After all, if there was an assault to be made, the Confederate artillery would not be the killing force storming the Federal heights. It would be enemy infantrymen, and they would be fighting like swarms of angry bees agitated out of a disturbed hive.

Hunt was determined to prepare for the ominous activity he was witnessing: "I [inspected] the whole line, ascertaining that all the batteries . . . were in good condition and well supplied with ammunition. As the enemy was evidently increasing his artillery force in front of our left, I gave instructions to the batteries and to the chiefs of artillery not to fire at small bodies, nor allow their fire to be drawn without promise of adequate results; to watch the enemy closely, and when he opened to concentrate the fire of their guns one battery at a time until it was silenced; under all circumstances to fire deliberately, and to husband their ammunition as much as possible."[22]

As boldly as the Confederates were positioning their artillery for the cannonade, Colonel Alexander wondered why the Federal artillerymen did not open up with a bombardment on his Southern batteries sufficient enough to break the intent of the Confederate plan. The Southern artillerymen went about their activities and in full view of the Union army. It was a sound military tactic for artillery to break up an enemy massing their guns as they were attempting to concentrate. The day before, for example, A. P. Hill's artillery had enfiladed the Federal guns when they were attempting to concentrate. Colonel Walker, Third Corps chief of artillery, later reported: "On the 2d, the battalions of Pegram, McIntosh, Lane, and a part of Garnett's battalion, under Major Richardson, were put in position, on the right of the Fairfield turnpike, about 1 mile in advance of the position of the previous day, and, later in the day, Poague's battalion was also put in position still farther to the right. From this position a fire was opened at intervals, enfilading the enemy's guns when they were attempting to be concentrated, and also diverting their attention from the infantry of the First Corps."[23]

For July 3, the Federal guns had a chance to respond with the same opportunity as Hill's guns. Colonel Alexander recalled, "For 9 hours—from 4 A.M. to 1 P.M. we lay exposed to their guns, & getting ready at our leisure, & they let us do it." Alexander quizzically wrote: "The enemy very strangely interfered with only an occasional cannon-shot, to none of which did we now reply, for it was easily in their power to drive us to cover or to exhaust our ammunition before our infantry column could be formed. I can only account for their allowing our visible preparations to be completed by supposing that they appreciated in what a trap we would find ourselves. Of Longstreet's 83 guns, eight were left on our extreme right to cover our flank and the remaining 75

Forward center position of Alexander's Confederate guns facing the Union center on July 3. Copse of trees in center background. (AC)

Alexander's Confederate guns from right forward position on July 3. Copse of trees in center background. (AC)

were posted in an irregular line about 1300 yards long, beginning in the Peach Orchard and ending near the northeast corner of the Spangler wood."[24]

There was wisdom to Colonel Alexander's puzzlement. Without knowing the outcome, many tacticians would expect an army to protect itself from menacing enemy movements *before* they became a threat. Batteries of artillery were most vulnerable as they were in the process of preparing for action. Batteries presented themselves as such large targets, it took only minutes to disable them. Crippling just one horse in a team stopped the rig until it was cut out of the harness, and every halt increased the danger of being overwhelmed by additional enemy fire and being forced out of action without ever shooting back.

Alexander's surprise at what amounted to an Union artillery truce against Longstreet's guns was probably due, in some part, to his expectation that the Union army had its normal overabundance of artillery ammunition that could be wasted on such tempting targets. While the Army of the Potomac did have an overabundance of artillery ammunition, most of it was twenty-five miles away in Westminster, Maryland. Resupplying could not be accomplished quickly. Hunt was concerned about his *local* ammunition supply. In this regard, on the morning of July 2, before the artillery reserve arrived, Hunt had heard some disturbing news from General Meade:

> [Meade] informed me that one of the army corps—the third [sic]—had left its whole artillery wagon train behind, and that other corps,—not known—were also short of ammunition. He was much disturbed; and feared that taking into account the expenditures of the previous day, there would not be enough to carry us through the battle. . . . [With the special wagon train of 20 extra rounds], I was therefore enabled to reassure General Meade, but it was absolutely necessary for us to economize ammunition by restricting its use to the production of positive material effects, and strictly necessary purposes. There was certainly none to throw away in puerile endeavor, to scare the enemy or unnecessary ones to keep up the coverage of our own troops.[25]

Only half of the ammunition train was up by the evening of July 2, forcing units to rely on other artillery units, mainly the artillery reserve, for support.

Other observations that must have been puzzling Colonel Alexander as his guns were positioned relatively unmolested included the combat engagements in the distance or on the ground adjoining the left of his growing artillery line near the Confederate center. Many troops were fighting at other parts of the field. On the Union right flank, Culp's Hill was heavily engaged until 11 A.M. Elsewhere, the artillery traded shots and participated in playful fire with their counterparts. Intermingled with the artillery fire was the constant sniping of skirmishers and sharpshooters down the lines. Near the left of Alexander's line, there was battle action taking place, some of it quite fierce. A few hundred yards from Alexander, in front of the Union center where many of the Confederate infantry would pass in the assault on July 3, the battle heated up to more than a skirmish with artillery and infantry units engaged in the fight for the Bliss farm.

Hunt's grave concern over shortages of Federal artillery ammunition combined with the view of the enemy artillery's buildup threatening the Union line must have been a compelling predicament to ponder. It is puzzling why the Federal guns were allowed to use precious ammunition by engaging in a "sideshow" event such as the Bliss action and yet not breakup the vulnerable and tempting targets offered by Alexander's guns as they were wheeled into position. Alexander observed the artillery as it opened up in the melee at the Bliss buildings: "At least 100 guns, on the two sides, got into a duel which lasted nearly a half hour & then finally died out. I would not let one of my guns fire a shot. For myself, I think it was a mistake to use that much ammunition prematurely if it could have been avoided. This duel made a great deal of noise while it lasted, & many writers have imagined it to have been part of the cannonade to prepare the way for Pickett."[26]

On the Union side, General Hancock was either less impressed than Alexander in viewing this action at the Bliss farm or he did not emphasize the impact it produced on the ammunition supply of his artillery. Hancock merely said, ". . . the artillery of the corps was frequently and successfully engaged with that of the enemy." Hancock's remaining ammunition supply, of course, would later be the central issue in the quarrel with Hunt.[27]

After the morning actions of July 3 settled down, the conspicuous buildup of the Confederate artillery was completed. The result—General Meade, his corps commanders (whose cannons were within range of the newly placed Rebel batteries), and General Hunt, through their inaction, tacitly allowed the Confederate artillery to array itself unmolested and gain firepower superior to the Union guns. The Army of the Potomac's defending artillery line was now facing, what seemed, impossible odds.

View of Bliss farm in center distance from the left flank of Alexander's Confederate guns on July 3. (AC)

With fewer guns to reply to this dominant force, Hunt's mental wheels were turning to determine a way to counter this threat. He calculated a response:

> . . . Some of the guns on Cemetery Hill, and Rittenhouse's on Little Round Top could be brought to bear, but these were offset by batteries similarly placed on the flanks of the enemy, so that on the Second Corps line, within the space of a mile, were 77 guns to oppose 150 . . . It was of the first importance to subject the enemy's infantry, from the first moment of their advance, to such a cross-fire of our artillery as would break their formation, check their impulse, and drive them back, or at least bring them to our lines in such condition as to make them easy prey. There was neither time nor necessity for reporting this to General Meade. . . .[28]

A threatening predicament now faced the Army of the Potomac. It is apparent that one of the greatest Union gambles made in choosing the right defensive tactic at the battle of Gettysburg, or at least one choice made with the greatest restraint, was ignoring the massive buildup of Confederate artillery on the morning of July 3 in order to save ammunition for defense against a possible assault. This deliberate choice of action, or, in this case, nonaction, is a prime example of how ammunition levels affected decisions in the way battles were fought and the extreme conservation measures that were imposed which greatly altered the outcome. Holding back the artillery fire against a growing artillery threat was an option attached with grave consequences. One can only see the brilliance in this risky move because the outcome is now known.

But if theorists termed this Federal inaction a mistake, it turned out to be the best one made that produced such outstanding results for Meade. Had the Federal guns interrupted the artillery preparations prior to the cannonade, Pickett's Charge would probably not have occurred. Halting Southern artillery preparations would have eliminated the close-up infantry encounter and, in doing so, the Army of the Potomac would have lost the unique circumstance that inflicted the blow that turned the Army of Northern Virginia back.

While the results of Pickett's Charge are now history, the Confederates came dangerously close to breaching the Union center. A different climax begs for another point to consider. In the aftermath, there would have been a great deal of reflection and condemnation had the Confederate artillery been allowed to position their guns unmolested *and* if the Confederate infantry had broken through the Union center successfully on July 3. General Hunt's reputation, as well as the Union high commands', would have had to withstand the charges of negligence for not destroying the Confederate artillery threat as it was allowed to grow unhampered under their watchful eyes. The Hunt–Hancock controversy would have taken on an additional twist and an interesting dialogue on whom to blame for such negligence.

Preparations

Arrival

Many words could be used to describe the environment of working with an artillery battery in battle. Physically, it was a stressful, strenuous, dangerous, and very dirty job. But even before a gun crew fired its first round in a battle, one of the most difficult tasks was simply getting to the battlefield and into position. Accounts relating to the difficulties of artillery pieces being moved to their destinations are infrequent. One example, however, illustrates the frustrations encountered by a battery on the march. In his 1883 article, Captain William L. Ritter, 3rd Maryland Artillery, C.S.A., described "an artillerist's troubles" at Jackson, Mississippi:

> On account of the darkness and the crookedness and roughness of the road, one of the gun carriages ran against a tree, and occasioned an unwelcome delay, as the enemy was in pursuit and not far behind. The piece had to be unlimbered, the gun carriage run back, the piece limbered up again, and a cautious drive around the tree made. This mishap having been overcome, others followed. The battery had not gone far before another gun ran against a stump; and soon after, in crossing the branch near Stone Bridge, a wheel slipped into a deep chuck hole on the side of the road. The cannoneers had to unlimber again, to pull the piece out. Owing to the detentions the rest of the battery got a mile ahead. The Captain sent back four horses to assist in pulling the piece up the hill, near the bridge; and instructed the officer in charge of the bridge not to fire it till the last gun had crossed. The bridge had just been fired, however, and was already in flames when the gun crossed over.
>
> Again, when near the railroad, the battery encountered a boggy place, in which Lieutenant Ritter's piece stuck fast. The horses were untrained and balky, and refused to pull, while the driver could not well see which way to move, because of the darkness.[29]

Burdened with heavy equipment pulled by horses, the artillery branch, when operating off the road, was substantially less mobile than infantry or cavalry. Moving a battery around was highly restrictive and limited by terrain features, daylight, or weather. Infantry soldiers could run through the woods, jump a ditch or stone wall, and climb a fence. A battery commander, however, had better look at the ground and its obstacles before crossing over it. Each cannon with a full complement of ammunition weighed about four tons.

The worst time to position an artillery battery was during combat. If the battle was underway, the ground was most likely pockmarked with crater holes, or crowded with soldiers, and otherwise strewn with wreckage, wounded, and dead. It was a continuous challenge to overcome the restrictions created by moving heavy equipment without the use of roads. In addition to surmounting terrain impediments and the debris of battle, the heavy load of an artillery battery often had to be moved about handicapped with the difficulty of managing horse teams terrorized by the gunfire.

Gun Placement

Upon arrival on the battlefield, if time permitted, commanders or their chiefs of artillery proceeded to select firing positions for their guns. Artillery's proper application required a great deal of time in studying the layout of the ground and how to use terrain features to the best advantage. Anticipating the enemy's movements and possible attack points also had to be considered. If artillery was to be used to its fullest capacity, infantry commanders had to know its limitations and capabilities. Correct tactics called for using artillery in a more defined purpose than simply scattering guns along an infantry line to support or boost its firepower; such a distribution of cannons along a line was rarely practical.

Placement of a battery and readying it to operate depended on several factors. As a safety precaution, the immediate vicinity around the battery had to be examined for exposure to potential enemy threats such as buildings, sunken roads, and any features that could shelter enemy troops. Placing a battery near woods, for example, occupied by enemy troops and within rifle range of their sharpshooters, was deadly to artillerymen and their horses. The preferred positions were in hilly or rolling terrain with moderate height, an open view in front, and at sites which allowed a range of barrel elevations for hitting targets. Rolling terrain in front of a battle line was preferable to flat terrain. Enemy shellfire that struck an undulating surface near its high point usually ricocheted over the defenses. The corresponding dust kicked up could not be seen by the enemy to correct the accuracy. Consequently, ammunition was wasted. If practicable, a battery could operate behind the crest of a hill with their gun muzzles pointing over the top but with the hill providing some protection from enemy fire. This protection also concealed the ammunition limbers and caissons. Terrain features to avoid were ditches, hedges, marshy grounds, etc., or anything that could restrain maneuverability.[30]

The most important consideration of gun placement was the effectiveness that could be produced from the battery's firepower. Effectiveness was best achieved by placing guns at coordinated points and allowing the concentration of several batteries to mass their fire on selected targets. Gun positions were also to be chosen to cover anticipated points of attack and locations that exposed the enemy to the longest periods under fire.[31]

To insure success, it was best for guns to be placed where targets could be hit in depth. Since the depth of an opposing line was characteristically shallow, firing straight into the line or perpendicular fire caused the least damage; artillery fire could kill far beyond the shallow enemy line it was directly facing. The best effect was achieved by arranging the guns where they could produce an enfilading crossfire which swept the length of enemy lines. There was a much greater benefit to exposing the enemy to the type of fire that could penetrate a line at an angle and hit more targets. As the angle of fire changed away from the perpendicular, the destructiveness increased to its maximum, which took place when firing was directed into the side of a line.

With the wide usage of rifled guns and their accompanying long ranges, converging artillery fire could play a vital role in damaging the enemy. This crossfire was especially true at Gettysburg, and with regard to weaponry the Federal army had the greater potential to do it. The Army of the Potomac possessed more rifled guns than the Army of Northern Virginia: 210 Northern rifles compared to only 137 Southern guns. In theory then, the Federal army could expect to arrange its artillery to create a more destructive crossfire and also win the counter battery contest at long range, more secure from a counterstrike.[32]

Crossfiring, besides the benefit of increasing the damage, directed a battery's guns at an enemy force that was approaching a point of the defending line *other than their own*. This created a psychological advantage in which gun crews could operate coolly. They were not the ones at risk and consequently their fears of being overrun were diminished. On the down side, though, if a large portion of a battle front were under attack and a battery's position was threatened, a battery commander had to overcome a strong and instinctive inclination to address such threats on his own front. Allowing crossfiring did not provide such protection. Without proper discipline and training, it was difficult to ignore their own front and use their resources against an enemy that was not directly threatening it.[33]

A battery took up a lot of space. According to regulations in the Federal *Artillerist's Manual*, a battery in line of battle covered an eighty-two-yard front and a depth of thirty yards. It needed elbow room to operate. The horse teams of each piece, in particular, needed turning room to maneuver to perform the movements necessary to service the gun. The battery also needed a space small enough that artillerymen could perform under the watchful eye and respond to the orders of the battery commander and yet large enough to avoid making it too easy for the enemy guns to hit. In general, it was recommended that artillery pieces be spaced according to the distance from enemy artillery in a manner that did not offer too many targets packed into one area. The idea was to calculate the maximum margin of error allowed enemy gunners and place the guns where, if an enemy shot missed its intended cannon targeted, it did not hit the piece next to it.[34]

The terrain of the Gettysburg battlefield provided challenges to each army in the placement of artillery. Although the entire lines needed a proper artillery defense, commanders had to choose gun positions with the realities of what the terrain provided and in conjunction with how they chose to position their troops. The shape of each army's line of battle resembled the now famous fishhook formation. The Confederate army occupied the exterior hook and the Union army had the interior line.

With the terrain of Gettysburg, selections for placing artillery by applying the principles of gun placement also had to be compromised with practicality. In examining the ground, the town itself was an obstacle. Buildings blocked artillery fields of fire for both sides. The low and level ground directly north of town was suitable for Confederate artillery positions, but their view of Union positions located on Cemetery Hill and Cemetery Ridge was obstructed by the town and the intervening higher ground Gettysburg sat upon. Any Southern guns located north of the town could only fire indirectly at Union targets. Long-range guns, however, could be placed on the more distant Oak Ridge to hit Union positions with direct fire.

The town also discouraged concentration of infantry troops. Structures impeded any coordinated advance and allowed sharpshooters to roam at will and at close range. The town's buildings provided innumerable safe havens for Confederate marksmen. Enemy sharpshooters presented a constant threat to the Federal infantry and the gun crews covering the streets leading to their positions. Despite this threat, the textbook recommendation that artillery avoid positioning near such places that could shelter enemy troops had to be overlooked. The streets pointing into the Union line on Cemetery Hill required an artillery defense, so in this case practicality won over guidelines for gun placement.

Gettysburg was also an obstacle that created a longer line of communication. The town interfered with the connective coordination needed between the Confederate artillery on Seminary Ridge and Lee's left flank, Ewell's Second Corps's artillery on Benner's Hill. The Confederate artillery on Benner's Hill east of town would join in the cannonade on July 3 but its isolation from other guns participating forced it to operate independently.

Benner's Hill was one of the few places on the Confederate left that provided open, level ground suitable for placement of artillery. This hill, however, was overshadowed by the heights of Cemetery Hill and Culp's Hill where the Union guns loomed to threaten any Southern guns that might be placed there. The greater part of the Confederate army occupied Seminary Ridge which provided many options for placement of artillery. If a gun duel occurred, Seminary Ridge provided terrain that allowed open fields of fire and the opportunity to place guns where they could create a deadly crossfire. This ridge extended over two miles with level ground for ease of maneuvering and provided an attractive platform for artillery. Some considered part of the ground weak because of the lack of shelter for the men, horses, ammunition chests, and their exposure to the Union guns on Cemetery Ridge. In retrospect though, except for horses, the resulting casualties proved that Seminary Ridge was not much more hazardous than the Federal gun positions on Cemetery Ridge.

In actuality, the nature of Seminary Ridge offered more shelter for Southern troops than Cemetery Ridge did for the Union forces facing them. The Federal positions were at a visual disadvantage. The lay of the ground spotlighted their presence. While Cemetery Ridge provided the Federals with superb firing positions, they were out in the open and had the potential to suffer full exposure to a crossfire from enemy artillery. The Federal line's vulnerability is still obvious today. If one views Cemetery Ridge from General Lee's equestrian statue on Seminary Ridge, the focal point of the Confederate attack against the Union center on July 3 presents the Union positions in a manner highlighted by the sky as a background. This backdrop would have silhouetted anyone standing near Cemetery Ridge's crest and, as long as the air was clear, assisted in aiming Confederate artillery. The Confederate line, on the other hand, was provided with a neutral tree-lined background that blended troops into the landscape or transformed objects into indistinct targets or otherwise interfered with Federal artillery aiming at specific targets.

Defensively, the most practical ground for setting up artillery fire on the battlefield was located at or near each army's center line of battle. The view of

Confederate gun position on Benner's Hill, east of Gettysburg, pointing at Union line on East Cemetery Hill. Culp's Hill is on the left. (AC)

Union guns on East Cemetery Hill pointing at Confederate gun positions on Benner's Hill (just below water tower). (AC)

the ground that lay between the centers was mostly open and it allowed early detection of enemy activity. Offensively, however, either army's center line of occupation offered an unattractive option to contemplate seizure. Between the two centers lay the open fields separating the two lines. Placing defending artillery to control this ground would not have required much deliberation. The intervening terrain was not perfect for defensive purposes but it did not have woods, steep ground, or many obstacles that could shield attackers if they crossed over it.

For a Confederate assault, undulations of the intervening terrain would offer temporary protection from enemy artillery for some advancing troops at longer range, but the open ground at mid-range offered exposure to artillery much of the time. The ground at closer range, except for the Codori farm buildings, fences, and some vegetation, allowed maximum exposure of all of the advancing troops. It would be a bold move for Lee to commit enough men to snatch Cemetery Ridge away from the Union army. Meade, as well, must have pondered the consequences of attacking such daunting ground as Seminary Ridge. Each must have weighed the costs required to overpower their opponent's valued position.

Overall, the ground occupied by the artillery in the Army of Northern Virginia and the manner in which it faced the Army of the Potomac, provided many opportunities for an offensive force to exploit. A striking advantage for many Confederate gun positions was the encircling effect produced against the Union line stationed at Cemetery Hill and Cemetery Ridge. With the exception of the town blocking part of the field of fire, the Southern artillery, with its rifled guns, could throw iron into the exposed Union lines from a surrounding three-quarter circle.

Colonel Alexander elaborated on the line's particular benefit: "[The exterior line] gave us one single advantage. It enabled us to enfilade any of the enemy's positions, near the centre of their line, with our artillery fire. Now, a battery established where it can enfilade others need not trouble itself about aim. It has only to fire in the right direction & the shot finds something to hurt wherever it falls. No troops, infantry or artillery, can long submit to an enfilade fire. But, both the infantry & artillery lines which we were to attack could have been enfiladed from somewhere in our lines near Gettysburg."[35]

A primary deficiency interfering with the Army of Northern Virginia's gun

View from Peach Orchard overlooking Southern line on Seminary Ridge (treeline in background) and distant fields crossed by Confederate forces on July 2 and 3. (AC)

The Union center position is in the distance as viewed from the Confederate center. (AC)

placement was the layout of the road network that led into their six-mile long, fishhook-shaped line. Unlike the parallel roads leading into the Federal lines, the primary avenues leading into the Confederate lines were perpendicular. In addition, there were few secondary roads interconnecting with the primary roads in between. E. P. Alexander observed: ". . . Communication from flank to flank even by courier was difficult, the country being well cleared and exposed to the enemy's view and fire, the roads all running at right angles to our lines, and some of them at least broad turnpikes which the enemy's guns could rake for two miles." The road network most certainly affected Lee's operations. It congested their efforts to reach the field. It checked efforts to communicate, shift troops, or move supplies overland. It also stifled movement of artillery pieces and generally interfered with their ability to operate against the Union army.[36]

The Confederate army's *external* fishhook-shaped line posed an additional obstacle. This great bugaboo of military tacticians would make it difficult or impossible to allow a unified effort over such geography. It would take a half day for one flank to assist the other and any Confederate maneuver near its front line would likely be in view of the Federals. Lee's front covered twice that of the Union's.

In addition, each of Lee's three artillery reserves was disbursed at different points to the rear. The reserves and other support troops awaiting orders to the front were stationed up to a mile in the rear. Therefore, the rear lines of communication necessary to move artillery and ammunition behind their front and then into their positions encompassed a line greater than six miles. Any guns "loaned" to another corps more than likely had a greater distance to travel than the Federal artillery reserve guns, and any movement was impeded by terrain with few and narrow roadways to access Seminary Ridge.

On the Union side, the terrain occupied by the Army of the Potomac had its own pros and cons for the placement of its guns. A benefit of being on the defensive was the Union army could squeeze more artillery pieces in a battle line that was half the length of the Confederate's. Although the arrangement made better targets to shoot at, it significantly increased Federal defensive firepower which would be needed to stop a massed assault. Theoretically, the Army of the Potomac could place 120 guns per mile to defend its battle line, while the Confederates could place only 45 guns per mile to defend its long line.

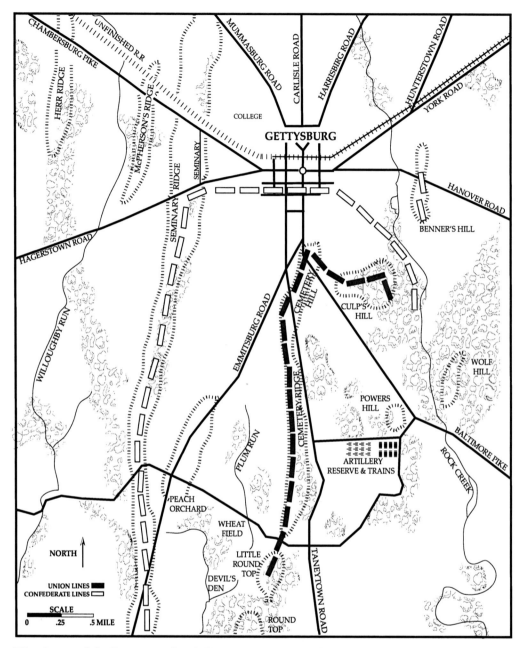

The Army of the Potomac's battle line was conveniently supplied by the network of roads paralleling the rear area. Interconnecting roads allowed rapid transfer of men and equipment. Note the central location of reserve artillery and supply train.
The Army of Northern Virginia's battle line was supplied by access roads which were mostly perpendicular to its front. This was beneficial for withdrawal, but in battle, the road network slowed delivery of ammunition and hampered the rapid movement of men and equipment to other parts of the line.

More important, the Union army had the *interior* line of the two positions. This arrangement allowed transfer of troops or equipment in a direct line to destinations, whereas exterior lines caused circuitous routes and time consuming movements to destinations. Since the Army of the Potomac was fighting a defensive battle, it needed the ability to gather rapid support to repel attackers, plug up gaps, or do whatever was necessary to avoid being overrun. Besides having the interior line, the internal configuration of the Union fishhook provided superior advantages over the ground occupied by the Confederate army. Any battle map of Gettysburg shows the tremendous advantage of internal access to the Federal front. Two main roads, the Taneytown Road and the Baltimore Pike, fed into Meade's army parallel and adjacent to the rear of its line of battle. Any support on these roads was just minutes from the front; and, in addition, there were secondary roads interconnecting to the main ones allowing total and, except for their own traffic jams, unobstructed movement for the entire length of the line.

Meade's good fortune gave him the ability to quickly shift reinforcements and resupply the front line from wagons parked in nearby fields or roads. He could also provide additional artillery and ammunition to the battlefront with a seemingly limitless supply from artillery reserve nearby. No point in the Union line of battle was more than a mile from the support of the invaluable artillery reserve which helped save the Army of the Potomac at Gettysburg.

The ground occupied by the Union army also had deficiencies. Although the Army of the Potomac possessed the advantages of a shorter internal line and easy support access from the rear, the terrain on which it had to deploy its artillery canceled out some of these benefits. Much of the ground it held was not suitable for artillery placement. Trees, soft or uneven ground, stone walls, fences, etc., restricted maneuverability on their line of battle. Visibility was restricted by belts of woods, thickets, or intervening ridges between the two battle lines. The Union line's flanks provided little room for enough guns to assist in their defense. The rugged nature of the Union ground posed greater difficulties for Federal batteries due to the promptness in which many were moved about. While many of the Southern cannons were moved about in a relatively unhurried manner, many of the Federal artillery pieces, on the other hand, were shifted during the battle without much deliberation and in a fast-paced, desperate atmosphere, non-conducive to proper gun placement.

Union gun positions on East Cemetery Hill. Culp's Hill is in background. (AC)

Union gun positions on East Cemetery Hill. Historic archway entrance to town cemetery is in center. (AC)

In describing the Federal line, Culp's Hill was on the northern end of it and anchored the Union right flank. First Lieutenant Muhlenberg, artillery brigade commander of the Twelfth Corps, described it: "The density of the growth of timber, the irregularity and extremely broken character of the ground, studded with immense bowlders [sic], prevented the artillery from taking position in the line proper of the corps." Enough artillery was available but there wasn't enough room for it. The hill was limited to positioning only two batteries on it, while the rest was held in reserve until later use.[37]

Adjacent to Culp's Hill was Cemetery Hill. This hill was the "curve" of the Union fishhook. The guns located there would serve Meade well on more than one occasion. On July 2, they wrecked Latimer's Confederate guns on Benner's Hill and on the third, they joined in a destructive crossfire against the left flank of the Confederate infantry assault, severely damaging the advance long before the attackers reached the Union lines on Cemetery Ridge.

Cemetery Hill, however, was overcrowded with Federal infantry and artillery. The Federal artillery squeezed its batteries into positions that exposed their line to a deadly flanking fire from multiple directions. It was unavoidable to position troops or batteries on Cemetery Hill and not offer a tempting target to enemy guns across the valley on Seminary Ridge or from Benner's Hill east of Gettysburg. The densely packed Union troops, interspersed with artillery pieces, and their numerous limbers and caissons made it easy for the Confederates to avoid the tedious job of aligning guns to obtain a crossfire.

Major Osborn's Eleventh Corps artillery had five batteries to squeeze together on Cemetery Hill. He stated that: "The crest of the Hill was so limited that even the guns I had were placed at half regulation distance. I at once appreciated that the admirable position taken by Howard [Osborn's commander] and especially the hill upon which he had placed his own [infantry] command was full recognized by the enemy as the point of greatest strength in the line. It was plain that Lee's primary object was to drive the artillery from that hill."[38]

In addition to his five cramped batteries, Osborn drew another two from the reserve. He described his artillery disposition:

> Nearly all the guns and all the caissons were among the graves. Each battery was
> in position as in park—fourteen feet between the guns—the limbers and caissons at
> proper distance in rear of the guns. The spaces between the batteries were greater

Ominous view of Federal guns on East Cemetery Hill. (AC)

Stevens's 5th Maine battery on the slopes of Culp's Hill. East Cemetery Hill is in background. (AC)

than the spaces between the guns of any one battery, but yet they were close together. No earthworks were thrown up to protect the men, nor could there have been without digging up the dead in the Cemetery . . . We made the best target for artillery practice the enemy had during the war. But there was another side to it. We commanded their guns as well as they did ours, with the advantage on the enemy's part of being more scattered. In addition to this we commanded the plain perfectly, with no timber intervening, over which the enemy's infantry must advance to the charge.[39]

Cemetery Hill was the most vulnerable part of the Federal line for the enemy's artillery to employ a crossfire. Because of the crowded Federal assemblage of men and artillery pieces, it required fewer Confederate guns to achieve a crossfire effect. Confederate guns could deploy without stirring too much and still place their guns in relatively safe firing positions.

Between the flanks of the Union army lay some of the best ground for Federal gun positions—Cemetery Ridge. Excluding the part of the line that faced the town, this ridge was where artillery had the elbowroom to maneuver and array its guns to create a deadly crossfire. The Union army could position its guns and ammunition behind the crest for safer operation. Here is where it could best repel an enemy bold enough to transit the wide-open fields on its front.

Extending down Cemetery Ridge towards the Union line's southern end, the ground slumped to lower ground. It was the least attractive ground on Cemetery Ridge. Much of it was unsuitable for placing artillery. This low section was marshy in places and its frontal field of fire was obstructed by an intervening ridge that concealed most of the Confederate line that faced it. This intervening ridge would precipitate the bloodiest day of the battle, July 2, and create a controversy that is still debated today. The lower ground facing this intervening ridge was the ground assigned to Major General Dan Sickles of the Union Third Corps.

At the southern end of Cemetery Ridge, the left flank of the Union army abruptly terminated at a precipitous hill—Little Round Top. With its open view on one side facing the enemy, Little Round Top possessed a good field of fire for long-range dueling, but it was not well-suited for close combat because of its steepness. Artillery could participate in its defense, but the cannon barrels could not be depressed to actually damage attackers attempting to take its summit. Little Round Top's slopes and summit also did not have much elbowroom to maneuver cumbersome equipment through and around the rugged terrain.

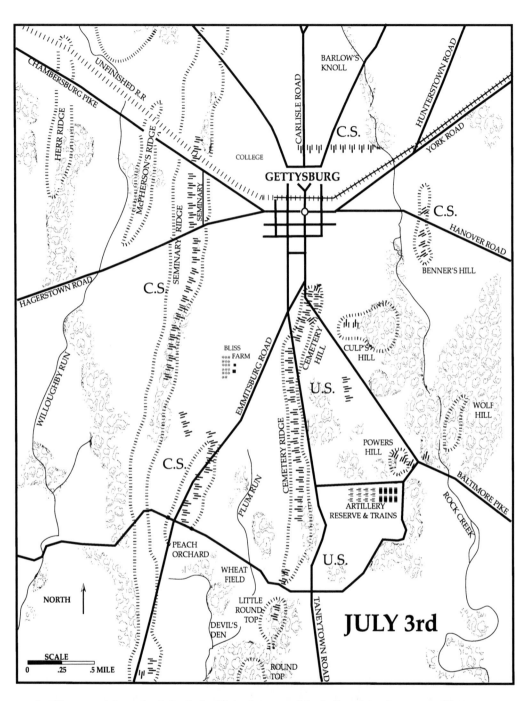

Artillery positions for July 3rd. Note the town blocked connective control between Confederate artillery batteries located on Seminary Ridge and Benner's Hill, a gap of 1 3/4 miles. Also, note the packed Federal positions on Cemetery Hill – vulnerable and easy targets for Confederate gunners.

With the Army of the Potomac's flanks anchored on Culp's Hill and Little Round Top, the ground on these prominent points offered little for an artillery officer to appreciate and provided few options in arranging proper artillery protection for the battle line. Tactically, and according to military theory, these flanks and any other anticipated point of attack needed a higher proportion of guns to repel any assailants. With the terrain features being what they were, infantry would have to protect this important ground on the flanks, mostly on their own.

While each artillery branch faced many problems, the greatest collective challenge for positioning artillery at the battle of Gettysburg was undertaken by the Army of Northern Virginia on July 3. Lee's eventual plan prior to the infantry assault was to arrange his artillery in a way to project an extended and concentrated fire into the Union center on Cemetery Ridge and other threatening points to soften up the enemy lines and pave the way for the advance. There were difficulties to overcome, however, in undertaking an offensive cannonade of such magnitude and duration.

An enormous obstacle in planning the offensive cannonade was how, in an unmanageable six-mile line, the Southern artillery firepower of different commands could be coordinated to cooperate in a combined effort and create a destructive crossfire to demolish common targets. The primary responsibility for arranging cooperation among the different artillery commands belonged to the chief of artillery, General Pendleton. Given the complexities of the plan, artillery's involvement on a broad front, and time limitations, this was an enormously difficult assignment.

To begin with, there was a great deal to prepare for but little time to do it. Artillery officers were busy moving up and placing batteries, insuring ammunition chests were full, and preparing final details for the opening signal shots. Time restraints prevented the preoccupied artillery officers of one command from surveying the ground of other artillery units with which they were expected to cooperate. General Pendleton was expected to expedite coordination but he had few staff to communicate instructions along the lengthy line and perform the necessary preparation duties.

The impediment of a long line lent itself to the breakdown of control between artillery units that were supposed to jointly participate. Loss of control had already happened on July 2 when lateral coordination broke down

Two Federal batteries were placed on the rugged face of Little Round Top. (AC)

Federal view from Little Round Top facing Confederate tree line in distance. Wooded ground in center and right was mostly open then or with low vegetation. (AC)

among the Confederate infantry forces advancing en echelon. Support troops, arriving either in a disordered fashion or not at all, prevented the exploitation of their gains. One example was General Wright's claim that his Georgia brigade pierced the left-center of the Federal line. Wright reported: "I have not the slightest doubt but that I should have been able to have maintained my position on the heights, and secured the captured artillery, if there had been a protecting force on my left, or if the brigade on my right had not been forced to retire." The lateral breakdown on July 2 allowed Federal commanders to maneuver and feed troops onto threatened areas of the battlefield and stop breakthroughs at critical moments. On July 3, unless sufficient staff were available to implement the comprehensive plan for Southern artillery, a recurrence of a breakdown in lateral coordination of Confederate artillery occupying exterior lines was even more likely.[40]

Having an exterior line, of course, was not a choice for the Army of Northern Virginia. Its burdensome length, in one respect, compensated for some of its shortcomings elsewhere. With regard to gun placement, their artillery could create a concentration of fire superior to Federal guns. Although the Confederate artillery was outnumbered it was opposing an enemy line that extended three miles. General Lee's 270 guns could, theoretically, bring 90 guns per *target* mile to bear against the enemy. Conversely, and also theoretically, the Union artillery's 370 guns faced a six-mile-long line, averaging only 61 guns per *target* mile—a comparatively weaker force if used against a broad front.

In view of all these circumstances, the Army of Northern Virginia was faced with a formidable task on July 3. With regard to judging the risks that were involved in undertaking the artillery action that day, it is difficult to formulate an opinion of Lee's plan by using only the same limited knowledge available to those commanders on July 3, 1863. We cannot easily isolate information we know now from information that the participants would learn only after the fact. We, of course, know the result of the operation. We have studied the terrain and read the verdicts on the plan's worth.

On the Union side, proper Federal gun placement to counter the Confederate artillery threat on July 3 was an altogether different challenge than what the Army of the Potomac experienced on the previous day. Compare the potential firepower of Federal artillery used on July 2 with how

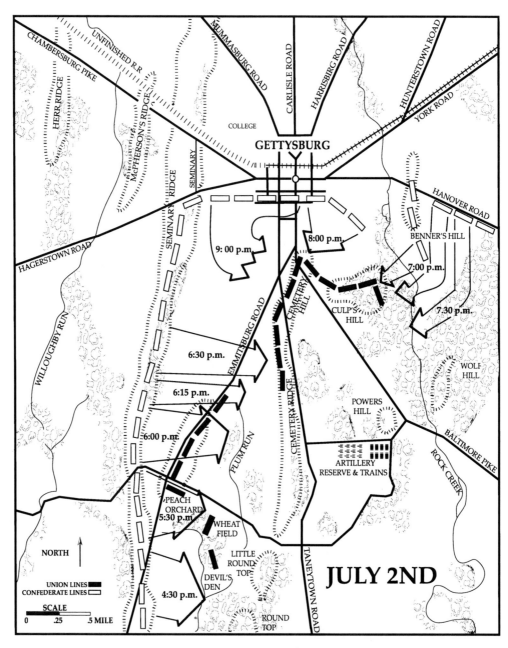

Compared to Pickett's Charge on July 3rd, Federal artillery operations on July 2nd involved defending attack points covering practically the entire Union line. Attackers approached in stages and in more dispersed formations. With little warning of an attack and limited time to respond, command style shifted more to crisis management precluding concerns for proper gun placement, cooperation with other artillery units, and other considerations appropriate for defending this type of attack.

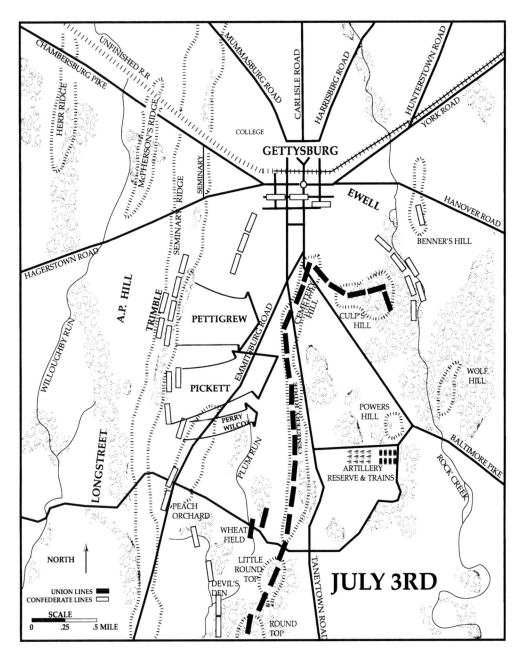

Compared to the Confederate attack against the Union line on July 2nd, Federal artillery operations on July 3rd involved defending the line on a much narrower front. Attackers approached in denser formations, increasing depth of damage. The assault was made in concert rather than in stages. Hours of Confederate artillery preparations on the morning of July 3rd signalled the probability of an attack. This pre-warning allowed time for the Union defenders to plan countermeasures against the anticipated enemy activity.

it was employed on July 3. The Confederate attack on the second was made on a broad front against a broad defensive line that involved half of the entire Union line. On July 3 the Confederate attack was made on a front half as broad as the one it made on the second and focused against a narrow defending front just a few hundred yards wide.

In the wide-front engagement of July 2, Federal artillery, not anticipating the attack nor preparing for it, had an exceptionally wide field of fire to operate against making it difficult to coordinate and concentrate its fire to stop the stubborn advances. Federal artillery on the second was also hampered considerably by wooded terrain, rolling ground, or heights too steep to depress cannon barrels to defend. After General Sickles moved his Third Corps forward to the Emmitsburg Road, the contact point between the two battle lines before the Confederate advance was much less distant than on July 3. Therefore, defending artillery had much less reaction time to stop any advance, even though a short bombardment took place before it began and forewarned that an assault was probable.

On July 3 conditions were much different. Although the Union line had a greater chance to be overwhelmed by sheer numbers in a more unified attack, the circumstances on July 3 gave the Federal defenders greater opportunities to help fend off the attack. Federal commanders knew the attack was probable because of the very visible Confederate artillery preparations going on across their front before the opening shot. The intense cannonade confirmed the imminence of the attack and the duration of the shelling allowed additional time to respond and make preparations to counter the impending threat. The Southern formations also presented more compacted targets than the multi-staged advances of July 2 and, as a result, provided a more focused field of fire for Union artillery. The terrain crossed over by the Confederate infantry on the third was also substantially more open than some of the ground contested the day before. The assault on the third exposed the enemy advance to artillery fire longer than on the second and, consequently, made the Federal positions ideally suited for creating a crossfire into the advancing and compressing Confederate columns gathering to pierce the Union center.

It is today, and was then, exceedingly difficult for commanders to do battle where large armies covered large areas of battleground. The difficulty was magnified by operating on unfamiliar terrain and with maps that were not designed for informing commanders about the details needed to fight a battle. At Gettysburg, commanders were, for the first time, learning the importance of the area's terrain features—the road network and how it interconnected, the hills, ridges, woods, etc.—in relationship to their battle lines as well as the enemy's. They were just learning the names of local terrain features such as ridges, hills, and farms, and commanders had to send orders for troops or batteries to go to these unfamiliar places—thus "Seminary Ridge" was confused with "Cemetery Ridge," for example. No one saw the whole battle, including the commanders, and no one left with a total knowledge of what happened.

★ ★ ★

In summary, proper gun placement relied on a combination of many things. Each battery was interdependent with infantry or cavalry units, or with other batteries to create an effective artillery force and carry out the plans of the army commander. Correct placement needed infantry commanders that were knowledgeable in the use of artillery or competent artillerymen skilled in the technical aspects of artillery operations, tactics, weapons' capabilities and limitations. Proper placement needed careful thought regarding how to use the terrain advantages, or how to protect terrain weaknesses, and consideration had to be given to anticipating the enemy's intentions.

Site Preparation

Once an artillery site was chosen, preparation had to be made for operating the guns. The ground in front of the batteries had to be cleared of any vegetation or obstacles that interfered with an open field of fire or shielded enemy troops within rifle range. The site had to also be prepared anticipating any movements during an action; it had to be ready for the advancement of the guns, if ordered, or for easy removal should a retreat be necessary.[41]

Although it was natural to seek shelter under cover of a tree line or behind a stone wall, it was actually safer to distance a gun crew from objects that could endanger it when their position was pounded by enemy shells. Buildings, fences, breastworks, etc. could protect as well as injure those seeking cover. If the guns at the battle of Gettysburg were placed near stone walls like many are located today on the battlefield, it subjected artillery gun crews to a dangerous and awkward area to operate. For one thing, the artillerymen loading the charge down the barrels needed some "dancing room" to maneuver the six-foot long sponge-rammer forward of the barrel. Secondly, locating a gun directly behind a stone wall was careless and against safety instructions. Directives stated: "Cover which makes splinters when struck by shot, such as masonry, wood stacks, &c., is objectionable. Artificial cover may be obtained by sinking the piece. This is done by making an excavation for it to stand in. The excavation should be one foot and a half deep in front, and should slope gently upward toward the rear. . . . The guns when so posted should not be placed behind wood or stone barricades. Such cover should be removed and the pieces sunk . . . , or earth parapets placed in front of them."[42]

For standing artillerymen, stone walls would not have offered much protection from the airbursts of exploding projectiles. Rocks would certainly stop bullets but a 12-pound ball colliding into a stone wall at several hundred miles an hour would have caused an unwelcome chain reaction. On impact, the

Using 6-foot rammers, artillerymen needed maneuvering room forward of the gun to load efficiently. Stone walls posed a serious threat from incoming rounds fragmenting the rocks. (AC)

The trail of the gun carried a prolonge rope, wound around the iron brackets on top. It had pointing rings and handles at the end for positioning, adjustable metal straps to secure implements, and bumper guards, rectangular metal plates to protect wood from limber wheels in sharp turns. (AC)

rocks would explode into shrapnel-like shards and be just as deadly as their iron counterparts; during the cannonade on July 3, one of the color guards in the 136th New York Infantry "had a fragment of a rock driven into his head, causing instant death."[43]

Falling tree limbs and tree splinters could be just as deadly. If artillery was positioned among trees, a gun crew's safety depended, to some extent, on the trees' variety. When exposed to artillery fire, it was preferable to be in a tree line of softwoods. An enemy solid shot passing through a pine tree, for example, made a clean round hole where a solid shot hitting a hardwood, such as an oak, splintered and broke the brittle wood into deadly fragments.

In addition, the type of soil was considered in the placement of the guns. Ideally guns were to be located on hard ground, where they could be easily placed and maneuvered by the fewest men. The recoil effects also were affected by the ground hardness. The gun needed freedom to recoil. Soft ground and a high elevation of fire increased the friction on the trail and, in turn, decreased the recoil of the piece. Decreasing the recoil could damage the carriage and it placed more explosive pressure on the barrel in turn increasing the force to burst the gun. On soft ground the trail could dig in so deep that the gun could flip over backwards or break the axle.

Despite the dangers of hampering a gun's recoil risks were taken; guns were tested to their limits. At the first battle of Manassas, for example, Cushing's Federal battery was positioned beyond the maximum range of his guns. He ordered his men to dig holes under the trails deep enough to allow firing at angles upwards of forty degrees—dangerously increasing barrel stress on his rifled guns by inhibiting their recoil reaction and creating an extra hazard for the gun crew.[44]

Artillery Support Placement and Threats on a Gun

After positioning the guns and preparing the site, each battery had to be protected either by its location or by infantry supports. Infantry troops, when supporting artillery, had to put enough space between themselves and the cannons to prevent them from being hit by enemy rounds that were aimed at their artillery. Placing infantry behind a battery was an unsafe situation. The cannons they supported attracted enemy artillery fire and any overshot could hit its unintended victims. In addition, if infantry combat occurred close to the artillery, a battery firing in front of support troops obstructed their field of fire; with this arrangement, a battery still in operation prevented any advance of their infantry until those guns had finished.[45]

Since a battery's self-protecting front was the least vulnerable to attack, infantrymen were generally not placed in front of cannons because of premature shell explosions and exposure to the shedded components of the projectile. Supporting infantry troops were better protectors on the flanks of a battery, more so than in front of, among, or behind it.

Because of the dual arrangement of infantry and artillery units sharing the battle line, each relied heavily on the other's resources during an action. Infantrymen expected their artillery to inflict long-range damage, provide protective comfort for them, and help prevent massed enemy lines from approaching their defenses. Artillerymen, on the other hand, needed infantry support when the fighting came within small-arms range, especially when the enemy was shielded by woods or anything that masked their presence, but in open ground as well.

When sharing a battle line's front, each infantry and artillery unit had to be prepared to interact and have a mutual understanding of how they would cooperate during different phases of the conflict. In a heavy assault, for example, a battery commander needed to know when to cease fire so his infantry supports could come into play on the battery's front. A cooperating infantry commander, with his supporting troops on the flanks, had to decide when to wheel his men forward to protect the guns and sweep the ground with a crossfire. Such maneuvers could not be performed well without a collaborative agreement beforehand, when plans were made in quieter moments. Support infantry needed to be placed close to the batteries, protect their exposed sides, and be ready to act if the guns were threatened with capture.[46]

If a defensive line was in jeopardy of being overrun, the support infantry was used to buy enough time for artillery batteries to safely remove their equipment from the field. Cannons were not supposed to be captured. Sacrificing artillery pieces, however, was sometimes deliberate and it usually happened under extraordinary circumstances. It was rare to have these weapons placed in situations allowing capture and, unless there were sound reasons for their loss, dishonor was attached to the unit involved. Guns were honorably lost, however, when protecting the safety of other troops providing that their captors paid dearly for them.

Sometimes artillery pieces were captured because of simple misunderstandings. At Gettysburg, for example, some of the last Federal units to retreat from Seminary Ridge on July 1, were Colonel Wainwright's First Corps batteries. Wainwright, unfamiliar with local landmarks, overheard some directions given to General Doubleday about holding Cemetery Hill. Not knowing that there was such a place, he assumed references to the *seminary* were used interchangeably with *cemetery* and supposed he already occupied it. While Federal infantry units were given the order to fall back to Cemetery Hill, Wainwright was "still under the false impression as to the importance attached to holding Seminary Hill." Wainwright commented, "A few minutes, however, showed me our infantry rapidly retreating to the town." While the infantry was in retreat and the enemy lapping in from two directions, the guns, now without supports, were left to their own fate. Limbering up, the cannons were pulled off the ridge, up Chambersburg St., three abreast, and at full gallop. The loss was one gun and four caissons.[47]

Different methods were used in responding to threats on artillery pieces. When retreat was imminent and capture of guns probable, the weapons had to be disabled in some manner to prevent the enemy from turning them against the withdrawing troops. Disabling the gun could render it inoperable either temporarily or permanently. Circumstances surrounding the gun's capture and the expectations of its retrieval determined the methods chosen to incapacitate the piece.

If recapture was probable, temporary measures were used. The most common temporary method of disabling a gun was spiking. Properly done this required a hardened steel spike with a soft point. It was hammered into the vent, level with the top of the barrel. The rammer was then pushed down the bore to bend the soft point of the spike resulting in the temporary closure of the vent hole that ignited the powder charge. If no spikes were available, rat-tail files, nails with the heads cut off, and even musket rammers were used. Although it took additional time, spiked cannons could still be fired even though access through the vent was cut off. Quickmatch, a slow-burning cotton fuse, could be laid from the muzzle back to the powder charge and then ignited.[48]

A spiked vent could be reopened providing the spike was not bent inside and there was access to the rear of the bore. Blowing out the spike also was possible. This was done by using a one-third charge, packed in the barrel with wadding, and a board with a groove on the underside for a length of quickmatch placed in the bore. In an iron gun, the clogged vent might be redrilled or a new one made nearby. In a bronze gun, sulfuric acid poured around the spike often reduced its tight fit enough to expel it with a charge. If nothing else worked, the vent-piece, which was a separate threaded part in many guns, could be removed and the blockage cleared or a new vent-piece could replace the damaged one.

Besides spiking the vent, other measures were used to temporarily disable an artillery piece. Options included damaging the elevating screw or taking the implements required to load the piece; destroying shell fuses; ramming a shot the wrong way and wedging it into the bore; or if time allowed, destroying the carriage by burning it or knocking the spokes out of the wheels.[49]

Disabling ammunition was another option in neutralizing an artillery piece. In the retreat on July 1 of Colonel Wainwright's guns just mentioned, battery commander Lieutenant James Stewart described the devotion to duty displayed by one of his artillerymen: "I found one of my men bursting the cartridges that were on one of the caissons, the rear axle of that caisson was broken and four of the horses had been killed. I inquired if any one had ordered him to remain and destroy the ammunition, and he said 'no; but the rebs are following us up pretty hard, and if the caisson fell into their hands, they would use the ammunition upon us.' I remained with him until he had destroyed the last round and then told him to keep with me."[50]

Not many cannons were captured permanently by either side during the battle of Gettysburg. General Pendleton reported five Confederate pieces were lost to capture or were disabled. This was offset by the Confederate reports stating that seven Union guns were captured (General Hunt said six were lost).

The reason that few Confederate guns were captured by the Union army at Gettysburg was partially due to the fact that the Union army, with the exception of retaking their positions on Culp's Hill on July 3, was totally on the defensive. Except during the Confederate retreat, the Federals had no opportunity to be in the close presence of enemy artillery in order to make a capture.

On the other hand, the Confederates, being on the offensive and given their initial successes, had greater opportunities to acquire Federal guns. But even though they captured substantial ground on July 1 and 2, a considerable amount of fighting occurred in wooded areas such as Herbst Woods, Culp's Hill, and the Round Tops, where few Federal guns were present. The Federal guns that were captured, for the most part, were captured temporarily. Union infantry troops in support would not let their lost guns be removed without the enemy paying a high price for such an honor.[51]

If permanent capture of a piece was probable, the gun's destruction was necessary to withhold it from enemy use. Any number of methods could be used to achieve this. Cutting or knocking off the barrel trunnions made the gun unusable; placing stress on the barrel beyond its capable firing limits was another method; loading the gun with a charge and packing the bore with sand would usually burst an iron gun. With bronze guns, bursting a shell in the barrel or firing broken shot would severely damage the bore. If time allowed, building a fire under the chase, the tapered portion of the gun barrel from the trunnions to the muzzle, and smashing it with sledgehammers could damage a bronze gun. Aiming the barrel at high elevations with multiple charges and projectiles could blow a barrel. Firing one gun against another also could bend or break a barrel beyond repair.[52]

Targets

After the guns and ammunition vehicles were positioned, the site preparation was completed, and protection arranged with supporting infantry, the next step was to select enemy targets. Published guidelines suggested the most effective target selection. When attacking, the artillery was to concentrate its might on the enemy strongpoints offering the most resistance. On the defensive, the artillery was to concentrate its firepower on the most dangerous threat at the moment, especially against infantry or cavalry.[53]

Targets were not always visible in a battle. Smoke, terrain, vegetation, buildings, etc. often concealed the intended target. But telltale signs such as reflections of small-arm gun barrels or bayonets, smoke drifting out of a tree line, or flame piercing through the dense smoke from belching cannons divulged enemy activity. Confederate Major George Randolph at Big Bethel could not see the Federals approaching but he knew when to open up with his artillery:

> Fire . . . was not opened upon them for ten or fifteen minutes, when from the number of bayonets visible in the road we judged that a heavy column was within range. The action then commenced by a shot from the Parrott gun, aimed by myself, which struck the center of the road a short distance in front of their column, and probably did good execution in its ricochet. At no time could we see the bodies of the men in the column, and our fire was directed by their bayonets, their position being obscured by the shade of the woods on their right and two small houses on their left, and somewhat in advance of them.[54]

Battery commanders frequently ignored prioritizing targets according to published guidelines. Disregarding directives and causing an irresponsible waste of ammunition produced from poor judgment did not go unnoticed. In general, authorities thought too much ammunition was wasted on suspected targets not visible, small groups of men, or objects of little consequence. There was also a great temptation for artillery units to battle it out with each other, consuming large quantities of precious ammunition in the process, and contributing little to the outcome of the battle; such contests were to be avoided, if possible, and *Instruction for Field Artillery* stated: "The effect of field artillery is generally in proportion to the concentration of its fire. It has therefore for its object, not to strike down a few isolated men, and here and there to dismount a gun, but by a combined and concentrated fire to destroy an enemy's cover; to break up his squares and columns; to open his ranks; to arrest his attacks, and to support those which may be directed against him."[55]

One precept believed that fire should be opened on enemy artillery as they were bringing their pieces around to form into battery. Another believed that artillery fire from several guns should be directed with angle-fire towards one gun to disable it rather than an uncoordinated fire at many targets, thereby diluting the effects of concentrated firepower.

When pieces were fired at troops, a converging fire directed at one point was designed to break the momentum of the attack, throw the enemy line into confusion, and breakdown the morale of the units. Federal ordnance instructions stated: "It is not the number of killed and wounded that decides a battle, but the panic and demoralization of those who remain; and this panic and demoralization are much sooner created and spread by concentrating the artillery fire on successive points than by distributing it over a wide space."[56]

Working a Gun

Firing

Proper positioning of a battery and proper site preparation was often a luxury when a battle was in progress. Roberts's *Handbook of Artillery* described the unbelievable quickness with which a battery could begin operations: "It could come into action and fire one round in 26 seconds, timing from the order 'action front,' to the discharge of one piece."

Loading and firing a gun required concentration and close attention to detail. The process included an orderly series of moves necessary to ensure the safety of the gun crew and the effectiveness of the gun's operation. After the gun had been properly positioned, the limber was placed six yards behind the gun and facing towards it. Upon receiving the order to fire from the battery commander, the gunner took over operational control of his piece and gave all the executive commands. He pointed the gun, communicated orders he received such as ammunition types, and also, if needed, estimated the proper fuse time to synchronize the projectile's detonation.

After evaluating the time setting for the next fuse, the gunner yelled the number of seconds or target distance to the gun crewmember who was preparing fuses at the limber. When time allowed, during a slow-firing mode, the gunner was also responsible for checking the proper fuse setting.

When given the order to fire, the gunner gave the command to load, bent over the trail to verify the proper direction and elevation, and stepped aside to observe the effects of the projectile. After firing, he then had the gun moved back into place from its recoil.[57]

When the round was fired, reloading was accomplished by sponging and ramming. The man who sponged the barrel first had to observe the vent to insure that it was closed; if the vent was not closed, he would discontinue sponging and give the command, "stop vent!"

Closing the vent was the most important safety precaution in loading a gun. This deprived the bore of oxygen to feed any burning debris remaining, and it prevented a current of air from passing out of the gun during sponging and ramming the round. Any air movement in the bore had to be suppressed. The rammer sponge fit the bore snugly and thus acted as a piston. Failing to close the vent properly would allow the sponge to force smoldering cartridge bag remnants, such as pieces of thread or paper, into the vent. Any hidden sparks in the vent created a dangerous condition when the powder bag was inserted. Carelessness was likely to cause a premature explosion and produce catastrophic injuries to the rammer. The vent had to be closed from the time the sponge entered until the charge was inserted; this included the moments during the removal steps of the sponge and rammer as well. If the vent was not sealed during this stage, removing the sponge sucked air and any debris from the vent back into the bore and rekindled any lit sparks or debris remaining.[58]

The thumbstall, a protective leather accouterment, was used to close the vent. It looked like the thumb and wrist portion of a glove. Its purpose was to protect the thumb from severe burns caused by escaping hot gases. The thumbstall was pressed against the vent when the piece was sponged and loaded. Sometimes, in desperation, a gun was loaded without the use of a thumbstall.

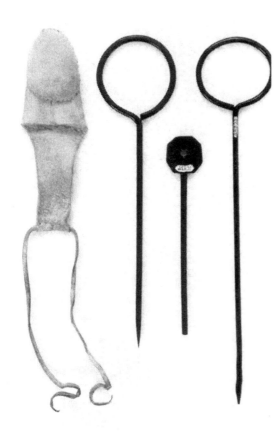

The thumbstall protected a thumb from heat while stopping the vent.
The priming wire pierced the cartridge bag.
The vent-punch and gimlet cleared obstructions. (GNMP/WDC)

The experience was excruciating. One example involved Lieutenant Alonzo Cushing, Federal battery commander. Although he was already mortally wounded as Pickett's Charge reached its climax on Cemetery Ridge, he was heroically assisting his artillerymen in loading a gun. The only available thumbstall was a lump of burned leather, worthless and worn out. Without hesitating, Cushing dutifully plugged the gun's vent with his unprotected thumb as the barrel was being sponged. In his last moments of life, his faced flushed with agony, he grabbed his injured finger after the searing-hot gases burned his thumb to the bone from the sponging of the barrel.[59]

Next in the loading process, after closing the vent with the thumbstall, the sponge was introduced to the barrel. Sponging cleaned the barrel, cooled it, and most important, extinguished any remaining sparks from the previous shot. Rifled guns could hide sparks in the barrel grooves and this made it especially important to perform the sponging step properly. The sponge was dipped into a bucket of water, spun around to remove excess water, forced to the bottom of the bore, and twisted to remove cartridge remmnants. Wet sponging the barrel was preferable to dry sponging in extinguishing smoldering bag embers, but this method formed a paste of charred matter that was difficult to remove.

This plaque at the Gettysburg National Military Park depicts artillerymen of Battery K, 1st New York Light Artillery, Artillery Reserve, sponging the bore, thumbing the vent, and carrying ammunition. (AC)

After sponging, the ammunition was introduced to the bore with the powder bag seam to the side. This alignment was done to prevent the thick-stitched seam from resting under the vent and interfering when the bag was pierced. The ammunition was then rammed down the barrel. A potential hazard contributing to barrel stress for any artillery piece, rifled or smoothbore, was the position of the ammunition in the barrel after ramming. Extreme care was needed to ram the projectile completely to the rear of the bore. If loaded properly, the exploding propellant gas pressure was transmitted immediately to the projectile and forced it from the barrel. If ramming did not push the ammunition completely to the rear of the bore, a space existed between the powder and rear of the barrel. This created a dangerous situation. In this case, when the cartridge ignited, the *entire* powder charge was converted into a gas *before* the projectile moved; its full power was developed prematurely. Consequently, the full explosive force of the gas "crashed" into the stationary projectile before its inertia was overcome. The explosive force, suddenly stopped in its tracks, exerted a powerful strain on the cannon with the potential of bursting the barrel.[60]

After ramming, the powder bag was pierced with a rigid instrument called a vent pick or priming wire. The friction primer was placed in the barrel vent and a twelve-foot lanyard was then attached to it. The friction primer was inserted in the vent and covered with the left hand, keeping the lanyard slack to prevent accidental firing. After the men were clear of the wheels, the command of "fire" was given and the lanyard was pulled.

Aiming Devices

Different methods and implements were used in aiming a gun. One device, the quadrant, considered an old-fashioned tool, was sometimes used to measure the degree of elevation of the barrel in relation to the perpendicular and was used in conjunction with the *Table of Fire*. The *Table of Fire*, pasted inside the limber lid, listed the degrees of elevation, ranges, and times of flight for various projectiles and was used to calculate accuracy of fire.

Information regarding the value of the *Table of Fire* and the importance of its use compared to using the skilled estimates of the gunner as an alternative is sketchy. The table did not consider the fact that guns of the same model and caliber made by a different manufacturer did not perform the same. Some tables did not provide information precise enough to calculate accuracy of fire properly. A Confederate artillery sergeant named Humphreys described the shortcomings of his *Table of Fire*: "The elevation, range and time of flight were all three given in round numbers. This was probably the best our ordnance department could do; but it was our place as artillerymen to modify these tables to suit ascertained facts, and to construct tables for the pieces that had none."[61]

Reliance on using the *Table of Fire* under battle conditions was different than practiced training. Sergeant Humphreys stated: "They would go through the motions of obtaining the range and correcting the errors in assumed cases; but when it came to actual firing in the face of the enemy, they would cast all that to the winds, and begin to fire with nervous haste, taking careless aim and guessing haphazard at the necessary correction, so that they were liable after one error to err the next time as much or more in the opposite direction."[62]

Artillery pieces used a variety of sights. One type of sight was the breech sight. This brass sight was marked with degrees of elevation and an adjustable bar to line up and aim with the muzzle sight. To aim properly, the breech sight had to be in the absolute vertical. To achieve this another implement, the gunner's level, was required. Artillery pieces more often than not operated on

The quadrant measured the degree of elevation of the cannon barrel. (AC)

Table of Fire for Napoleon gun. Charts like these were usually pasted on the inside of the limber chest lid. (GNMP/WDC)

TABLE OF FIRE. LIGHT 12-POUNDER GUN MODEL 1857.

SHOT. Charge 2½ Pounds.		SPHERICAL CASE Charge 2½ Pounds.						
ELEVATION In Degrees	RANGE In Yards	ELEVATION In Degrees	TIME OF FLIGHT Seconds			TIME OF FLIGHT in Seconds	RANGE In Yards
0°	323	0°50'	1"	300	0	0"75	300
1°	620	1°	1"75	575	0 30	1"25	425
2°	875	1°30'	2"5	635	1°	1"75	615
3°	1200	2°	3"	730	1°30'	2"25	700
4°	1325	3°	4"	960	2°	2"75	785
5°	1680	3°30'	4"75	1080	2°30'	3"5	925
		3°40'	5"	1135	3°	4"	1080
					3°45'	5"	1300

Use SHOT at masses of troops, and to batter, from 600 up to 2,000 yards. Use SHELL for firing buildings, at troops posted in woods, in pursuit, and to produce a moral rather than a physical effect; greatest effective range 1,500 yards. Use SPHERICAL CASE SHOT at masses of troops, at not less than 500 yards; generally up to 1,500 yards. CANISTER is not effective at 600 yards; it should not be used beyond 500 yards, and but very seldom and over the most favorable ground at that distance; at short ranges (less than 200 yards) in emergency, use double canister, with single charge. Do not employ RICOCHET at less distance than 1,000 to 1,100 yards.

CARE OF AMMUNITION CHEST.

1st. Keep everything out that does not belong in them, except a bunch of cord or wire for breakage; beware of loose tacks, nails, bolts, or scraps.
2d. Keep friction primers in their papers, tied up. The pouch containing those for instant service must be closed, and so placed as to be secure. Take every precaution that primers do not get loose ; a single one may cause an explosion. Use plenty of tow in packing.

(This sheet is to be glued on to the inside of Limber Chest Cover.)

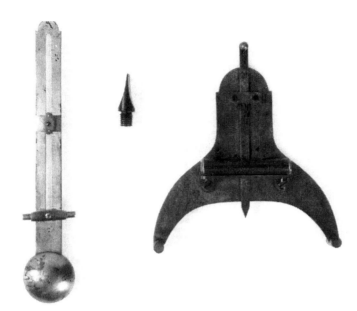

(Left) *A pendulum-hausse was a free-swinging rear sight supported by a seat on the barrel breech.*
(Center) *A muzzle sight was the front aiming sight.*
(Right) *A gunner's level located the proper position for the breech sight.*
(GNMP/WDC)

uneven ground and the gunner's level indicated the perpendicular. The gunner's level, however, and the quadrant, mentioned above, were rarely used in the field, at least by Federal artillerymen. The quarterly inventory report, *Summary of Ordnance and Ordnance Stores on Hand in the Artillery Regiments,* for the Union army's entire artillery force dated June 30, 1863, lists only a handful of these two devices.

A more popular type of sight that was in service on a broad scale, the pendulum hausse, eliminated the need for the gunner's level. This brass sight rested in a cradle at the rear of the barrel and used an adjustable slider and graduated scale marked with degrees of elevation to achieve proper range. The pendulum hausse was free-swinging and weighted with lead at the bottom to obtain a vertical line with the earth which allowed the gunner to aim properly, even though the gun carriage was positioned on ground that was not level.

Parrott rifles used a brass stadia sight. It consisted of a movable sight which slid up or down on a brass rod which had graduated markings. The device called a tangent sight, was mounted on the right hand side of the barrel. An eyebolt was installed in the reinforcing band and held the sight while the front sight was located at the top of the rimbase at the trunnion. The reason Parrott guns used this type of sight was because of the thick reinforcing band at the breech end. This raised part of the barrel required a much taller muzzle sight which made it much more susceptible to breakage.

Besides gun sights, other aiming devices were used to maximize the accuracy of artillery fire. At Gettysburg, an interesting invention was used in Captain Greenleaf Stevens's 5th Maine Battery. To estimate the ranges to potential targets, one of Stevens's lieutenants, Edward N. Whittier, spent the time calibrating the distance by manipulating an instrument called a *"French ordnance glass."* Lieutenant Whittier referred to this instrument and its connection with Gettysburg in an address delivered in 1891. Little information, however, is known about this device. Attempts to research a drawing of what it looked like or information on how it was used have proven unsuccessful. There are no references to it in the entire Official Records unless it is referred to by another name. This device was described by Whittier as being the "nearest approach to a range-finder for light artillery at that time in use" and was a precursor of modern artillery-fire-direction equipment.[63]

Another device described in the *Artillerist's Manual* whose usage appears doubtful was a hand-held stick known in France as a *"stadia"* (different than the stadia sight mentioned above). To estimate distance, this small stick was held vertically at arm's length. By bringing the top of the stick level with the top of a man's head and noting where the man's feet lined up with one of the graduated markings on the stick, a correlation between distance and height was presumed to calculate range. Noting the ordinary height of an infantry soldier, these graduated markings were derived by how he appeared at different intervals of distance. Since lengths of arms and heights of soldiers varied, the stadia stick's precision was questionable. General Gibbon, author of the *Artillerist's Manual*, described this device as "not very accurate except for short distances."[64]

Aiming

Aiming was mostly accomplished with the gunner observing the target and using direct fire. Sometimes, as mentioned earlier, indirect fire was used where the gunner could often judge the location of the target from smoke generated by enemy fire, dust created from troop movements, or reflections of metal. If the target was not visible, aiming improvisation also included the help of signal stations and balloonists to guide the gunner. The art of aiming, more often than not, consisted of skilled judgment rather than scientific calculation. The *Artillerist's Manual* pointed out the requirements needed: "In order to become proficient in the use of firearms, a man must either learn the principles upon which his arm is constructed, as well as those governing the inflammation of the powder and the passage of the projectile through the air; or he must, from long actual practice with the arm, understand the result of these principles. It is evident that a combination of the two will produce the best marksmen in the shortest time."[65]

Hitting a target successfully required thorough training, planning ahead, careful observation, astute estimating ability, and a thorough understanding of the elements that reacted on the projectile in flight. One aspect of training men to be good marksmen required them to be able to measure distances by pacing it off. The *Artillerist's Manual* called for training men in recognizing and correctly estimating ranges:

> In order to estimate distances by the eye, spaces were measured off, and men placed at points along the line to show their appearance at the different distances. . . . The distances are then paced, and, finally measured. In these different operations the men are made to notice different parts of the body and equipments, which become indistinct as the person is removed farther off. On a clear day, and with ordinary sight, at from 190 to 200 yards, every part of a man's body can be seen; and, although the details of dress and figure begin to grow indistinct, the grades of the officers can be recognized at these distances. From 400 to 480 yards, the face can no longer be distinguished, but the head, body, arms and movements, as well as the uniforms and muskets, can.
>
> At 600 yards, the head and upper and lower parts of the body can be made out; and of the uniform, the accouterments and white pantaloons only can be seen.
>
> From 750 to 800 yards, the body appears as an elongated form. Extended arms can be seen in profile, as also the legs of men in motion. The uniform can no longer be distinguished at 900 yards; but the files can be seen, as well as the movement of troops, and the dust thrown up by a projectile ricocheting on dry ground. From 1,100 to 1,200 yards, the files can scarcely be distinguished, and the troops appear like solid masses, the movements of which can be still followed.[66]

Preplanning any anticipated enemy troop movements was also an integral part in producing successful artillery fire and made the aiming process much easier. Artillery officers with foresight and opportunity laid out correct ranges by premeasuring distances to potential targets before any action began and by firing a few rounds to confirm the effects.

On Marye's Heights at Fredericksburg, Virginia, for example, the Confederate artillerymen fired with deadly results. They had premeasured the exact ranges to possible points of conflict such as the avenues that would feed enemy troops from the town, or anyplace that would promote the massing of infantry for an assault, or areas where shelter would seem likely.[67]

At Gettysburg, before the action occurred, Stevens's 5th Maine Battery, located on the slopes of Culp's Hill, estimated the distances to potential targets by using his range-finding device, mentioned above, and accurately premeasured potential targets. Calculations such as barrel elevations and fuse lengths were determined. These measurements were completed in a calm atmosphere and not in the midst of a battle, which naturally distracted from the concentration and precision necessary for accurate performance. When permission was received to fire a test round from Stevens's position, the one attempt landed squarely on its target—a clump of trees at the Culp farm. Lieutenant Whittier described the outcome of their preparations: ". . . As quickly as the enemy [Hay's and Hoke's Confederate brigades] appeared, even while his lines were forming, the battery opened with case-shot, each one bursting as if on measured ground, at the right time, and in the right place in front of the advancing lines."[68]

Range could also be estimated by observing the enemy's artillery piece and noting the time it took between the flash and report of the gun and multiplying the seconds by the velocity of sound—about eleven hundred feet per second, depending on the temperature.

Another integral part of aiming successfully was viewing the effects of the artillery round. Close observation of the projectile's degree of success on hitting the target was essential for improving accuracy. It made no sense to continue firing without attempting to correct the aim. Observation, however, was complicated for several reasons. Thick clouds of white smoke from enemy artillery positions, as well as from friendly guns, gradually obscured the ability to correct the aim and assess any damage on the targets. When other guns were also firing toward the same target, it was nearly impossible, with any degree of certainty, to determine the accuracy of a specific gun crew and which gun hit where. A way of judging one's own accuracy was the degree of accuracy shown by the enemy's guns. On Cemetery Hill, July 2, Union artillery commander Thomas Osborn noted that if his guns were not doing the intended damage the enemy would soon discern the range and hold it. Conversely, if the enemy's guns were off target, Osborn's guns were probably doing their job.

Ironically, the degree of difficulty in hitting a target, in certain cases, could increase substantially when using a highly accurate rifled gun instead of a less accurate smoothbore. With the increased range of the rifled gun, target observations were often made from firing positions located well beyond the range of a smoothbore. This simply made the target much more difficult to see through a denser atmosphere caused by the added distance.

Velocity differences between smoothbore and rifled guns also made aiming more difficult for rifled cannons. With smoothbore ammunition, after the initial velocity rapidly decreased, soldiers could actually see the comparatively slow-traveling projectiles as they curved in their fall toward their target. Although smoothbore projectiles had a greater initial velocity because of their much greater charge, the blunt round shape quickly slowed down the ball by the air resistance acting upon it. This reduction, in turn, allowed the ball to be visually tracked; at maximum range, a smoothbore projectile's striking velocity was only about one-third of its muzzle velocity and less than half the average velocity of a rifled projectile. According to *The Ordnance Manual for the Use of the Officers of the Confederate States Army*, a smoothbore spherical case projectile, for example, using a 2½-pound charge, had an initial velocity of 1,485 feet per second or 1,013 miles per hour. At 1,500 yards the velocity had rapidly worn down to 486 feet per second or 331 miles per hour.[69]

Conversely, the pointed rifled projectiles retained their velocity much longer than smoothbore ammunition. A 3-inch rifle projectile, for example, had a muzzle velocity of 1,232 feet per second or 840 miles per hour. At 1,500 yards, the velocity was down to 839 feet per second or 572 miles per hour. The smoothbore, therefore, retained only one-third of its original velocity while the rifled projectile retained two-thirds.[70]

But even though rifled projectiles were invisible in flight, their bursting shells flashed brightly leaving a soft puff of white smoke as their signature and earmarking their accuracy for the next round; even non-exploding rifled projectiles kicked up dust for the artillerymen to gauge their aim. Rifled projectiles became visible, however, if they tumbled out of control. It was not unusual for the projectile to fail in taking the rifled grooves of the barrel or to have the spin wear off. As a result, the shell flew erratically towards an unpredictable destination.

An eyewitness to the cannonade on July 3, Federal General John Gibbon, described the visual performance of incoming projectiles: ". . . The whole air seemed filled with rushing screaming and bursting shells. The larger round shells could be seen plainly as in their nearly completed course they curved in their fall towards the Taneytown road, but the long rifled shells came with a rush and a scream and could only be seen in their rapid flight when they 'upset' and went tumbling through the air, creating the uncomfortable impression that, no matter whether you were in front of the gun from which they came or not, you were liable to be hit."[71]

There were other enormous variables besides those just mentioned and, as discussed earlier, included inconsistent fuse reliability and the lack of precision range estimating when time fuses were used. In addition, every time the gun was fired the information gained from observing the hit of the previous shot was lost when the recoil moved the gun's position. The vibration of the piece also affected accuracy. Care had to be taken to reset the elevation of the barrel. In the retreat from the battle of Resaca, Captain William L. Ritter, 3rd Maryland Battery, C.S.A., described the results of enemy gunners overlooking this step of resetting the elevation: "A heavy fire was kept up for about an hour with telling effect. This was evident from the fact that the enemy's shots were continually rising; this was a sure sign that they were becoming excited. The elevating screw of a cannon is depressed by the impact upon it of the breech at the moment of firing, with the effect of course, of elevation the muzzle, and causing the shot to rise higher and higher. The screw should be run up after each discharge of the piece—something that in the tumult of battle a gunner might easily forget."[72]

During the battle of Antietam, Federal General John Gibbon noticed: "In the midst of this pandemonium I happened to look at this gun and noticed that the cannoneers had carelessly allowed the elevating screw to run down and every time the piece was fired its elevation was increased until now its missiles were harmlessly thrown high over the heads of the enemy in its front."[73]

The reaction of a gun's recoil on the elevating screw and the failure to make

The elevating screw adjusted the range. Vibration of the piece could move the elevating screw and change the range if left unchecked. (GNMP/AC)

constant adjustments to reset the elevation could have been a contributing factor causing Confederate guns to overshoot the Federal lines on July 3.

Forces uncontrollable by artillerymen included performance of projectiles due to wind and weather conditions. Wind increasingly influenced the projectile's flight path as the round lost velocity and, in turn, its ability to resist wind forces. Variations of wind velocities along the trajectory of a projectile made it more difficult to control accuracy than a steady wind. Rifled projectiles which have their center of gravity away from the middle of the round allowed the wind to react unevenly on the length of the body. Humidity changed the speed at which gunpowder converted from its solid state to a gas propellant. Fuses burned at different rates. As a result, the trajectory and the timing of the bursting charge varied. Changes in temperature and barometric pressure also shifted the range. Even the rotation of the earth affected accuracy, and it varied depending on the latitude which has different rotational velocities. This influence caused a projectile to drift to the right in the northern hemisphere. The degree of drift depended upon latitude, range, and time of flight.[74]

Inconsistency of ammunition was another uncontrollable factor. Variability was chiefly caused by the quality of materials and non-uniformity in manufacture, storage, care in transportation, and handling. Any slight deviation and often undetectable variations in uniformity of manufacture affected the performance of the projectile. No two mills, for example, made powder the same way. Different batches from the same mill produced different results. Consequently, the propellant force and the burn rate of the powder varied the projectiles' performance.

On one occasion, Brigadier General William Barry, chief of artillery, U.S.A., suspected that condemned ammunition sent back to the arsenal was accidentally reissued. Another instance occurred in Cowan's battery during the battle of Fredericksburg. Captain Cowan stated: "I examined several case shot, and found one without any powder filling, and another filled with, apparently, iron filings or rust."[75]

Transportation and handling affected powder cartridges. The long journey to Gettysburg, the condition of the roads, the constant movement, and lack of any cushioning suspension system for carriages carrying the ammunition supply certainly jarred and most probably altered the explosive reaction of some of the gunpowder. The Federal *Artillerist's Manual* described the result of hard handling: "When the cartridges have been a good deal knocked about, the dust formed by the crushed grains obstructs the interstices between the grains, and, the charge fuzing instead of exploding, the velocity of the ball is diminished." Variation in ramming pressure altered the results also. Hard ramming in the loading process, for example, affected velocity. Packing the grains tighter reduced the space between the grains for the reaction and this altered combustion.[76]

It became all-important for each artilleryman to learn, as best as he could, the subtle characteristics manifested by his gun as a host of other often uncontrollable factors interfered with the success of an artillery battery. There was a lack of uniformity in cannon barrel manufacture. Projectiles, also expected to be of uniform manufacture, were supplied with slightly different weights or diameters. The net effect from all the variables produced different ranges between like-model guns that had the same caliber, same angle of fire, and same charge. Wear and tear on the barrel also altered performance. Changes in windage affected the trajectory of the projectile and influenced the gun's accuracy. Continuous firing caused windage to change. Increased firing caused the barrel to heat up and, as a result, changed its dimensions; as the heat increased, the bore diameter of the gun tube expanded and made the bore slightly larger, while the unheated projectile's diameter remained the same. Consequently, the loading of the projectile had a looser fit and the windage was increased.

In cases where specialty ammunition, such as hot shot, was used, a projectile smaller than the bore diameter was also necessary to overcome the effects of heat expansion. Hot shot, not used at Gettysburg, was a solid projectile. After being heated to a white or red-hot temperature, it was fired at wooden structures or ships. Splintering wood made it more combustible, and, after a time, the smoldering debris ignited to a flaming fire. In the case of hot shot, the projectile's heat expanded its diameter, greater than the diameter on the cooler bore of the barrel, and made it difficult or impossible to load. In this case, it was a reaction of heat on the projectile and not the barrel that could interfere with the necessary windage.[77]

With all the variables gunners had to deal with in aiming a cannon, success in hitting the target with a solid shot was more predictable than using explosive projectiles, especially at greater distances. Other projectiles had internal components that were not always arranged symmetrically and consequently caused deviations in their trajectories. Solid shot was heavier than shell and, with a more fixed center of gravity, resulted in greater stability to the ball's trajectory and made it more resistant to the external forces that caused deviation.

The actual trajectory of a solid ball fired from a smoothbore, however, differed from its predicted trajectory. This deviation was caused by the ball's eccentricity when manufactured. Eccentricity is the degree of difference between the imperfect center of gravity in the ball's finished state and its actual center of gravity. A slightly off-centered ball, along with other factors such as its position in the gun, the air motion, and other external forces produced deviations, which caused the ball to revolve around an uncertain and variable axis; these factors created an imperfect trajectory.[78]

The greatest and perhaps least considered handicap in aiming artillery accurately during a battle was the lingering presence of smoke. Cannons and also small-arms were magnificent generators of this haze. Thick white clouds were produced even during moderate fighting. This elusive, but important, factor obstructed views more than trees. When the smoke factor was removed from the battlefield by the introduction of smokeless, high explosive powder in twentieth-century warfare, the casualty rates from artillery fire skyrocketed.

Smoke had a major effect in the way Civil War battles were fought. It placed limitations on the way everything operated or moved. Although smoke blocked the ability of artillerymen to see enemy targets, it also blocked their own presence from the enemy as well. At the start of a cannonade, any discomfort or uneasiness felt by gun crews most likely originated from the dilemma that, to operate their piece, they had to present themselves to the enemy as the most visible targets. Relief would not come until their own guns began belching a welcome smokescreen to hide their presence. Smoke at least created the sense that the enemy's intent was less personal, that enemy guns were not pointing at individuals.

Aiming with the unavoidable presence of smoke was made particularly difficult during large-scale cannonades like that on July 3 at Gettysburg. Because of the smoke, Union observers could only snatch brief glimpses of what was happening in the enemy line. Captain Charles A. Phillips, Battery E, Massachusetts Light Artillery, reported: "About 1 o'clock the enemy opened a heavy fire from a long line of batteries, which was kept up for an hour, but beyond the noise which was made no great harm was done. Having received orders from General Hunt and from you not to reply to their batteries, I remained silent for the first half hour, when General Hancock ordered us to open. We then opened fire on the enemy's batteries, but in the thick smoke probably did very little damage."[79]

After the cannonade and all the guns slackened, the Confederate infantry columns formed for the assault. The fields they were about to cross were laden with smoke and, for the moment, made the men invisible. The sheltering atmosphere created by the smokescreen must have been an appreciated substitute for their hushed guns; smoke postponed casualties and allowed them to draw closer to their objective. But soon the smoke dissipated and they were transformed into visible targets and forced to maneuver in clear view of enemy artillery. This changed condition must have provided little of the reassurance and protective feeling that their now silent artillery fire had just contributed to their fighting spirit.

In retrospect, the result of the cannonade on July 3 was modest. It was characteristic of what large-scale bombardments were known to produce. The Federals, for example, viewing the aiming skills of the Confederate gunners, were not impressed with their performance. Commanders surveyed the enemy's accuracy and appraised the cannonade's effects. Colonel Wainwright observed that "the enemy fired full three shots to our one. I have never known them to be so lavish of ammunition. Lee must have given special orders, and have placed much reliance on this fire." Wainwright deemed the results "not very effective, nine tenths passing over our men."[80]

Just south of the Union center, Lieutenant Freeman McGilvery, brigade commander of the Federal artillery reserve, had been in the midst of the iron storm. He reported: "The enemy opened a terrific fire upon our lines with at least one hundred and forty guns. This fire was very rapid and inaccurate, most of the projectiles passing from 20 to 100 feet over our lines."[81]

Although the cannonade pounded away with a fury, and considering the volume of fire and its duration, both forces suffered relatively little from the artillery fire. Damage was sustained, but many shots were too high, did not explode properly, or were otherwise ineffective. In the Union line near the copse of trees, Major Sylvanus Curtis, 7th Michigan Infantry, witnessed the effects of the Confederate projectiles bouncing towards them: "Nearly all the shot and shell struck in front and ricocheted over us, or passed over us and burst in our rear." While many of the aiming elevations of the Confederate guns may, in fact, have been correct, incorrect or faulty fuse settings may have created the appearance of overshooting. The object of explosive rounds using timed fuses was to detonate them *above* and *before* they reached the enemy lines. Any late detonations or duds would create the false impression that the aim was too high. In addition, some explosive shells apparently had the wrong fuse settings. One Confederate noted that some of the artillerymen near Heth's division were setting the fuses for their explosive projectiles to detonate at a mile and a quarter, while the distance between the two lines was less than a mile. Failure to reset the elevating screw, moved from the vibration of the piece, also could have been a factor in firing too high. Another possibility was the lay of the land. Firing at

Cemetery Ridge made it impossible to view any rounds landing in the rear of it and thereby provided no point of reference to make the proper adjustments.[82]

After two hours of raging artillery fire which hurled thousands of missiles across the fields, the Confederate cannonade failed to achieve its objective. The focal point of the attack in the Federal center was damaged but it was repairable. Replacement batteries and fresh gun crews were being rushed up to the front in time to receive the attack. Elsewhere in the Union line, the Southern cannonade apparently had not silenced a single Union gun on Cemetery Hill, McGilvery's line on the left-center, or Little Round Top. It was this firepower that could be brought to bear against the assaulting lines with their vulnerable flanks and envelop them with a withering crossfire.

The cannonade of July 3 did not produce the decisive effect intended. Its failure was undoubtedly caused, in part, by the multitude of aiming limitations that hampered the most skilled and ardent gunners in performing their work at hand. To what degree, no one can calculate.

Timing & Choosing Projectiles

For an army in combat, the timing of artillery fire and choice of targets relied on opportunity and the intent of the commander's battle plan. The artillery, in performing at its best, was to cause substantial damage to obstacles, demoralize enemy troops, and, in turn, interrupt enemy battle plans and make their opponents easy prey for infantry or cavalry to finish the task.

Timing was important in choosing when to open fire and instructions guided when a battery should begin to shoot. Commencing fire because the targets were in range was justifiable only when at least a quarter of the shots were hits. Within six hundred yards, rapid fire was to be used, "but only at a decisive moment when the rapidity [should be] increased to its greatest limit."[83]

Besides timing, frequency of fire was also an important consideration. The rate of fire depended on the intensity of the battle, instigated by one side and responded to by the other, and also the degree to which the accompanying peril threatened the participants or swayed the fight. If called on, cannons could fire two aimed shots per minute with shot or shells, or four charges of canister per minute at close range. Aiming cannons loaded with canister was not as important due to the wide pattern this ammunition projected as well as its typical use in moments of close-range desperation where timing no longer mattered and the concern for wasting ammunition had completely disappeared from their "things not to do" list.

Frequency of fire was supposed to be determined by knowing the quantity and type of ammunition on hand for immediate use and also the range of the targets. Since range was a factor, artillerymen needed to distinguish between the maximum range of their piece and its effective range. There was a distinct difference. As the range increased, so did the lateral deviation or drift of the round, and, in turn, the chances of hitting the target decreased. A 12-pounder smoothbore cannon, for example, firing a solid shot at only six hundred yards would have a horizontal deviation of about three feet. At twelve hundred yards, a typical operational range for Gettysburg, the deviation increased to about twelve feet. The other projectiles fired by the 12-pounders produced an even greater deviation. Although a gun crew's piece might deliver the projectile to the target area within its maximum range, the round may well have drifted beyond its effective range and the chance of hitting the target was negligible. It made no sense to even try if the chance of success was slim.[84]

Firing beyond the effective range was not only a waste of ammunition that would most likely be needed at a more critical moment, it also bolstered the morale of the enemy. When no damage was inflicted on the enemy by artillery fire it increased their confidence, it created a false sense that the aggressor's firepower was impotent, and, if the missed targets happened to be troops in an attack, it allowed them to advance with increased audacity.

Smoothbores could, on occasion, increase their effective range by ricochet firing. This phenomenon achieved some advantages that could not be accomplished by the projectile's normal trajectory. Ricochet firing was important in cases where projectiles had to reach behind enemy obstacles or when it was necessary to extend a cannon's effective fire beyond the limits of its normal range. Best accomplished over level, hard ground, ricochet firing was a deliberate effort of a gun crew to aim low in order to "bounce" the projectile over terrain and gain altitude in order to increase its range. The ricochet effects were often better than direct fire because the bouncing effect decreased the ball's velocity as the projectile skipped across the terrain. Too much velocity on a ball hitting targets with little resistance caused a small hole with little damage. A ball with little velocity fractured, split and splintered objects, and scattered dangerous fragments.

A more defined type of ricochet firing was "horizontal" or "parallel" or "rolling" fire. With the barrel parallel to the ground, the line of sight struck the ground just seventy-five yards in front, causing the projectile to skim the ground with a number of bounces but not passing higher than the muzzle. This type of firing was supposed to be more efficient in striking targets at longer ranges, but it depended on the hardness and flatness of the terrain.[85]

An added benefit of ricochet firing was its visual impact on the enemy. A ball speeding along the ground at high velocity ricocheted and kicked up corresponding dust clouds on its deadly path. Understandably, this effect created terror in its recipients. As a consequence of this visible performance it becomes apparent that ricochet firing affected morale greater than a ball passing through the line.

Ricochet firing was used at Gettysburg but its destructive value appears negligible. Controlling a ricocheting projectile was a difficult art. Skipping a ball was especially hard to do over uneven ground, where it randomly ricocheted as the gunner attempted to hit a target with the right bounce. The rolling terrain at Gettysburg most certainly interfered with the ability to predict the proper bounce needed to hit targets. Much of the ground capable of allowing ricochet firing had crops which characteristically contained softer ground and, in turn, suppressed the bouncing effect. Trees, stone walls, and miles of fence were also present to deflect any well-aimed ricochet shot.

Besides range considerations, frequency of fire was also determined with a conscious effort to control the expenditure of ammunition. In battle, the artillery branch did not have a free reign on the consumption of ammunition. Artillery ammunition was by far the bulkiest item carried in an army's inventory and the most difficult to replenish. Its use was restricted because of the heavy burden in manufacture and the large transportation effort required in replacing it. Because of the immense quantity of artillery ammunition required and the cubic feet of space it occupied, an enormously disproportionate share of vehicles and animals were used to transport this vital supply as compared to transporting small-arms ammunition.

The concern for expending ammunition reached far beyond the battery level. There were published circulars and orders with detailed instructions reminding artillery officers of the manner in which ammunition was to be used. General Henry Hunt pleaded with artillery officers to be mindful of the consequences of wasteful usage: "At a time when all the resources of the country are taxed to the utmost to provide the Army and Navy with munitions of war, the ineffective expenditure of ammunition, in addition to other evils, diminishes greatly the efficiency of fire to which the artillery might attain; the excessive demand giving us, in many instances, imperfectly constructed and hastily inspected projectiles, instead of carefully manufactured and approved ammunition. If the expenditure of ammunition continues to be as extravagant as heretofore, it will be impossible to keep the army supplied."[86]

The importance of safeguarding the supply of ammunition during battle is revealed in a somewhat amusing confrontation at Gettysburg. Major Osborn, commanding Eleventh Corps artillery, encountered a concerned General Meade over his use of ammunition. Osborn commented:

> While this fire on Cemetery Hill was at its very height, General Meade rode into the batteries at great speed followed by two or three staff officers. As he came within hearing he shouted, "Where is Major Osborn?! Where is Major Osborn?!" As he came near me, I answered him. He then shouted, apparently greatly excited, "What are you drawing ammunition from the train for?" I said some of the ammunition chests were giving out. He then said, "Don't you know that is in violation of general orders and the army regulations to use up all your ammunition in battle?" I replied that I had given that no thought and that General Hunt had directed me to draw what I might require from the ordnance train. He then said, "What do you expect to do here?" I replied that I was expected to hold the hill, and that I expected to do so, if the infantry would stand by me . . . He then rode off with as great a speed as he had come.[87]

During artillery operations, "generally, the rate of fire should be much less than one shot per minute." The *Artillerist's Manual* warned: "By wasting ammunition, the supply destined for a whole campaign may be expended in a few hours of firing." Theoretically, in the Army of the Potomac, excluding the horse artillery, if each of its guns fired one round per minute it had an ammunition supply to allow four and three-quarter hours of firing time. In comparison, the Army of Northern Virginia could fire for only three and one-third hours—a 40 percent smaller inventory of ammunition. This was a lopsided difference for an army on the offensive which habitually used more ammunition.[88]

Six months after Gettysburg, the Army of the Potomac's Artillery Headquarters issued General Order No. 2 addressing the wasteful expenditure of ammunition. It said:

> Rapid firing at large bodies and opening at long ranges are . . . causes of waste. In small skirmishes between 300 and 400 rounds per battery are expended; the fire, according to the reports, frequently averaging, and sometimes exceeding, one round per minute for each gun. In general engagements, batteries have been known to expend all the ammunition in their chests in a little over an hour and a half.
>
> An officer who expends ammunition in this manner proves his ignorance of the proper use of his arm, and a want of capacity for the command of a battery. He also incurs a heavy responsibility by throwing a whole battery out of use, and should be held to answer for the consequences.
>
> There has been an improvement in this consumption of ammunition. It is not so much the loss of the ammunition that should be considered—limited as is the amount which an army can transport—as the loss of effect from too distant and too rapid firing.
>
> In no case, except when firing canister at short ranges, should the rate exceed one round from each gun in two minutes; and that rate should only be reached at critical moments, when the distance, numbers, and formation of the enemy are such that the fire is sure to be effective. At all other times, one round in four to six minutes is as rapid firing as should be permitted.
>
> The value of the rifled cannon consists principally in its accuracy. Accuracy requires careful pointing, with close observation of the effect, and these require time. Twelve shots in an hour at an object over 1,000 yards distant, the time being spent in careful loading and pointing, will produce better results than fifty shots will ordinarily produce from the same gun in the same time. If a heavy artillery fire is required it should be obtained not by rapid firing, but by bringing a large number of guns into action, and firing each with greatest accuracy attainable.[89]

In actuality, with the excitement produced in battle, any sense of time most likely seemed surrealistic and difficult to place in context when survival in the presence of the enemy was uppermost in the artillerymen's minds. The men felt better when they fired quicker. It relieved stress, occupied their time, and gave them a sense of doing something to counteract the damage inflicted by the enemy. This temporary remedy for stress, however, had to be tempered with the necessity of saving enough ammunition to sustain the battle at critical moments in order to win the fight or at least, prevent disaster.

Unless there were extraordinary circumstances, artillery officers who used up all their ammunition in a short period could be dishonored and subjected to an accusation of having a cowardly desire to leave the battle scene.

Union Major Osborn witnessed the premature flight of one battery: "I . . . saw [a] battery with all the men mounted on the ammunition chests at full speed, the horses running down the Baltimore Pike, the drivers whipping their horses at every jump. I never saw the battery again, and as it did not belong to my command, I did not report it to the proper superiors. Doubtless, the Captain reported to the commander of the Reserve Artillery that he was in the hottest of the fight and that he and all his men were heroes. At all events, the giant monument on Cemetery Hill stands to the credit of that battery."[90]

William H. McCartney, 1st Massachusetts Battery, reported that from this battery, "I caused to be collected, from a piece of woods directly in the rear of the ground which had been occupied by said . . . battery, 48 rounds of 3-inch projectiles, perfect; 22 rounds having been found near the position which had been occupied by one limber."[91]

Cowardice was certainly not the case with the gallant Alonzo Cushing who commanded the Federal battery in the Angle and the focus for Pickett's men. During the great cannonade, when Cushing's artillery rounds were quickly depleting, he asked his chief of artillery, Captain Hazard, for more ammunition. "Young man!" Hazard responded, "Are you aware that every round you fire costs $2.67?" (This was relatively inexpensive when compared to the most expensive projectile manufactured by the Tredegar Iron Works. This Southern firm produced a 7-inch, steel-tipped, wrought-iron bolt, weighing 115 pounds. Following the duel between the *Monitor* and the *Merrimac*, it was developed for piercing armor plate. Each projectile cost Tredegar $53.40 to make but the navy paid $95—a handsome profit.)[92]

Days after Gettysburg, General Meade's assistant adjutant general, Seth Williams, issued a circular for the benefit of those who scurried off the battlefield after their ammunition was depleted, pointing out the existing order regarding consumption of this vital resource:

> Attention is called . . . forbidding batteries to be withdrawn from the field because of a want of ammunition. This was done in several instances in the recent battle, and in one instance, a large quantity of ammunition was found upon the ground so abandoned. As rapidly as ammunition is expended, caissons will be emptied by transfer to other chests; and as soon as two caissons at most are emptied, they will be sent to

the trains for supplies. Wagon-loads can no longer be sent to batteries. The privilege of thus sparing the labor of battery horses has been abused to the injury of the service. The practice of taking a number of rounds of shot, shell, and shrapnel from the chests, and bringing them near the gun when in action, is positively prohibited. Proper pointing gives ample time under all circumstances for procuring ammunition, one round at a time, from the limber chests; the only exception is in the case of canister at close range. Large quantities of ammunition have been left upon the ground as a result of the bad practice referred to.[93]

The timing of artillery fire had to take into account not only the immediate supplies in the limbers and caissons, but also the proximity and accessibility of the reserve ammunition supply. In the Union line on July 3, for example, although extra artillery ammunition was nearby, Hunt's concern also included its accessibility. He knew that if the enemy guns opened up on the Federal defenses it would be difficult to supply ammunition under a heavy artillery barrage. In fact, attempts were made by using wagons and caissons from the artillery reserve. The rear of Cemetery Ridge, however, was thoroughly blasted by projectiles of every description. This created a terrible atmosphere of danger and a moonscape of potholes big enough to effect the transport of artillery ammunition by these heavy vehicles. Hunt said, "It was of vital importance that when *his* fire ceased, *we* should have in the chests a sufficient reserve of ammunition to sustain a rapid and effective fire from all our batteries on the advancing Infantry [sic] from the moment it emerged from the woods."[94]

Undoubtedly, the greatest restraint shown in expending ammunition, as discussed earlier, occurred with the Federal artillery that faced the Confederate guns and participated in the cannonade on July 3. After observing the Confederate buildup all morning long, General Hunt immediately proceeded along the lines giving his assessment of the situation and instructions to the artillery officers. If a cannonade were to open, Hunt instructed, "[the battery commanders] *would not return the fire for fifteen or twenty minutes at least.* . . . and to concentrate our fire on that point (where most guns were) firing slowly, deliberately and making target practice of it."[95]

Besides his concern for developing an effective response to any anticipated Confederate cannonade, Hunt's experience evoked other considerations. His conservative approach of using a muted artillery response to enemy cannons was also due to his awareness of a common ruse used to deflate the firepower advantage of an opponent—an offensive cannonade preceding an assault designed "to induce us to throw away our ammunition *in reply*, previous to his assault, so that his infantry might pass without serious injury or disorder over the half mile and more of his advance that was beyond our effective musketry range." The plan to deal with the imminent action, now facing the Union center, was clear to Hunt. It was of the first importance to have his line in the best possible condition to meet the assault.[96]

Once the Confederate guns opened, it took steely discipline to hold back the Union artillery in reply during a cannonade with the magnitude and intensity that has since received such historic significance. The Union troops on Cemetery Ridge must have felt helpless at first and, no doubt, experienced that "sinking feeling."

The Federal gun crews were needed most in the minutes before their blue-clad infantry would take over the fight in close-up combat. This was where the impending charge reached its climax and this was where it had to be smashed and defeated. Hunt was insistent on the artillery remaining detached and not getting drawn into a wasteful gun duel. His adamant stance on this point bordered on the obsessive.[97]

Artillery's Effects

What was it like to experience the sights, sounds, and excitement of artillery fire? A witness to the beginning of the cannonade at Antietam described his ordeal and what he saw in such vivid detail as to place the reader in the midst of the battle:

> Smoke from a distant battery appeared: Puff—Puff, Puff, Puff—Puff, Puff, and after an interval the sound reached them in the same rhythm: Pum—Pum, Pum, Pum—Pum, Pum. A caisson blew up with a silent orange flash throwing fire and splinters high into the air. . . . Then the sound of the explosion came with an identity of its own, a soft brushing shock-wave felt on the forehead and cheek, a slight jarring under the feet. . . . The walking wounded started coming back—men with shocked, staring faces. . . . On top of the ridge, just at the edge of safety, one of the hobblers sat down to pull off a shoe. Behind him a round, black object came bouncing along like a rubber ball; there was a soft smashing sound; the man collapsed with odd violence

into the semblance of a large bloody rag doll; and the solid shot bounded again, sailing lazily over the heads of the Maine soldiers.[98]

Mr. Wilkeson, reporter for the *New York Tribune*, who was at General Meade's headquarters, described the opening scene of the cannonade on July 3 at Gettysburg:

In the shadow cast by the tiny farm house, sixteen by twenty, which General Meade had made his head-quarters, lay wearied staff officers and tired correspondents. There was not wanting to the peacefulness of the scene the singing of a bird, which had a nest in a peach tree within the tiny yard of the whitewashed cottage. In the midst of its warbling a shell screamed over the house, instantly followed by another, and another, and in a moment the air was full of the most complete artillery prelude to an infantry battle that was ever exhibited. Every size and form of shell known to British and American gunnery shrieked, whirled, moaned, whistled, and wrathfully fluttered over our ground. As many as six in a second, constantly two in a second, bursting and screaming over and around the head-quarters, made a very hell of fire that amazed the oldest officers. They burst in the yard—burst next to the fence on both sides, garnished as usual with the hitched horses of aides and orderlies. The fastened animals reared and plunged with terror. Then one fell, then another—sixteen lay dead and mangled before the fire ceased, still fastened by their halters, which gave the expression of being wickedly tied up to die painfully. These brute victims of a cruel war touched all hearts. Through the midst of the storm of screaming and exploding shells an ambulance, driven by its frenzied conductor at full speed, presented to all of us the marvelous spectacle of a horse going rapidly on three legs. A hinder one had been shot off at the hock. . . . During this fire the horses at twenty and thirty feet distant were receiving their death, and soldiers in Federal blue were torn to pieces in the road, and died with the peculiar yells that blend the extorted cry of pain with horror and despair.[99]

Another eyewitness, Union Brigadier General John Gibbon, commented:

. . . About 1 o'clock on Friday, a single gun on the opposite side of the valley went "Bang," and there was a whirr of a shot. Presently another "bang" and then "bang," "bang," "bang," "bang," until it was impossible to count the shots; and, along with these reports came every kind of bustle, whirr, whistle, and shriek that man has heard or can imagine; the most terrific of all proceeding from some elongated missile, which ceasing to revolve around its axis, dashed "promiscuously" through the air, becoming visible on such event. The twelve-pound shots were also to be seen as they came; and the worst of it was that every shot seemed to be coming straight to hit you

Artillery damage, below right diamond-shaped air vent, can still be seen in Trostle barn. (AC)

Today, a number of structures like this one around Gettysburg exhibit artillery shells in walls once damaged in the battle. (AC)

A casualty of war. Artillery fire could sometimes kill or wound thirty to forty soldiers by a single shot. (MCMOLL/USAMHI/WDC)

between the eyes. Horses were the greatest sufferers here, for the men lay down and escaped; but the poor brutes had to take it standing.[100]

The physical effects of artillery fire were diverse and the destructive force released by the different types of artillery ammunition varied. In his *Artillerists Manual*, Federal General John Gibbon wrote: "The precise effects of a single ball cannot be accurately stated. Cases are cited where thirty or forty men have been disabled by a single shot; but it is a laid down as a principle, that a 6- or 12-pound ball will go through six men at 800 yards' distance." In the Peninsular campaign, Federal artillery Captain John Smead saw the effects of a rifled shot: "An empty camp-kettle, standing a few yards in rear of the battery, had a Parrott shot through both sides without moving or upsetting it."[101]

John Worsham, 21st Virginia Infantry, witnessed the effects of artillery shot at the second battle of Manassas:

I heard a thud on my right like some one had been struck with a heavy fist. On looking around I saw a man at my side standing erect with his head off; a stream of blood squirting a foot or more from his neck. By the time I turned around, I saw three others lying on the ground, all killed by the same cannon shot. The man standing was a captain in the 42nd Virginia Regiment, and his brains and blood bespattered the face and clothing of one of my company, who was standing in my rear. This was the sec-

254

ond time I saw four men killed by the same shot during the war—the other time being at Cedar Run a few weeks before—each time the shot struck as it was descending. The first man had his head taken off, the next was shot through the breast, the next through the stomach, and the fourth had his bowels torn out.[102]

Even if the projectile missed, its side effects could be stunning or worse. During the New Madrid campaign, a brush with death for John Ferguson, 10th Illinois Infantry, left an indelible memory. A shell from a Confederate gunboat landed near him and exploded: "I thought for a short time that I was killed. I was perfectly serviceable but could not move or scarcle breath attal; it was caused by the pressure of the air striking me with such a force, that I was left without power to move for a minnot."[103]

A non-explosive shot could be deadly even if it just brushed past a lucky soldier. With it came a wave of compressed air that could sear the skin and was capable of tossing bodies about or stunning anyone in its wake. On July 1 at Gettysburg, L. A. Smith, first lieutenant in the 136th New York Infantry, witnessed such an event: "Just as we came up the slope and passed over the brow of Cemetery Hill we saw an artilleryman killed. As he was carrying ammunition from the caisson a cannon ball passed to the right of our regiment and so close to the man that he whirled around and around and fell upon his face dead. The concussion killed him."[104]

If shot did not injure anyone, it could easily terrorize soldiers on the receiving end by reminding them of their proximity to instantaneous death. Joshua Chamberlain, in reminiscing about the battle of Fredericksburg, recalled that: "The air was thick with the flying, bursting shells; whooping solid shot swept lengthwise our narrow bridge, fortunately not yet ploughing a furrow through the midst of us, but driving the compressed air so close above our heads that there was an unconquerable urge to shrink beneath it, although knowing then it was too late."[105]

Eyewitnesses graphically described the physical effects of artillery at Gettysburg. Col. E. P. Alexander wrote: "Capt. Carlton [of Troop's Georgia Battery], taking position on a pretty grassy slope, had a 20 [pounder] rifle shell knock one whole buttock off a lead horse in making a turn. I never saw so much blood fly, or so much grass painted red before, & the pretty drill Carlton was wishing to show off was very much spoiled."[106]

During the cannonade of July 3, Federal General Oliver Howard and his

Meade's headquarters just behind the Federal center position on Cemetery Ridge. (AC)

artillery chief, Colonel Thomas Osborn, viewed the impressive power of the Confederate bombardment. One of the first Confederate artillery shots smashed into the Federal gun positions on Cemetery Hill. Osborn witnessed its effects: "I saw one shell go through six horses standing broadside." Caught in this barrage on Cemetery Hill, General Howard reported: "At about 1 P.M., a terrific cannonade opened upon us . . . hurling into the cemetery grounds missiles of every description. Shells burst in the air, in the ground to the right and left, killing horses, exploding caissons, overturning tombstones, and smashing fences. There was no place of safety. In one regiment twenty-seven were killed or wounded by one shell . . . "[107]

Lieutenant Colonel Charles H. Morgan, stationed at General Meade's headquarters when the July 3 cannonade began, wrote:

> "Army headquarters were visited with such a shower of projectiles that sixteen horses belonging to the staff and escort were killed before the officers could get away and 'they stood not upon the order of their going.' One of them, seeing his horse badly wounded by a piece of shell, rushed into the house for his pistol to put the poor brute out of pain and coming out, put two bullets into a fine uninjured horse belong-

ing to Capt. [James S.] Hall, signal officer of the 2d corps, and would probably have emptied his revolver as he was a poor shot, had not Capt. Hall interfered."[108]

On the Confederate side of the field, a member of the Crenshaw Artillery saw the devastation thrust on the animals: "Ripped open and disemboweled" by the jagged pieces of metal, the beasts let out all-too-human screams as they collapsed to the ground. "[It] was enough to try the stoutest heart."[109]

E. P. Alexander witnessed the brutality of artillery on the human form: "I remember one with the most horrible wound that I ever saw. We were halted for a moment by a fence, and as the men threw it down for the guns to pass, I saw in one of the corners a man sitting down and looking up at me. A solid shot had carried away both jaws and his tongue. I noticed the powder smut from the shot on the white skin around the wound. He sat up and looked at me steadily, and I looked at him until the guns could pass, but nothing, of course, could be done for him."[110]

Shortly after the battle of Gettysburg ended, Robert Carter, 22nd Massachusetts Infantry, upon inspecting the aftermath of July 2 near the Peach Orchard, commented on the effects that artillery cast upon the enemy soldiers:

> Our tour extended across the swale, inside our picket lines now occupied by the Pennsylvania Reserves, which had been swept by the 5th and 9th Massachusetts batteries. The scenes of that spot, as the fast-quickening daylight revealed its dreadful horrors to our astounded gaze, still linger on our memories. Masses of Kershaw's and Wofford's brigades had been swept from the muzzles of the guns, which had been loaded either with double-shotted, or spherical case, with fuses cut to one second, to explode near the muzzles. They were literally blown to atoms. Corpses strewed the ground at every step. Arms, heads, legs and parts of dismembered bodies were scattered all about, and sticking among the rocks and against the trunks of trees, hair, brains, entrails, and shreds of human flesh still hung, a disgusting, sickening, heart-rending spectacle to our young minds. It was indeed a charnel-house, a butcher's pen, with man as the victim.[111]

An artillery gun drill. (MCMOLL/USAMHI/WDC)

VII

Artillerymen

Gun Crews

*A*rtillerymen performed under the most trying conditions. Loading and firing cannons in battle required close attention to following safety precautions, alertness to obeying instructions, and precision teamwork. To achieve teamwork, when a campaign was not underway, artillery commanders were required to take the necessary measures to train gun crews. Each artilleryman also had to be prepared to perform the duties of others at the piece when they became casualties. *Instruction for Field Artillery* stated: "Each recruit has to learn different duties, and to handle different implements from those he was previously engaged with; and these again vary with the several natures of ordnance and machines which an artilleryman must use. It is impossible that such a variety of exercises can be well executed, or even remembered, unless the recruit is made to comprehend the object of the various duties he is called upon to perform."[1]

In winter quarters, while the infantrymen were practicing on the drill fields, artillerymen were busy in the course of instruction for field artillery. According to the Army of the Potomac's General Order No. 2, training "will embrace the tactics, orders, &c., in force, and also the subject of ammunition, its description, and mode of preparation." Men were also taught the care needed to avoid the extravagant expenditure of ammunition.[2]

Comparatively, operations for artillerymen in a Union battery were in general simpler to perform than those in a Southern battery with respect to training the gun crew and handling the artillery pieces. This was primarily due to the Army of the Potomac's organizational arrangement where practically all of the batteries contained uniform weapons. In a Confederate battery of mixed pieces, gun crews had to adapt and learn the operation and performance of different pieces within the battery. As previously mentioned, the guns and ammunition performed with distinctly different behavior. Rifled guns, for example, were more complicated to fire than smoothbores. They required longer times to load and needed more attentiveness to safety. Compared to smoothbore barrels, sparks were more prone to hide in the recessed grooves of rifled guns, making them harder to extinguish in the haste of loading.

Beyond the problems associated with mixed pieces, all artillerymen operated their guns under the most trying conditions: they toiled in stifling heat; they were subjected to the deafening roar of their guns and also the explosions of enemy shells falling within their ranks; they worked their guns in the midst of exploding metal fragments and sparks showering down upon them and on their high-explosive inventory of ammunition. Because of the noise, communication within the gun crew was often done through hand gestures, head nods, exaggerated facial expressions, or motions such as tapping the trail or muzzle. As the battle intensified, thick sulphurous smoke choked their lungs and irritated the lining of the nose and throat. Their muscles were strained to the limits from the repetitive motions of returning the heavy recoiled cannons to their firing positions. Ammunition needed carrying and horses tending.

Artillerymen fired their pieces often unsheltered and, until the guns generated enough of a smokescreen, were openly visible to the enemy. Until the atmosphere thickened, the enemy's gun crews pinpointed their location from the smoke and flames belching from their guns while the infantry took cover in places the gun crews wished they could hide.

As the battle progressed, the precision teamwork and efficiency of the gun crew diminished as exhaustion set upon the battered artillerymen, or as they took on casualties. One engagement could decimate a battery in equipment and the skilled gun crew needed to operate it. Captain Osmond B. Taylor, Virginia battery, described the toll taken on his men on July 2 in just a few hours of fighting:

> I lost at the first position one of my best gunners (Corpl. William P. Ray). He was killed while in the act of sighting his guns. He never spoke after receiving the shot, walked a few steps from his piece, and fell dead. I had also while in this, my first position, the following men wounded: Vincent F. Burford, badly bruised on shoulder; Silas C. Gentry, cut on the wrist; Joseph Moody, cut in the face and bruised on the back; Byrd McCormick, shot through the calf of the leg by a bullet from a spherical case; Edward J. Sheppard, wounded badly in heel, and several others slightly wounded. I had killed in the lane while going to my second position another excellent gunner (Corpl. Joseph T. V. Lantz). He had both legs broken above the knees; lived but a little while. His only words were, "You can do me no good; I am killed; follow your piece." While in my second position, I had two men wounded: Hill Carter Eubank, shot through the leg. Eubank was a very promising youth, about eighteen years of age; left the Military Institute at Lexington, Va., to join the army; was brave and attentive to his duties. The other (Claiborne Y. Atkinson) struck on the leg by a piece of shell; seriously wounded.[3]

To continue battery operations, manpower losses could be sustained, but only to a certain point. Neither army carried spare artillerymen that were unassigned to a battery and waiting to rush in to restore the decimated gun crews. Batteries, low in manpower, often had to rely on infantrymen as replacements. When this happened, the infantrymen that a regimental commander would be willing to loan to a battery to operate a gun, when his primary responsibility was to his regiment's success, were most likely his most worrisome men. The likely candidates might be the greatest laggards, skulkers, under-performers, or any soldiers that needed watching in battle. Such cases resulted in placing incompetent individuals around a gun that needed a team of skilled men to make it work and an awareness of the safety precautions necessary to stay in one piece.

Firing multiple rounds, for example, required altering the ammunition to prevent injury to the gun crew. Federal General John Gibbon recalled what one unskilled soldier did: "After the battle [Antietam] Lieutenant Stewart told me that, after the order was given to load with 'double canister', he noticed one of our volunteer cannoneers placing both *complete* charges in the gun and directed him the next time to knock off the cartridge of the extra charge against the hub of the wheel (as is usually done). The man did as he was told but in his excitement, he got his finger under the edge of the heavily loaded tin canister and nearly mashed it off. Stewart said every canister after that, went in to the gun just as it came from the arsenal."[4]

Despite the inherent dangers in working the guns, infantry soldiers sometimes had the opportunity to operate an artillery piece on their own. They were untrained in artillery safety precautions, yet they probably had some awareness through observation of the hazards involved from previous combat experience. One incident, though difficult to imagine, that illustrates the apparent disregard of common sense in the heat of battle took place during the Appomattox campaign. Brevet Major M. Barber, U.S.A., reported on the capture of two Confederate pieces by infantrymen and their attempts to turn the guns on the fleeing Rebs: "Being unable to procure primers the pieces were discharged by firing a musket into the vent of the piece. In this manner, twelve rounds were fired, when a section of artillery coming up, the guns were turned over to its commander." Where did these men stand to ignite the cartridge and avoid the recoil?[5]

For gun crews, coping with their vulnerable predicament during artillery operations was an enormous challenge. Mentally, performance required more independent discipline than infantrymen. For one thing, artillerymen did not have the same relationship with each other in battle that infantrymen experienced. The kinship was not less of a bond, but it was one derived from different experiences. Infantry troops, for example, fought close to one another, and all had common tasks or performed identical motions. They loaded and fired their weapons the same, they had uniformity of movement in battle, they marched at the same pace, etc. Their physical closeness provided each soldier with strength and moral support. The "touch of the elbow" forged the "brothers-in-arms" into a collective determination that empowered the regiment to act as one. Infantry troops also often had the option of concealing their presence from the enemy during artillery bombardments.

Artillerymen, on the other hand, did the opposite. They operated without the intimate connective support of their comrades, and each performed a specialized duty with different movements. They were physically spread out during operations, and their work was most likely performed in view of the enemy, unsheltered from incoming missiles. This made coping with the hazardous situation more difficult and required artillerymen to possess character with a more independent disposition.[6]

Artillerymen's self-reliant disposition often inspired them to remain at their posts beyond what many might consider a more sensible departure. At Gettysburg on July 2, for example, Confederate infantry overran Federal guns on East Cemetery Hill; while many of the Union infantrymen retreated to the rear, the defending artillerymen resorted to hand-to-hand fighting in order to save their pieces. Just as gutsy were the Union artillerymen of Stewart's battery who lined the Baltimore Pike and held up fence rails to stop the runaways; gutsier still, Stewart's men robbed food from the retreating men in the midst of the struggle to save the hill. In another example, at the height of Pickett's Charge, Union Captain Andrew Cowan, 1st New York Independent Battery, witnessed an unusual scene juxtaposed amidst the brutal fighting taking place:

> I was on the crest a moment, after my guns had been pulled back and in that instant I saw [Union Brigadier General Alexander] Webb behind Cushing's [Union] guns surrounded by a number of officers and men and the colors of two, or perhaps three of his regiments. A great many men and officers too were running away as fast as legs could carry them, and had been for two or three minutes before. James Plunkett, a Vermonter, attached to my battery, fought and cursed them and finally I saw him hit one fellow over the head with a coffee pot. The bottom burst in and I shall never forget seeing the fellow running away with the pot, down over his head and face. Webb gallantly rallied his men, and the strength of the enemy was so nearly spent that victory was ours.[7]

Although artillerymen required a more independent disposition than infantry soldiers, their work was highly dependent on the interactions of the gun crew firing their piece. This teamwork, combined with the conscious effort to observe safety precautions in their hazardous environment, required their total concentration and probably helped to form cohesive bonds among a battery's members and helped them to cope with the situation at hand. Captain B. C. Manly, Company A, 1st North Carolina Artillery, described the cool manner in which one of his cannoneers defused a potentially dangerous situation during the Gettysburg campaign: "I deem it but justice . . . to mention an act of coolness by Private H. E. Thain, by which many lives were probably saved. Thain was acting No. 6 at one of the guns, and, while adjusting a fuse-igniter, it accidentally exploded, and ignited the fuse already in the shell. He seized the shell, and ran with it several yards from the limber, at the same time drawing the burning fuse from the shell with his fingers."[8]

For artillery officers to operate in battle, it required extraordinary mental discipline and concentration. Union Major Osborn described what it took to perform on July 3: "This terrific artillery battle, which all knew was the immediate forerunner of victory or defeat, was [exceptionally pressing to the human condition] . . . During such time, the force of will which an officer must bring to bear upon himself in order not only to control his men but also govern himself, is wonderful. He must by sheer force of will shut up every impulse of his nature, except that of controlling the officers and men subject to his command. He must discard all care of his personal safety and even his own life. The most difficult person to control is always himself."[9]

Osborn also shared an introspective and personal experience that disclosed his great respect for self-control in battle:

> While the artillery fire was at its highest, [Captain Wadsworth, a son of General Wadsworth] came to me with some directions and to make some inquiries for headquarters. I was at the moment on a nice horse thoroughly accustomed to me. His horse was the same. We halted close together in the midst of the batteries, the horses headed in the opposite directions and our faces near together. Neither horse flinched. The forelegs of each horse were in line with the hind legs of the other, and we stood broadside to the enemy fire. While we were talking, a percussion shell struck the ground directly under the horses and exploded. The momentum of the shell carried the fragments along so that neither horse was struck nor did neither horse move. When the shell exploded, I was in complete control of my nerves and did not move a muscle of my body or my face. Neither did Wadsworth, but I dropped my eyes to the ground where the shell exploded, and Wadsworth did not. I never quite forgave myself for looking down when that shell exploded under us. I do not believe that

there was a man in the entire army, save Captain Wadsworth, who could have a ten pound shell explode under him without looking where it struck.[10]

Another artillery officer, Lieutenant Wheeler, 13th New York Battery, described the mental challenge he endured during the three days at Gettysburg. After exposure to frequent fire and pushed to the limits of physical endurance, he described his feelings as being ones of overriding joy. With the imminent chance of death a constant companion, Wheeler acknowledged that the "danger was so great and so constant, that it took away the sense of danger" and that this feeling was substituted with "joyous exaltation, a perfect indifference to circumstances." He felt his experience at the battle of Gettysburg was the most enjoyable time of his life. Having thought about his experience months later, however, he reasoned that his initial reaction was somewhat due to his command responsibilities which focused his attention on operating the guns and, consequently, raised his mental awareness to its highest state.[11]

The epitome of concentration was displayed at Gettysburg on July 3. Gun crews up and down the Union line were responding to the commands barked out by their gunners. "Sponge–thumb the vent–ram–correct the aim–trail right–trail left." A Federal lieutenant noticed one of his gunners: "[He was lying] stretched along the trail, setting off his elevations by one, two, and three finger breadths . . . Suddenly a round shot carried away the head of No. 1, and his body fell across the gun breech—blood and brains spattering and splashing the gunner from head to waist. Deliberately, the gunner wiped the ugly mess from his face, cleared his eyes, lifted the corpse from the gun, laid it on the sod, resumed his post and continued operations with scarcely the loss of a count." In later years, the same lieutenant, then a regimental commander, used this incident to describe self-control to his young officers: "That was discipline—the discipline that every man must acquire before he can call himself a field artillerymen."[12]

When times were quieter, being in the artillery branch did have its small rewards. Colonel Charles Wainwright, artillery brigade commander, First Corps, commented:

> Almost every day . . . I have been obliged to remark . . . how superior is the position of a light battery officer to even a colonel of infantry, so far as comfort goes, in times of general discomfort. They have a mechanic and tools always close at hand,

265

and their little cart to carry the mess-chest, a bag each, and the company desk, while either a tent is struck in on top of the forage wagon or if their battery is in position, they have their paulins. All these enable them to go through such a month as this last with quite as much comfort as a general officer with his spring wagon, and at times he is better off, as their cart, being ordnance property and part of the battery, is never sent to the rear, but moves with the battery at all times.[13]

Chiefs of Artillery: Hunt vs. Pendleton

In comparing the two chiefs of artillery at the battle of Gettysburg, history books ordinarily recognize General Hunt as performing superbly well and General Pendleton receives a rather dismal appraisal. Perhaps, according to many historians, Pendleton should not have been Lee's chief of artillery. Critics who compare him with Hunt, however, must recognize the different predicament each was placed in at the battle of Gettysburg.

To begin with, General Hunt, acting on behalf of General Meade, exercised authority over almost 30 percent of the Army of the Potomac's guns—the artillery reserve. He could and did have an active control which influenced the outcome of the battle. In contrast to Hunt, General Pendleton organizationally did not control one single cannon nor did he exercise a level of power that was even close to what Hunt was given. In *Lee's Lieutenants*, Freeman said: "Pendleton had neither the prestige nor the authority to assure employment of all the guns as one weapon under one leader. He appears in the campaign more as a consultant than as a commander." In this respect, the title "chief of artillery" is not comparable to Hunt's as this title intimates that each chief's duties and power of authority were the same, when in fact, they were not.[14]

In addition, the Union army fought almost totally on the defensive where most of the action took place and where Hunt operated. Historic accounts naturally focus on those areas of higher interest produced from close-up action. That is where the drama and suspense occurred and where the fate of the battle was determined. Hunt, for most of the battle it seemed, lived in the saddle. His participation was one of the most active; overall, it would be difficult to name an officer from either side who was more involved in the fight than Hunt. He seemed to be everywhere on the line to supply fresh batteries needed to fill holes in the front, and the timing of his presence at critical locations was instrumental in winning the battle. Hunt was subjected to the intense pressure of keeping the entire army supplied with artillery ammunition. This anxiety consumed his efforts as well as the attention he devoted in cautioning artillerymen not to be wasteful with their artillery fire.

Hunt's valor in battle was inspirational. Lieutenant Colonel Charles Morgan, Hancock's inspector general and chief of staff, witnessed Hunt's involvement during Pickett's Charge: "During the thickest of the melee, General Hunt, Chief of Artillery of the Army, rode down to the front of Webb's brigade, and emptied his revolver at the enemy, had his horse killed under him and retired."[15]

Pendleton's activities during the battle, on the other hand, were greatly overshadowed by Hunt's very visible involvement. Pendleton operated at long range from the action. The circumstances under which he participated did not expose him to the dangers and heroic opportunities that Hunt experienced in the close-up contests. In this regard, the spotlight draws itself to the performance and great deeds accomplished by General Hunt.

At Gettysburg, with the burden of the high command on their shoulders, both Lee and Meade depended highly upon their chiefs of artillery for the overall coordination of their army's firepower. To accomplish the wishes of their commander, however, each was confronted with incredible problems.

Pendleton was burdened with the tremendous challenges and high expectations of others, particularly on July 3. The job assigned to him for arranging the proper artillery coordination was nearly impossible to achieve. It was doubly more difficult than the Union's since Pendleton had to survey a line twice as long. If flank to flank contact was necessary, any instructions or communication sent out by horseback and returned with a response was a half day's ride. Even if Pendleton was centrally located, he had few men on his staff to accommodate such a task. The liaison required by Pendleton or his staff added to the difficulty of basic communications. This coordination included distributing orders or information and arranging firepower by detaching guns from one corps' jurisdiction and assigning them to another. These responsibilities took staff power and time to accomplish the work.

A great difficulty facing Pendleton's Confederate gun placement for July 3, not to be overlooked, was the spontaneity of General Lee's final plan. Lee's original intent for July 3 was not to attack the Union center, but to renew the attacks of July 2 and exploit the partial successes won against the Federal flanks. The participants in this original plan were to include a simultaneous

View of ground traversed by Pickett's division from Federal center. (AC)

Union guns on left-center overlooking the path of Pickett's men. (AC)

attack with General Ewell striking the Federal right on Culp's Hill and General Longstreet attacking the Union left. The exact points of attack in Lee's plan against the Federal left are inexact and controversial, but the point to be made is that the eventual attack against the Federal center was a substitute for the original plan and not part of it.

Lee's final plan was unavoidable. The original planned attack of July 3, the continuation of the July 2 action, was under way against the Union right flank on Culp's Hill at 4:30 A.M. and was precipitated by the Union attack there trying to regain the defenses they had lost on the second. Lee's original plan, however, was already obsolete before it began. While General Ewell's troops on the Confederate left were ready, those under General Longstreet on their right were not. They would not participate for several reasons: when the fighting began on Culp's Hill they were not in position to make the simultaneous attack with Ewell; the men, whose energies and numbers had been thoroughly used up from the heavy fighting on July 2, were not in a condition to participate; and if they did participate, their right flank would be dangerously compromised. General Lee stated: "General Longstreet's dispositions were not completed as early as was expected, but before notice could be sent to General Ewell, General Johnson had already become engaged, and it was too late to recall him. . . . General Longstreet was delayed by a force occupying the high, rocky hills on the enemy's extreme left, from which his troops could be attacked in reverse as they advanced. His operations had been embarrassed the day previous by the same cause, and he now deemed it necessary to defend his flank and rear with the divisions of Hood and McLaws."[16]

Lee was then faced with a battle plan only halfway implemented but now underway on Culp's Hill and too late to stop. If his renewed attack on Culp's Hill was part of a diversionary plan, like it was on July 2, any new plan then adopted by General Lee complicated the unfolding events. Lee either had to write off Culp's Hill as inconsequential to the overall design for July 3 and move on to prepare for a new proposal, or, if he valued the positive results that could be produced from the Culp's Hill action, it would take time for Lee to appraise the operation's success while it was in progress.

General Lee was a deliberate planner, but he also responded well to the changing challenges of a battle and was not prone to impetuosity. It would be uncharacteristic of General Lee to commit forces to his first plan but then make an impulsive decision by altering it, and without waiting until the battle had matured or until its outcome was evident. However, Lee was most likely concocting an alternative to the faltering original plan even before word was received that it was failing. Details of any new plan's preparation needed deliberation, discussion, reviewing maps, surveying ground, and then the information had to be disseminated.

After canceling the original battle plan for July 3, Lee chose to assault the Union center. The precise time that General Lee changed his plan is unclear, and for the day ahead time was running out. But it would have been most difficult for Pendleton to rearrange the entire artillery line to properly support the infantry after a sudden and drastic switch in plans with different objectives. After all, E. P. Alexander's guns of Longstreet's Corps were prepared to do battle against a different target. Alexander later commented on this change of plans: "Early in the morning General Lee came around, and I was then told that we were to assault Cemetery Hill, which lay rather to our left. This necessitated a good many changes of our positions, which the enemy did not altogether approve of, and they took occasional shots at us, though we shifted about, as inoffensively as possible. . . . "[17]

Confederate artillery officers undoubtedly relied on their chief of artillery to examine the ground to "recognize & know how to utilize his opportunities" and coordinate the event. During the artillery preparation, Alexander saw no attempt to coordinate Confederate fire. In his observation of Pendleton, he commented: "The chief of each corps only sees his own ground. I never had an idea of the possibility of this [coordination] being done at the time, for I had but the vaguest notion of where Ewell's corps was. And Ewell's chief doubtless had as vague ideas of my situation & necessities."[18]

In *Lee's Lieutenants* Freeman corroborated Alexander's assessment of poor coordination and commented: ". . . There was scant liaison. The powerful artillery of the Third Corps was not used heavily at the time it would have been most useful. To the extent that the artillery of the Second Corps was employed on the day of the charge, Colonel Tom Carter's was the one battalion that was effective. In Hill's and Ewell's Corps, Alexander computed that fifty-six guns were not used, and that of the eighty-four employed, eighty were parallel to the line of the enemy, though an enfilade of part of the Union position would have been possible."[19]

Alexander does, however, testify that Pendleton was in his presence, giving instructions, and assessing artillery preparations, which counters his condemnation of him: "Not very long after sunrise Gen. Pendleton came up & paid me a visit and commended all of my arrangements. . . . Now the orders which I received, both from Longstreet & Pendleton, were quite specific, & were carried out to the letter . . . & even more effectively, I think, than could have been reasonably expected beforehand."[20]

Pendleton's report of his activity on July 3 characterized his role as being fully involved. His account stated that "by direction of the commanding general, the artillery along our entire line was to be prepared for opening, as early as possible on the morning of the 3d, a concentrated and destructive fire, consequent upon which a general advance was to be made." Pendleton visited the lines to oversee the preparations and made necessary adjustments. He wrote: "[For the 1st Corps,] the battalion and battery commanders were also cautioned how to fire so as to waste as little ammunition as possible. . . . To the Third Corps attention was also given. . . . as did those of the Second Corps, each group having specific instructions from its chief."[21]

Some participants attributed the lack of coordination as the chief reason for the operation's failure on July 3, and inevitably someone had to be assigned responsibility for the artillery's role in it. Since participation in the cannonade was so encompassing, it was unlikely to allocate blame for poor coordination or inadequate preparation down to the lower commands; at that level, preparation duties were mostly devoted to local tasks. At mid-level, Confederate artillery officers of different commands were preoccupied with their own deployment problems in arranging batteries; Colonel E. P. Alexander, for example, started at 3:00 A.M. They had no opportunity to examine the ground occupied by other commands for chances to cooperate. E. P. Alexander blamed the disappointing artillery performance squarely on the Army of Northern Virginia's artillery's commander: ". . . The fault of this lay primarily with General Pendleton, General Lee's chief of artillery. He was too old & had been too long out of army life to be thoroughly up to all the opportunities of his position."[22]

While Pendleton took the brunt of Alexander's criticism regarding coordination, Alexander also attributed the coordination failure partially to insufficient staff organization "but principally it was due to the exceedingly difficult shape in which our line was formed, the enemy occupying a center and we a semi circumference, with poor and exposed communications along it."[23]

Besides Pendleton, there were few commanders that possessed such little authority relative to the assigned responsibility yet received so much blame for the outcome. Pendleton was singled out and condemned for such poor coordination on the third. Yet on July 2 the coordination of the en echelon attack by the Confederate infantry at the southern half of the field was at least as faulty. Most of the repercussions for the July 2 attack, however, focused the blame on commanders at the brigade level when, in fact, the responsibility for proper coordination had to originate with commanders higher up. Those infantry commanders higher up, in contrast to Pendleton, possessed the unquestionable authority over infantry troops where, in comparing Pendleton's predicament, this chief of artillery had no such authority to control the guns over which he received so much grief.

While the intent here suggests an effort to exonerate Pendleton and paint him as an unsung hero, it is merely an attempt to analyze the job under the conditions in which he was asked to perform in order to judge fairly the blame he was assigned. Few, if any, Civil War battles burdened an artillery commander greater than the responsibility of organizing and coordinating a general cannonade of such magnitude as at Gettysburg.

The Confederate artillery organization did not provide its chief of artillery with the authority and a staff that was adequate to allow proper preparation for the general cannonade that took place on July 3. As a "consultant" to the artillery, Pendleton, unlike some others, was not in a powerful position afterward to embark on a crusade in order to overcome condemnation. Assigning blame elsewhere would have pointed some of the criticism in an uncomfortable direction. That was not in the cards, lest it be too contentious.

Union artillerymen in action on July 2, 1863. (AC)

VIII

Summary

*T*he battle of Gettysburg graphically illustrated the artillery branch's state of the art and multifaceted challenges at mid-point in the Civil War. This engagement provided yet another valuable lesson in artillery's evolution in the pursuit for improvement.

When reviewing artillery's role during the battle and judging the artillery branch's performance, it must be recognized that some of the major factors that affected artillery operations, discussed in this work, contributed to the outcome of the battle. Some of the principle factors were uncontrollable, at least at the army level. One uncontrollable factor, for example, was the South's deficiency in resources for waging war. The Confederate government could not outfit its army with the necessary skilled manpower and equipment as well as the U. S.

government could. Secondly, new technology was, for the most part, not a controllable factor at the army level. Other than captured materiel, each army's artillery branch was supplied with materiel tested, approved, and procured by the ordnance department. In this respect, neither force at Gettysburg had control over the potency and reliability of weapons, ammunition, and other combat essentials that it received from its ordnance department.

In retrospect, attaining consistent quality and reliability for artillery pieces and related supplies was never fully realized during the Civil War. And the Confederate artillerymen, compared to their Union counterparts, undoubtedly suffered more from uncertainty in the performance of their equipment and supplies because of persistent problems in manufacturing or access to raw materials. The frequency of the participants' complaints, pointing out reliability problems, indicate that this issue was widespread and, as cited in previous examples, was not isolated to just the Confederate army. The reliability issue appears to be an important influence affecting the ability to fight at the battle of Gettysburg. The trustworthiness of just a few items such as ammunition, gunpowder, or shell fuses, when needed at critical moments, could help determine the outcome of the battle. The reliability factor, then, was as important as any weighty decisions made by any army commander.

Other factors that affected the artillery operations at the battle of Gettysburg *were* controllable at the army level. With regard to new technology, some local controllability did exist. It was in an army's best interest to exploit any new technology available or at least learn to adapt to its shortcomings. Rifle technology, for example, altered artillery's lethality. On one hand, rifled guns extended killing power beyond the range of smoothbores. But when an army chose to increase the number of its rifled guns at the expense of smoothbores, it sacrificed its artillery force's killing power at close-range. The technologic control, in this case, was in the hands of army commanders who affected changing the ratio of rifled guns to smoothbores.

Each army also had control of designing its artillery organization. The Army of Northern Virginia, for example, chose to form batteries containing four guns, even though there was greater efficiency in batteries containing six guns. The Union army's six-gun batteries needed fewer command personnel, they contained a larger pool of trained artillerymen to draw from or interact within the unit during operations, and they required less duplication of administrative duties. Six-gun batteries also provided more flexibility in fire-power and possessed a greater ability to share ammunition by having two more guns with their accompanying limbers and caissons.

More important, each army had control in equipping its batteries with specific models of artillery pieces. At Gettysburg, the Confederate artillery, as stated earlier, contained a large number of mixed batteries, while the Union artillery contained only one battery with mixed guns. Mixed batteries created an increased burden of supplying specific ammunition for each model of gun. In addition, batteries mixed with long-range and short-range guns could be useful when different ranges were needed, but this usually occurred in small-scale actions. In large-scale actions, however, when artillery was used on a broad front, uniformity of guns became increasingly important. Uniformity allowed placement of batteries in order to take advantage of the ability of long-range guns to achieve oblique or crossfiring and, at the same time, allowed placement of batteries to take advantage of the killing power of short-range guns to stop an infantry assault.

When used on a broad front then, some mixed-gun batteries that remained in the main battle line of the Army of Northern Virginia were working at cross-purposes, and an efficient firepower could not be acquired with the best gun placement. Efficient firepower was needed most in cases of large-scale cannonades like July 3, where the rapid expenditure of ammunition occurred and most likely the greatest gamble in forcing the battle to a successful conclusion took place.

Another controllable factor at the army level was the authority that each commander had in designing his artillery reserve. With respect to the battle of Gettysburg, the Army of Northern Virginia's Artillery Reserve provided close support by being attached to each of three corps, but it had no general pool of unattached guns for use by the army when a broad-front action took place. This structure consequently created jurisdictional problems and provided less freedom to react quickly to imminent actions.

The Army of the Potomac, on the other hand, had the freedom of movement with its large unattached artillery reserve. Special mention of the reserve's contribution to the success of the Union army at the battle of Gettysburg must be given to this important force. One would be hardpressed to name an organization that did more to save the Army of the Potomac and help win the battle. Over 80 percent of the Federal artillery reserve's guns were committed to action during the battle, often rushed in at decisive moments. Without the presence of the Federal reserve, the outcome of the battle would not be as we know it.

Another crucial controllable factor held by each army at the battle of Gettysburg was the selection of the manner in which to conduct the fight. Although combinations of circumstances essentially defined the method in which to fight, each army commander had a choice whether to initiate the fight or avoid it altogether. After the action began, each could commit forces for combat or disengage them at the appropriate moment. Each could choose to operate offensively or defensively.

Lee in reality, however, was forced to fight offensively. He was operating in enemy territory, far from his supply base. Consequently he had limited time to achieve his goals, as the longer he stayed the chances of victory diminished. The Union army, in contrast, could easily replenish itself with supplies and its troop strength grew larger by the day.

Meade, on the other hand, was prone to fight defensively. The circumstances he faced were, to say the least, intimidating. Awakened in the early morning hours of June 28, just three days before the battle, he was suddenly placed in command of the Army of the Potomac. Before he awakened, he was controlling ten thousand men; in the glimmering hints of dawn, he was responsible for an army approaching one hundred thousand. He was unfamiliar with commanding an army of such size and generally unversed on how well each of his army's forces could fight. He assumed command while the army was in motion and scattered. He had no time to select his own staff, and three days hence had to face a legend, Robert E. Lee. Understandably, Meade felt he would make fewer mistakes in fighting defensively rather than offensively.

Despite the obstacles confronting each army at Gettysburg, both commanders derived substantial benefits from their respective choice in taking either an offensive or defensive role. A number of factors generally suited the manner in which each chose to fight. These influences included terrain features, the shape and length of the line each held, and the potential firepower each force could develop when deploying its artillery.

Since the Army of Northern Virginia took an *offensive* role at Gettysburg, the ground they occupied for that purpose was better than that occupied by the Army of the Potomac. Although the length of the battle line was a major hurdle, with exterior lines Lee had the elbowroom to maneuver an army on the offensive. This layout created more options in choosing the point of attack, Lee's force was comparatively dispersed along the front and less prone to damage, and, theoretically, his artillery firepower per target mile was greater than the Union's. Lee's exterior line also made his army directly accessible to the mountain passes for withdrawal.

In comparison, Meade's ground, with its internal configuration and quick access to rear support, was more suited to a *defensive* army. With this role, Union forces could and did react quickly to the unknown plans of the enemy at any place in the line. Feeding men and guns onto the field at the right place and time saved the Army of the Potomac at Gettysburg. Had the offensive/defensive roles been switched, while the respective armies held the same ground, the results would be unimaginable.

However with regard to artillery, fighting offensively carried with it some extra burdens not associated with defensive fighting. For one thing, aggressive behavior called for bombardments or cannonades to prepare the way for the infantry to attack. The more belligerent an aggressor became in undertaking a preparatory cannonade, the more it consumed ammunition.

Aggressive cannonades also brought forth ironies to their purpose. Designed to severely punish the enemy, heavy bombardments in effect subdued artillery's killing power. This effect was the inevitable result created when offensive cannonades caused the defenders to respond in kind with their artillery. In doing so, the targets were quickly masked because of smoke generated from the enemy's response as well as smoke from their own artillery. The result reduced artillery's killing power or, at the very least, caused random damage rather than intentional damage.

Offensive fighting included other burdens regarding artillery. Cannonades more than likely divulged the attacker's intentions that an assault was imminent, they pinpointed the object of the attack, and consequently allowed the enemy to discern the purpose of the action and react accordingly. In addition, if the results of a cannonade were ineffective, the defending troops would not be terrorized but instead had their spirits raised with a sense of invincibility and determination to hold their ground.

Another impediment regarding the offensive use of artillery, and an additional irony, was due to the use of "advanced technology" ammunition. Because of the unpredictability of explosive projectiles detonating within their own lines, artillery often resorted to firing solid shot only over its advancing men when they were forward of the guns. Offensive artillery, then, temporarily lost its full effectiveness.

In contrast, when artillery was used defensively, it enjoyed the benefits that were the burdens of the offensive force. The defenders could take cover or hide in the smoke of the cannonade. They could await the enemy's plans to develop and respond accordingly. In addition, defensive artillery was able to freely choose the most effective type of explosive projectiles, since few of the defending troops would be forward of their artillery pieces. Consequently, artillerists were less concerned over injuring their own soldiers with unreliable ammunition. Lastly, when the fighting was close up, defensive artillery had a greater opportunity to use the deadliest ammunition in its inventory—canister. The Army of Northern Virginia's artillery, being on the offensive, fired canister only on a few occasions at Gettysburg.

Another controllable factor affecting the use of artillery was the manner in which the level of firepower was regulated. Ammunition supplies were finite. This factor created limits for an army to fight battles in both duration and intensity. Choosing to fight with grand cannonades, such as on July 3, seemed a logical tactic to prepare the way for an infantry assault, but it was a risky venture with serious penalties if it failed. Cannonades habitually wasted ammunition and quickly emptied the ordnance wagons. A sparse supply of ammunition, caused from combat or inaccessibility to it, affected combat decisions in how current actions were fought and also in planning future actions. Remember the unbelievable restraint shown by Federal commanders in allowing Confederate batteries to build their artillery line unhampered on the morning of July 3 and General Hunt's deep concern for adequate ammunition supplies? Or the Hunt/Hancock dispute on whether the artillery was to hold fire or open up during the July 3 cannonade? Short supplies of ammunition also affected choices in target selection, rate of fire, etc., and, more important, diminished the army's participation in lesser artillery actions where the more decisive outcomes often occurred.

Despite the many problems confronting the artillery at the battle of

Gettysburg, all in all, there was a great deal that went right as well. There are numerous examples depicting artillery operations the way theorists envisioned how artillery should have influenced the outcome. On July 1, for example, Hill's and Ewell's Confederate artillery joined in a concerted effort with their infantry to drive the Union First Corps and Eleventh Corps from west and north of Gettysburg. On the Federal side, its artillery put up a tenacious but unsuccessful stand on Seminary Ridge, and shortly afterward its defensive firepower helped control the retreat through the streets of town. On July 2 in another concerted Confederate action combining artillery and infantry, Longstreet's guns moved aggressively forward to confront Sickles's Third Corps. The joined Southern forces pushed Sickles's men back from the Peach Orchard and the Emmitsburg Road; but this was after Sickles's defiant guns and batteries from the artillery reserve, some without infantry support, exacted a heavy price for the ground gained by the Southern advance. To the rear of this action, yet another stubborn and crucial Union effort took place back in the main Federal line as reserve guns stopped a breakthrough that could have spelled disaster for General Meade. And on another part of the Federal line, unyielding Federal artillerymen resorted to swinging handspikes and rammers to stave off the Confederate infantry that were among their guns on Cemetery Hill. Accounts of these heroic actions would outshine the troublesome environment of operating with less-than-perfect materiel.

July 3rd–Preparation

Artillery actions on July 1 and 2, for the most part remain free of controversy from the should've/could've critics. The Confederates on July 3, however, were presented with a set of circumstances entirely different than the first two days of battle. Time was running out for General Lee: supplies and manpower were reduced significantly; the Federal positions were strengthening; the Confederate attack plan changed; and Lee was to employ the use of his artillery on the grandest scale yet.

July 3 best illustrates the challenges encompassing the artillery at the battle and deserves a recap of circumstances surrounding this historic event. There was no greater gamble made at Gettysburg that relied so heavily on the artillery as the instrument in contributing to the success of the battle than the cannonade preceding Pickett's Charge. Failure of the Confederate offensive cannonade on July 3 is still being analyzed today and the conclusions are not free from controversy. While it is impossible to assign a quantitative value to each factor in assessing how individual elements contributed to the outcome, it is beneficial to review the ingredients that helped determine the result.

To begin with, the scope of the plan was in itself a major stumbling block to executing it successfully. The operation's magnitude spawned a host of obstacles. Length of line and coordination, calling for a barrage of cannon fire that included many commands to interact as one, have already been discussed. There were other impediments to a unified attack. The town of Gettysburg itself aggravated any coordination problems. Gettysburg blocked fields of fire for any Southern artillery located directly north of the town. With this gap created by the town, there was some loss of firepower potential, and it also destroyed any connective control along this sector between Confederate batteries on Seminary Ridge and the isolated guns of the Second Corps artillery located east of town. The gap between the Second Corps guns on or near Benner's Hill east of town and the next nearest Confederate guns on Seminary Ridge measured one and three-quarter miles. By losing connective control, it promoted the piecemeal approach to any offensive move and diminished the shock effect of Confederate artillery on the impending attack. This, in turn, gave the defenders more opportunity to deal with the attack on their terms. They could recover from the initial shock, discern the enemy's intentions, and pick when and where to use their firepower to overcome the assault.

Despite the shortcomings presented by the shape and length of the line in effecting coordination, there were options presented by the terrain which derived a substantial benefit in arranging artillery firepower. The Confederate artillery had more choices to place guns where they could obtain the best converging fire against their intended targets. Colonel E. P. Alexander later criticized General Pendleton for not exploiting the combined potential of Confederate firepower against this vulnerable portion of the Union defenses: "Gen. Lee's chief [of Artillery, General Pendleton] should have known, & given every possible energy to improve the rare & great chance to the very uttermost. Only one of Ewell's five fine battalions . . . participated in our bombardment at all. It only fired a few dozen shots, for, apparently it could not see what it was doing. But every shot was smashing up something, &, had it been increased & kept up, it is hard to say what might have resulted. . . . That neglect was a serious loss. Every map of the field cries out about it."[1]

Undoubtedly, the Confederate artillery dispositions that preceded Pickett's Charge could have inflicted greater damage on the Union lines on Cemetery Ridge. The bulk of the Confederate firepower was placed almost hub to hub on Seminary Ridge, in a row parallel to the Union line, and any of the guns shooting at Federal targets perpendicularly were firing with the least effective angle of fire. If Confederate efforts were to be worthwhile in such positions, firing perpendicularly to the Union gun line required pinpoint accuracy into the shallow enemy line. Pinpoint accuracy would have been nearly impossible on the smoke-laden fields.[2]

Because of inadequate preparation to concentrate firepower, Confederate guns failed to neutralize the major threat against their advancing infantry, the artillery fire from the Federal flanks. Southern guns, which might have enfiladed the Federal batteries playing upon the advancing Confederate infantry, either fired straight to the front or missed destroying the lethal guns planted on the flanks of the Union center. Artillery fire emanating from the undamaged Federal center's flanks was instrumental in wearing down the advancing flanks of the grand assault.

Altering Lee's battle plan with eleventh hour changes on the morning of July 3 impeded adequate artillery preparations. This condition was further aggravated by the conscious effort to position Confederate artillery in a restrained manner in order to avoid unnerving the watchful enemy. Confederate guns were moved about in deliberate slowness to avoid agitating an enemy artillery force that was wound up like a powerful spring, waiting to release its coiled energy. It would only take a few words from any of the Federal commanders, whose scrutinizing eyes inspected the enemy buildup, to end the plan before it even started.

The defensive forces on the other hand, were either stationary, dug in, at rest, or merely preparing and waiting for any anticipated offensive moves then being unveiled by enemy batteries that were positioning along the Federal front.

July 3rd – Aftermath

All in all, the physical damage inflicted by the artillery from both sides on July 3 was out of proportion to the noise. Only afterward could commanders assess their artillery's performance. They would eventually come to realize that the disappointing results were typical of grand cannonades. In 1909, David G. McIntosh, a major at Gettysburg commanding a Confederate reserve artillery battalion, reviewed the effectiveness of the cannonade:

> The impression that any very serious effect had been produced upon the enemy's lines by the artillery fire proved to be a delusion; the aim of the Confederate gunners was accurate, and they did their work as well as could be, but the distance was too great to produce the results which they sanguinely hoped for. Previous experience should have taught them better. It is not a little surprising that General Lee should have reckoned so largely upon the result. Both sides had been pretty well taught that sheltered lines of infantry cannot be shattered or dislodged when behind breastworks, by field artillery, at the distance of one thousand yards and upwards.
>
> The soldier who has been taught by experience to hug tight to his breastworks, and who knows that it is more dangerous to run than to lie still, comes to regard with stoical indifference the bursting missiles which are mostly above or behind him.[3]

Although the Confederates lost a sizable number of horses, troop casualties were comparatively small, around three hundred fifty men. These losses were spread through their ranks in such a way as to appear minor. Such poor results from the Federal guns blasting into the Southern ranks must have boosted the waiting Confederate infantrymen's morale and raised their sense of invincibility.[4]

As to Federal casualties, many eyewitnesses provided accounts of the cannonade describing the brutal results of its shellfire, but few of the regiments, in fact, suffered from its effects. General Alexander Webb, whose Federal infantry brigade occupied the area of greatest fire, reported about fifty casualties. Total casualties around him probably were not more than two hundred. General Caldwell's division was located along the left-center of Cemetery Ridge. "With all his artillery," Caldwell observed, "[it was] the most fearful fire I have ever witnessed . . . But one of my men was killed and very few wounded."[5]

With the sense of sight diminished by the smoke and the sense of hearing overworked by the deafening reverberations of the explosions, it was difficult to assess accurately what was happening. The sound effects of the cannonade combined with an unusually large expenditure of ammunition were deceptive. Although the full effects of the Confederate artillery fire were not visible from Southern positions, the noise and visual effects caused some observers to overestimate the potential damage incurred in the Union line. Confederate Major Eshleman, commanding the Washington Artillery, was confident his guns were doing their job: "My men stood bravely to their work, and by their steady and judicious firing caused immense slaughter to the enemy."[6]

General Pendleton's viewpoint was similar: ". . . The effect was necessarily serious on both sides. With the enemy, there was advantage of elevation and protection from earthworks; but his fire was unavoidably more or less divergent, while ours was convergent. His troops were massed, ours diffused. We, therefore, suffered apparently much less. Great commotion was produced in his ranks, and his batteries were to such extent driven off or silenced as to have insured his defeat but for the extraordinary strength of his position."[7]

For others in the midst of the Federal lines, however, viewing the spectacle and seeing the actual results of the cannonade left them unimpressed. One viewed it as a "waste of powder." Another wrote: "Viewed as a display of fireworks, the rebel practice was entirely successful, but as a military demonstration, it was the biggest humbug of the season."[8]

General Hunt stated: "[Confederate artillery fire] instead of being concentrated on the point of attack, as it ought to have been, and as I expected it would be, was scattered over the whole field." At Appomattox, Colonel Long of Lee's staff, who had formerly served in the artillery with Hunt, told Hunt, ". . . when the fire became so scattered, [I] wondered what you would think about it!"[9]

The cannonade, despite its scattered appearance was, in fact, most destructive to the Union batteries near the intended point of attack, the center, and also behind the front line of Cemetery Ridge. Captain John Hazard, commanding a Second Corps artillery brigade in the Federal center, reported:

> Battery B, First New York Artillery, was entirely exhausted; its ammunition expended; its horses and men killed and disabled; the commanding officer, Capt. J. M. Rorty, killed, and senior First Lieut. A. S. Sheldon severely wounded. The other batteries were in similar condition; still, they bided the attack. . . . So great was the loss in officers, men, and horses, that it was found necessary to consolidate Light Company I,

First U.S. Artillery, Battery A, Fourth U.S. Artillery, and Batteries A and B, First Rhode Island Light Artillery, thus reducing the five batteries that entered the fight to three.

The greatest praise is due to the gallantry and courage of the officers and men of the brigade, of whom one-third were either killed or wounded. The fire under which they fought on the afternoon of July 3 was most severe and terrible . . . [10]

To some Union observers, probably because of the smoke, the focal point of the enemy's cannonade was not apparent. Some eyewitnesses viewed the incoming missiles as being scattered along the line. They were unable to assess the location where any concentrated damage was inflicted. The side effect of "diffused" Confederate fire tended to confuse the Union commanders in discerning the object of the impending attack. Thomas W. Hyde, a staff officer for General Sedgwick, said: ". . . We all knew that it was intended as the prelude to an infantry attack, but where the attack would be was in doubt, as the Confederate fire did not seem to us to be concentrated on any particular part of our line. That is where they were in error, as the whole of their fire directed on the Second Corps would have given their attack a much better chance."[11]

Tactically, the necessary concentration of fire was not adequately prepared. This in general resulted in a diffused fire against important targets that withstood the onslaught of the bombardment. Despite the intensity of Confederate artillery fire, Confederate damage to enemy artillery units on the flanks of the Union center was negligible. On the Federal right-center, Major Osborn's battery commanders on Cemetery Hill reportedly lost only two men, several were wounded, and there was no report of any guns put out of action. On the Union left-center, Lieutenant Colonel Freeman McGilvery, commanding his thirty-nine guns, reported that the enemy guns inflicted "but comparatively little damage to our immediate line." He also did not report any guns put out of service.[12]

This is not to say that the flanks of the center were ignored as targets. Major Osborn testified to this fact:

I judge that the guns of not less than one-half mile of this front were concentrated on our position, besides several batteries on our right, which enfiladed our position, excepting Captains Taft's and Huntington's batteries.

Our artillery endured this fire with surprising coolness and determination. No battery even showed a disposition to retire, and several times during the cannonading we silenced several of their batteries, but at a moment's cessation on our part, they would reopen upon us. The fire was extremely galling, and by comparing the rapidity with which the shells fell among and passed by our guns with the rapidity with which our guns replied, the number of guns playing on the hill was very much greater than the number in position there; probably double.[13]

Undoubtedly, the Federal artillery's own smoke concealed their location and interfered with the aiming skills of the Confederate gunners. It's ironic, however, that Hancock's guns, located in the Union center and replying without restraint, generated the most smoke to mask their presence but yet suffered the heaviest casualties. In contrast, those batteries located on the flanks fired in a subdued manner, generated less smoke, made them more visible targets, but suffered comparatively little. When the infantry attack was underway, the undamaged guns on the left and right of the Federal center were poised to start working on the advancing columns. Major Osborn, artillery brigade commander on the right of the Federal center, commented:

> The left of the charging column rested on a line perpendicular to our front, then stretching away to the right beyond our view, thus offering an excellent front for our artillery fire . . . The whole force of our artillery was brought to bear upon this column, and the havoc produced upon their ranks was truly surprising.
>
> The enemy's advance was most splendid, and for a considerable distance the only hinderance [sic] offered it was by the artillery, which broke their lines fearfully, as every moment showed that their advance under this concentrated artillery fire was most difficult; and though they made desperate efforts to advance in good order, were unable to do so, and I am convinced that the fire from the hill was one of the main auxiliaries in breaking the force of this grand charge.[14]

Colonel McGilvery, commanding the reserve guns on the Federal left-center, wrote of the Confederate advance: "These three lines of battle presented an oblique front to the guns under my command, and by training the whole line of guns obliquely to the right, we had a raking fire through all three of these lines. The execution of the fire must have been terrible, as it was over a level plain, and the effect was plain to be seen. In a few minutes, instead of a well-ordered line of battle, there were broken and confused masses, and fugitives fleeing in every direction."[15]

While the left of the advance was considerably damaged, Colonel Taylor of General Lee's staff observed that the Federal artillery was ineffective on the right of the advance: "Pickett's troops did not appear to be checked by the batteries and only halted to deliver a fire when close under musket range....The charge was made down a gentle slope and then up to the enemy's lines, a distance of over half a mile, denuded of forests and in full sight of the enemy and perfect range of their artillery."[16]

T. M. R. Talcott, major and aide-de-camp to General Robert E. Lee, in citing a Federal view from Swinton's *Army of the Potomac*, stated:

> While crossing the plain, it received a severe fire of artillery, which, however, did not delay for a moment its determined advance . . . The first opposition it received was from two regiments of Stannard's Vermont brigade of the First Corps, which had been posted in a small grove to the left of the Second Corps in front of and at a considerable angle with the main line. These regiments opened upon the right flank of the enemy's advancing lines, which received also an oblique fire from eight batteries under major McGilvray [sic]. This caused the Confederate troops on the flank to double in a little towards their left, but it did not stay their onward progress.[17]

Whatever their effectiveness was, the Federal guns on both flanks of the Union center were, in fact, fully operational for the infantry assault. Confederate artillery fire that should have played against the Federal guns flanking the Union center, was either misapplied in the cannonade because of the failure to arrange the proper concentration of fire, or the gunners manning the Confederate batteries assigned to neutralize the Union batteries on the flanks of the Union center did not aim as well as those gunners shooting into the center where most of the damage occurred.

Blaming smoke as a major cause for the failure of Confederate artillery on July 3 seems too simple to accept but it must be considered, at least, as a serious influence in the ability to operate. How much did this elusive haze effect the planners' considerations? The pre-assault bombardment established itself as the greatest cannonade in the Western Hemisphere. This claim would include the presumption that the greatest amount of smoke accumulation would have accompanied it. How much did the Confederate artillery preparations reflect the futility of arranging their guns to hit common targets or achieve a crossfire when these battle-savvy commanders knew what it would be like minutes into this unprecented cannonade and that their targets would soon be nearly or totally invisible?

Colonel E. P. Alexander's note to general Longstreet, sent just before the cannonade, indicated what everyone should have expected: "I will only be able to judge of the effect of our fire on the enemy by his return fire, for his infantry is but little exposed to view and the smoke will obscure the whole field. If, as I infer from your note, there is any alternative to this attack, it should be carefully considered before opening our fire, for it will take all the artillery ammunition we have left to test this one thoroughly, and, if the result is unfavorable, we will have none left for another effort. And even if this is entirely successful it can only be so at a very bloody cost."[18]

Shortly after the cannonade began, General Hunt reported: "All their batteries were soon covered with smoke. . . . Thence I rode to the artillery reserve to order fresh batteries and ammunition to be sent up to the ridge as soon as the cannonade ceased." Captain Charles A. Phillips, Battery E, Massachusetts Light Artillery, on the left-center reported: "About 1 o'clock the enemy opened a heavy fire from a long line of batteries, which was kept up for an hour, but beyond the noise which was made no great harm was done. Having received orders from General Hunt and from you not to reply to their batteries, I remained silent for the first half hour, when General Hancock ordered us to open. We then opened fire on the enemy's batteries, but in the thick smoke probably did very little damage. By your orders, we soon ceased firing."[19]

Major McIntosh, C.S.A., later wrote of the disabling effects of battlefield smoke on the ability to maneuver men: "Wilcox reports that shortly after the advance began, he received successive orders to advance in support of Pickett: that he put his brigade in motion and advanced, 'near the hill upon which were the enemy's batteries and intrenchments [sic],' but that owing to the smoke of the battle he was unable to perceive a man of the division he was ordered to support, and being subjected to a severe fire, he determined to retire."[20]

The points that contributed to staging Pickett's Charge and bringing forth its conclusion are numerous and complex. The end of the search for answers resolving the issues surrounding this captivating episode of the battle appears nowhere in sight. Those that witnessed it were moved forever. Major Osborn's impression of this epic event reflected the respect he held for the men in gray: "Taking it all in all, Pickett's charge, although a failure, was the grandest of them all. Although they were our enemies at the time, those men were Americans, of our own blood and our own kindred. It was the American spirit which carried them to the front and held them there to be slaughtered. Phenomenal bravery is admired by everyone, and that Pickett's men possessed."[21]

Conclusion

Working as an artilleryman at the battle of Gettysburg was an exceedingly draining experience, both mentally and physically. Despite the hazards surrounding these men and the complex nature impeding their efforts, there were many instances where the artillerymen of both armies performed admirably as far as tactics, command decisions, heroism, and stubborn fighting. For whatever conclusions the reader arrives at in judging artillery's role and performance at Gettysburg, this engagement underscored the significance of the artillery branch's organizational strengths and weaknesses, the integrity of its weapons and ammunition, and the successes and failures of its tactics. Above all, the battle showed the myriad of obstacles that Civil War artillerymen had to cope with and adapt to in order to perform their duty. It also illustrated the innumerable variables that played a role in forcing the result of the three-day fight.

Major Scheibert, of the Prussian Royal Engineers, who witnessed the battle of Gettysburg from the Confederate side, wrote his views on the defeat of Lee:

> What a difference from the systematic advance of the army from the Wilderness to the assault of the breastworks at Chancellorsville, where a unity of disposition and a feeling of security reigned in all the ranks. At Gettysburg there was cannonading without real effect, desultory efforts without combination, and lastly, the single attack which closed the drama, and which I, from my outlook in the top of the tree, believed to be only a reconnaissance in heavy force. Want of confidence, misapprehensions, and mistakes were the consequences, less of Stuart's absence than of the absence of Jackson, whose place up to this time had not been filled.[22]

Colonel E. P. Alexander succinctly expressed his views on the Confederate defeat as well:

> I think it a reasonable estimate to say that 60 per cent of our chances for a great victory were lost by our continuing the aggressive. And we may easily imagine the boon it was to Gen. Meade . . . to be relieved from the burden of making any difficult decision, such as he would have had to do if Lee had been satisfied with his victory of the first day; & then taken a strong position & stood on the defensive. Now the gods had flung to Meade more than impudence itself could have dared to pray for—a position unique among all the battlefields of the war, certainly adding fifty per cent to his already superior force, and an adversary stimulated by success to an utter disregard of all physical disadvantages & ready to face for nearly three quarters of a mile

the very worst that all his artillery & infantry could do. For I am impressed by the fact that the strength of the enemy's position seems to have cut no figure in the consideration [of] the question of the aggressive; nor does it seem to have been systematically examined or inquired into—nor does the night seem to have been utilized in any preparation for the morning. Verily that night *it was a pie for Meade!*[23]

To those artillerymen from both sides who remained devoted to their branch, burdened with unreliable ordnance and unsafe weapons, performing under exposed and dangerous conditions, one cannot help but give the respect they deserve and also honor those who sacrificed their personal dreams of living a life with futures full of promise in exchange for their cherished cause that abruptly ended their existence.

Epilogue

For the remainder of the war, the artillery branch, including its role, its organization, the weapons it used, and ammunition supplied to it, remained substantially the same as at Gettysburg. There were some new innovations, but they did not significantly impact the course of the war. The Union army, for example, introduced Greek fire, an incendiary shell fired from cannons and the precursor of napalm. This innovation's initial results were unimpressive and it was received with such outrage, that it never was given widespread use.[1]

Another invention was the "stink-shell," the harbinger of one of the world's most dreaded phenomena—gas warfare. In June of 1864, Brigadier General Pendleton, still chief of artillery, C.S.A., inquired about this shell's possible use: "I saw noticed in a recent paper a stink-shell, and it seems to me such missiles might be made useful to some extent at least . . . The question is whether the explosion can be combined with suffocating effect of certain offensive gases, or whether apart from the explosion such gases may not be emitted from a continuously burning composition as to render the vicinity of each falling shell intolerable. It seems at least worth a trial."[2]

Information on whether stink-shells were designed to injure soldiers or that they were actually employed in a Civil War battle is unclear. In any event, it was only a matter of time before the war would expend its final bullet and fire its last artillery round.

At the war's end, the country reunited with one army to worry about and many things to contemplate for future conflicts. The military rule books required revisions to address the lessons learned, and new tactics were needed to deal with the innovations that changed warfare forever; rifled weapons, breechloading guns, and repeating rifles, for example, were now a permanent part of the military hardware.

In civilian life, the nation's resources were again directed to non-military enterprises. After four years of destruction, the country's efforts were consumed with restoration and Reconstruction. Railroad projects, postponed by the war, were renewed, and unfinished building and expansion proceeded.

In the process, the tranquility enjoyed in peacetime deflated the military might and scaled back the army's bulging numbers of soldiers. The army directed its attention to reconstruction, fighting Indians, or the tedium of manning remote outposts. The once powerful artillery branch slowly lost its edge and drifted into a period of neglect and stagnation. By the 1880s artillery officers complained about a lack of firing practice and shortages of artillery pieces. Some batteries contained guns of Civil War vintage and West Point cadets drilled with 3-inch rifles and Napoleons. Some efforts were made to convert 3-inch Ordnance rifles to breechloaders and also increase the weight of their projectiles. The bore was increased to 3.2 inches and a steel breech-block was added. Although this adaptation met with initial enthusiasm by ordnance boards up to 1881, the idea apparently was not implemented.[3]

"Turf wars" within the military added to the problem. Infantry officers squabbled with artillerymen over which arm should be assigned the Gatling gun. The debate over who should command artillery batteries in battle still was not resolved. Colonel John Tidball, well-known Civil War artillerist, mirrored Henry Hunt's persistent view on the matter—the objection in assigning batteries to infantry brigades or divisions. With longer-range guns, for exam-

ple, Tidball feared the underuse of artillery firepower by an infantry commander who occupied terrain that could not use all of the assigned guns, but
jealously held them from use elsewhere.[4]

During the 1890s the United States army wrestled with the technology confronting its future and how to counter new threats used against its forces. New
inventions in artillery weapons and methods of fighting continued to be
introduced; tactical experience learned from the Civil War and accompanying
textbooks became obsolete. With deadlier new arms in common use, it was no
longer viable to present troops to the enemy in a close-order battle formation.
However, the newly adopted and preferred tactic, dispersion, exchanged the
old problems associated with dense formations for new ones related to maintaining control of a scattered mass of men.

Artillerymen entered an era that introduced the forerunners of forward
observers. Long-range guns had the capability to hit targets beyond human
eyesight. Tacticians began to recognize the value of indirect fire. This new
method, however, had limitations in that it needed to depend on forward
observers and a reliable means of communicating information. Consequently,
indirect fire was slower and more difficult than direct fire. In addition, long-
range artillery allowed it to be placed away from the infantry troops it was
supporting. This separation eliminated the psychological value that had
boosted the morale of Civil War troops when guns, using direct fire, were
intermingled with them on the front line.

"Short recoil" weapons which required less re-aiming were evolving and
then transforming into guns with "long recoil" mechanisms. This advancement eliminated the exhaustive efforts required of the gun crew in retrieving
the recoiled gun. Guns with recoil mechanisms could also fire continuously
without re-aiming, and the rate of fire increased.

Artillerymen, near the end of the century, saw the introduction of smokeless powder. Paul Vielle, a French chemist, invented the first dependable
smokeless powder called nitrocellulose in 1884. Since there was no time lost
waiting for the smoke to drift away, smokeless powder allowed an increased
rate of fire. Smokeless powder also had a longer explosion time than the black
powder used during the Civil War. Increased explosion time was an advantage. The swifter reaction of Civil War gunpowder, for example, subjected the
barrel to greater explosive pressures. The rapid explosion drove the projectile

Projectile lodged in the bore of a 3-inch Ordnance rifle. Gun is located today at the clump of trees in the Union center at Gettysburg. (AC)

only a short distance before the friction of the barrel worked against it. In contrast, with the increased explosive time for smokeless powder, the propelling gas reacted on the projectile longer in the barrel to produce a greater muzzle velocity, longer range, and increased power. Barrels could then be made longer to take advantage of this characteristic and, at the same time, reduce the size and weight of the cannon, since the explosive pressure was not as great as that generated by black powder. This made field pieces used in the 1890s lighter and more movable than their forerunners.

Steel breechloading cannons with ranges much greater than smoothbores were also introduced. Rifled breechloaders, with effective ranges of four thousand yards, reduced the need for large batteries or maintaining an artillery reserve to create a concentrated fire. Artillerymen could attain massed fire by simply changing the direction of fire. Metallic cartridges increased the capability of artillery. They made loading simpler, helped contain the explosive pressure, and contained the primer. The Gatling gun, the Dynamite gun, and other innovative weapons all added to the artillery branch's firepower at the end of the century.[5]

Artillery's role in battle had become increasingly important since the early days of the Civil War. With new weaponry, ammunition and tactics, artillery would become the driving force that inflicted the majority of casualties in future wars. And in the final years of the nineteenth century, many of those forgotten Union and Confederate gun barrels, blessed by the touch of the brave men who served them, that once belched flame and smoke across the land, were being prepared for a peaceful return to grace the fields of Gettysburg and other battle sites for future generations to appreciate and ponder over.

❧ Appendix A ☙

Ordnance, arms, ammunition, and other ordnance stores procured and supplied to the Union army since the beginning of the rebellion, and the quantity remaining on hand in the arsenals June 30, 1863. [Official Records, Series 3, Vol. 3, 936.]

No. 1.—CANNON AND MORTARS.

	Field guns	Siege guns	Sea-coast guns and mortars	Total number
On hand at the beginning of the rebellion	231	544	1,508	2,283
Purchased since	2,734	546	418	3,698
Total stock	2,965	1,090	1,926	5,981
Issued from the arsenals during the same period	2,481	841	1,247	4,569
Remaining on hand at the arsenals June 30, 1863	484	249	679	1,412

No. 2.—CANNON-BALLS, SHELLS, AND OTHER PROJECTILES.

	Field	Siege	Sea-coast	Total #
On hand at the beginning of the rebellion	90,199	131,036	142,356	363,591
Purchased up to June 30, 1863	1,912,894	242,155	407,695	2,562,744
Total stock	2,003,093	373,191	550,051	2,926,335
Issued from the arsenals during the same period	1,528,578	138,298	78,710	1,745,586
Remaining on hand at the arsenals June 30, 1863	474,515	234,893	471,341	1,180,749

No. 3—ARTILLERY CARRIAGES.

**A Field B Siege C Sea-coast D Mortar beds E Caissons F Traveling forges
G Battery Wagons H Total number**

	A	B	C	D	E	F	G	H
On hand at the beginning of the rebellion	266	104	1,787	106	213	117	60	2,653
Purchased up to June 30, 1863	1,948	154	45	97	2,063	348	226	4,881
Fabricated at the arsenals	637	484	509	234	223	58	64	2,209
Total stock	2,851	742	2,341	437	2,499	523	350	9,743
Issued from the arsenals during the same period	2,492	698	1,719	207	2,139	431	285	7,971
Remaining on hand June 30, 1863	359	41	622	230	360	92	65	1,772

⤙ Appendix B ⤚

Principal Operations of the Federal Ordnance Department, ending June 30, 1863 [O.R. Series 3, Vol. 3, 931-33.] [From the report of George D. Ramsay, Brigadier-General and Chief of Ordnance, Oct. 27, 1863.]:

....An immense amount of material has been prepared and advanced to different stages toward completion at the arsenals, embracing iron and wood work for artillery carriages and implements, projectiles and ammunition of all kinds for cannon, bullets for small-arm cartridges, leather work for harness, equipments, and accouterments. A large number of artillery carriages and small-arms of every description, which had been disabled in service, have been repaired at the arsenals and refitted for service in the field.

The principal articles supplied to the Army during the [fiscal year ending June 30, 1863] were:

Field cannon of different calibers	1,108
Siege cannon of different calibers	288
Sea-coast cannon of different calibers	41

CANNON-BALLS, SHELLS, AND OTHER PROJECTILES.

For field artillery service	699,217
For siege artillery service	156,000
For sea-coast forts	84,530
Artillery carriages for field service	1,125
Artillery carriages for siege service	840
Artillery carriages for sea-coast forts	753
Mortar beds	207
Caissons, traveling forges, and battery wagons	1,040
Artillery harness for two horses, sets each	6,002
Gunpowder pounds	5,337,765
Ammunition rounds for artillery	1,089,863
Friction-primers	3,719,740

Also large supplies of tools, materials, and spare parts for repairing and replacing in the field worn or lost parts of artillery carriages, small-arms, accouterments, and equipments of all kinds.

The stock of such principal articles remaining on hand in store at the arsenals and depots at the close of the fiscal year ending June 30, 1863, were as follows, viz:

Field cannon of different calibers	484
Siege cannon of different calibers	249
Sea-coast cannon of different calibers	679

CANNON-BALLS, SHELLS, AND OTHER PROJECTILES.

For field artillery service	474,515
For siege artillery service	234,893
For sea-coast forts	471,341
Artillery carriages for field service	359
Artillery carriages for siege service	44
Artillery carriages for sea-coast forts	622
Mortar beds	230
Caissons, traveling forges, and battery wagons	517
Artillery harness for two horses, sets each	1,767
Gunpowder pounds	1,463,874
Ammunition rounds for artillery	2,274,490
Friction-primers	6,082,505

☞ Appendix C ☞

Principal Characteristics of Smoothbore and Rifled Artillery Used at Gettysburg

FIELD ARTILLERY

Smoothbores	Bore diameter (inches)	Material	Length of tube (inches)	Weight of tube (pounds)	Weight of projectile (pounds)	Weight of charge (pounds)	Muzzle velocity (ft./sec.)	Range at 5° elevation (yards)
Models of 1841-44								
6-pdr. Gun	3.67	bronze	60	884	6.10	1.25	1,439	1,523
12-pdr. Howitzer	4.62	"	53	788	8.90*	1.00	1,054	1,072
24-pdr Howitzer	5.82	"	64	1,318	18.40*	2.00	1,060	1,322
Model 1857								
12-pdr. Napoleon	4.62	"	66	1,227	12.30	2.50	1,440	1,619

*weight of shell

Rifles	Bore diameter (inches)	Material	Length of tube (inches)	Weight of tube (pounds)	Weight of projectile (pounds)	Weight of charge (pounds)	Muzzle velocity (ft./sec.)	Range at 5° elevation (yards)
10-pdr. Parrott [2.9-inch characteristics similar]	3.00	iron	74	890	9.50	1.00	1,230	1,850
3-inch Ordnance	3.00	"	69	820	9.50	1.00	1,215	1,830
20-pdr. Parrott	3.67	"	84	1,750	20.00	2.00	1,250	1,900
12-pdr. James	3.67	bronze	60	875	12.00	.75	1,000	1,700
12-pdr. Blakely	3.40	steel & iron	59	800	10.00	1.00	1,250	1,850
12-pdr. Whitworth breechloader	2.75	"	104	1,092	12.00	1.75	1,500	2,800

Source: *Notes on Ordnance of the American Civil War 1861-1865*

Endnotes

Preface

1. Pickett, Lasalle Corbell, "My Soldier." *McLure's Magazine* (New York: The S.S. McLure Co. 1908), Vol. XXX, Nov. to April, 1907-1908, 569.

Introduction

1. Fairfax Downey, *The Guns at Gettysburg* (New York: David McKay Company, Inc., 1958), 99.

Chapter I: From the Beginning

1. O. E. Hunt, ed., *Photographic History of the Civil War* (Secaucus: The Blue and the Grey Press, 1987), Vol. 3, unless otherwise noted, 56.
2. U.S. Army Military Museum, West Point, N.Y. Small Arms display.
3. L. Van Loan Naisawald, *Grape and Canister* (New York: Oxford University Press, 1960), 33; Robert U. Johnson & Clarence C. Buel, eds., *Battles and Leaders of the Civil War*, 4 Vols. (Century Company, 1884-89. Reprint, New York: Thomas Yoseloff, 1956). Vol. 3 unless otherwise noted, 259.
4. U.S. War Department, *The War of the Rebellion: A Compilation of the Official Records of the Union and Confederate Armies*, 70 vols. In 128 parts, Series 1, Vol. 33, page 582. Hereafter referred to as "OR, Vol.__, Part__, __." Unless noted, all references are from Series 1.
5. *Grape and Canister*, 32-3; James K. P. Scott, *The Artillery at Gettysburg* (Article from Association of Licensed Battlefield Guides, hereafter referred to as ALBG) file 4-19A.
6. *OR*, Vol. 5, 67.
7. *OR*, Vol. 5, 67–68.
8. General E.P. Alexander, "Confederate Artillery Service." *Southern Historical Society Papers*, hereafter referred to as *SHSP*, (Richmond, Va., February-March, 1883),Vol. 11, Nos. 2-3, 109.
9. Prof. W. LeRoy Broun, "The Red Artillery. Confederate Ordnance, the Difficulty in Supplying it." *SHSP*, Vol. 26, 368, 372.
10. James C. Hazlett, Edwin Olmstead, M. Hume Parks, *Field Artillery Weapons of the Civil War*, Second edition (Newark: University of Delaware Press, 1983), 101; Charles B. Dew, *Ironmaker to the Confederacy: Joseph R. Anderson and the Tredegar Iron Works* (New Haven: Yale University Press, 1966), 180–182.
11. J. W. Mallet, "Work of the Ordnance Bureau of the War Department of the Confederate States, 1861-5." *SHSP*, Vol. 37–38.
12. *Photographic History of the Civil War*, Part 3, 63; John Busey & David Martin, *Regimental Strengths and Losses at Gettysburg* (Hightstown, N.J.: Longstreet House, 1986), 230; *OR*, Vol. 19, Part 1, 951; Vol.27, Part 1, 242.
13. *Photographic History of the Civil War*, 56.
14. "Confederate Artillery Service." *SHSP*, Vol. 11, 104.
15. *OR*, Series 4, Vol. 1, 292–293; William Bradford Williams, *History of the Manufacture of Explosives for the World War, 1917-1918* (Chicago: University of Chicago Press, 1920), 107–109.
16. Victor S. Clark, *History of Manufactures in the United States, 1860-1893* (New York: Peter Smith, 1929 edition, reprinted 1949), Vol. 2, 35; OR, Series 3, Vol. 4, 582.
17. *OR*, Vol. 21, 1,046.

18. Robert H. Gruber, *Summary Statements of Quarterly Returns of Ordnance and Ordnance Stores on Hand in Regular and Volunteer Army Organizations 1862-1867, 1870-1876* (National Archives Microfilm Publications Pamphlet Describing M1281, 1984), 1.

19. Kenneth W. Munden & Henry Putnam Beers, *The Union*. (Published for the National Archives and Records Administration by the National Archives Trust Fund Board, 1986), 15.

20. The Union, 15.

21. Francis A. Lord, *Civil War Collector's Encyclopedia* (Secaucus: Castle, div. of Book Sales, Inc.), 20.

22. *Civil War Collector's Encyclopedia*, 20.

23. "Confederate Artillery Service." *SHSP*, Vol. 11, 112-13.

24. Frank E. Vandiver, ed., *The Civil War Diary of Josiah Gorgas* (University AL.: University of Alabama Press, 1947), 90–91.

25. *OR*, Vol. 24, Part 2, 186.

Chapter II: Organization

1. Allan Nevins, ed., *A Diary of a Battle*, The Personal Journals of Col. Charles S. Wainwright 1861-1865 (Gettysburg, PA: Stan Clark Military Books, 1962 reprint), 129; *Grape and Canister*, 148; OR, Vol. 25, Part 2, 472.

2. *OR*, Vol. 27, Part 1, 571.

3. *OR*, Vol. 33, 582.

4. John Gibbon, *Personal Recollections of the Civil War* (Dayton, Ohio: Press of Morningside Bookshop, 1978), 148.

5. "Confederate Artillery Service." *SHSP*, Vol. 11, 99.

6. *OR*, Vol. 11, Part 3, 40; *Grape and Canister*, 30.

7. E. P. Alexander (Gary W. Gallagher, ed.), *Fighting for the Confederacy* (Chapel Hill: The University of North Carolina Press, 1989), 251.

8. *Battles and Leaders of the Civil War*, 305.

9. *OR*, Vol. 25, Part 2, 614.

10. David L. & Audrey J. Ladd, eds., *The Bachelder Papers—Gettysburg in Their Own Words* (Dayton: Morningside House, Inc., 3 Vols: Vols. 1 & 2, 1994, Vol. 3, 1995.),Vol. 2, 795. Hereafter referred to as *BP*.

11. *Battles and Leaders of the Civil War*, 259; U. S. Government Printing Office, *Report of the Joint Committee on the Conduct of the War*, Vol. 4 (Wilmington, NC: Broadfoot Publishing Company, 1999), 89, 92.

12. *BP*, Vol. 1, 433.

13. *Grape and Canister*, 424.

14. *BP*, Vol. 1, 441

15. Herb S. Crum, ed., *The Eleventh Corps at Gettysburg, The Papers of Major Thomas Osborn, Chief of Artillery* (Hamilton, NY: Edmonston Publishing, Inc.), 79–80.

16. Archer Jones, *Civil War Command and Strategy* (New York: The Free Press, 1992), 29–30.

17. *OR*, Vol. 27, Part 1, 884.

18. *OR*, Vol. 27, 480.

19. *BP*, Vol. 2 , 814.

20. *BP*, Vol. 1, 431–432 and footnote 113 on 432.

21. *OR*, Vol. 27, Part 1, 373.

22. *BP*, Vol. 2, 791, 795.

23. *BP*, Vol. 2, 794, 803.

24. *BP*, Vol. 1, 443–444.

25. *Battles and Leaders of the Civil War*, Vol. 3, 375.

26. *BP*, Vol. 1, 426–427.

27. *OR*, Vol. 11, Part 3, 40.

28. *BP*, Vol. 1, 426–427.

29. *BP*, Vol. 2, 809.
30. *OR*, Vol. 27, Part 1, 238.
31. *OR*, Vol. 27, Part 1, 239.
32. *BP*, Vol. 1, 426, 427 [footnote 104].
33. *BP*, Vol. 1, 430–431.
34. *BP*, Vol. 1, 431.
35. *BP*, Vol. 1, 427 [footnote 103, 104: appeared as margin notes, in a different handwriting than original letter].
36. *BP*, Vol. 1, 426.
37. "Confederate Artillery Service." *SHSP*, Vol. 11, 103.
38. *Battles and Leaders of the Civil War*, 386.
39. *OR*, Vol. 25, Part 2, 614.
40. *Regimental Strengths and Losses at Gettysburg*, 233.
41. "Confederate Artillery Service." *SHSP*, Vol. 11, 99.
42. *OR*, Vol. 5, 67.
43. Wilbur Sturtevant Nye, *Here Come the Rebels* (Baton Rouge: Louisiana State University Press, 1965), 14.
44. *Photographic History of the Civil War*, Part 3, 60.
45. *OR*, Vol. 25, Part 2, 615; Joseph Roberts, *The Handbook of Artillery for the Service of the United States* (New York: D. Van Nostrand, 1863), Fifth Edition, Revised and Enlarged, Part 14, Rifle Cannon–The Parrott Rifle Gun, Item #10.
46. *OR*, Vol. 25, Part 2, 838.
47. *BP*, Vol. 2, 796.
48. *BP*, Vol. 2, 797.
49. *OR*, Vol. 27, Part 1, 167–168, 241; *Regimental Strengths and Losses at Gettysburg*, 111, 148, 170, 191.
50. *OR*, Vol. 27, Part 1, 874.
51. Capt. M. W. Hazlewood, "Pickett's Men in the Gettysburg Charge." *SHSP*, Vol. 23, 232.
52. *Fighting for the Confederacy*, 260.
53. *OR*, Vol. 27, Part 1, 750–751, 874.
54. "Confederate Artillery Service." *SHSP*, Vol. 11, 99–100.

Chapter III: Artillery Technology

1. Prepared under Col. Josiah Gorgas, Chief of Ordnance, *The Ordnance Manual for the Use of the Officers of the Confederate States Army* (First Edition, Press of Morningside Bookshop, 1976), 378; *The Handbook of Artillery for the Service of the United States*, Part 7, Windage, Item #2.
2. Robert V. Bruce, *Lincoln and the Tools of War* (Bobbs Merrill Company, Inc., 1956), 126; Thomas S. Dickey & Peter C. George, *Field Artillery Projectiles* (Mechanicsville, VA: Arsenal Publication II, 1993), 322; M. C. Switlik, *The More Complete Cannoneer* (Museum and Collector Specialties Co., third edition, 1990), 172.
3. John Gibbon, *Artillerist's Manual*, 1860 reprint (Glendale, N.Y.: Benchmark Publishing Co., Inc. 1970), 24–25.
4. *Artillerist's Manual*, 83; *Field Artillery Weapons of the Civil War*, 98.
5. Ordnance Bureau, *The Field Manual for the Use of the Officers on Ordnance Duty* (Ritchie & Dunnavant, 1862; reprinted by Thomas Publications, 1984), 12–13; *Artillerist's Manual*, 83–84; *The Ordnance Manual for the Use of the Officers of the Confederate States Army*, 26.
6. *OR*, Series 3, Vol. 4, 469.
7. *Artillerist's Manual*, 84.
8. *Artillerist's Manual*, 60; The Ordnance Manual for the Use of the Officers of the Confederate States Army, 26.
9. Harold Leslie Peterson, *Notes on Ordnance of the American Civil War 1861-1865* (Wash. D.C.: The American Ordnance Association, (1959), 10; Attack and Die, 60.

10. John Gibbon, *Artillerist's Manual*, second edition, revised and enlarged (Dayton: Morningside, 1991), 455.
11. *Field Artillery Weapons of the Civil War*, 196.
12. *Fighting for the Confederacy*, 304.
13. Grady McWhiney and Perry Jamieson, *Attack and Die* (The University of Alabama Press, 1982), 60, 122.
14. Paddy Griffith, *Battle Tactics of the Civil War* (Yale University Press, 1989), 169.
15. Wayne Stark, *Civil War Cannon Costs* (Internet Address: http://www.cwartillery.org/art-cost.html).
16. *OR*, Vol. 10, Part 2, 362; Vol. 21, 1048; *OR*, Series 4,Vol. 3, 733; Charles B. Dew, *Ironmaker to the Confederacy: Joseph R. Anderson and the Tredegar Iron Works*, 189.
17. James C. Hazlett, Edwin Olmstead, M. Hume Parks, *Field Artillery Weapons of the Civil War* (Newark: University of Delaware Press, second edition, 1988), 91.

Chapter IV: The Guns, Equipment, and Animals

1. *Artillerist's Manual*, 65; *Regimental Strengths and Losses*, 234; Dr. Jay Luvaas & Col. Harold W. Nelson, eds., *The U.S. Army War College Guide to the Battle of Gettysburg* (Carlisle, PA: South Mountain Press, Inc., 1986), 207; *The Field Manual for the Use of the Officers on Ordnance Duty*, 6.
2. *OR*, Vol. 46, Part 2, 1,266–1,267.
3. *OR*, Vol. 1, 370.
4. *OR*, Vol. 38, Part 1, 121; Vol. 38, Part 3, 413.
5. *Field Artillery Weapons of the Civil War*, 52, 123; Warren Ripley, *Artillery and Ammunition of the Civil War* (New York: Promontory Press, 1970), 161; *OR*, Vol. 36, Part 1, 284, 508, 532; Vol. 51, Part 2, 759.
6. *Field Artillery Weapons of the Civil War*, 120.
7. Jack W. Melton, Jr. & Lawrence E. Pawl, *Introduction to Field Artillery Ordnance 1861-1865* (Kennesaw Mountain Press, 1994), 162.
8. *OR*, Vol. 21, 195.
9. *OR*, Vol. 28, Part 1, 31–32.
10. *OR*, Vol. 18, 191; *OR*, Vol. 46, Part 2, 1,266.
11. *OR*, Vol. 18, 193–194.
12. *Attack and Die*, 122–123; *Artillery and Ammunition of the Civil War*, 110; *Field Artillery Weapons of the Civil War*, 109.
13. *Attack and Die*, 59.
14. *Field Artillery Weapons of the Civil War*, 196; "Confederate Artillery Service." *SHSP*, Vol. 11, 109.
15. *OR*, Vol. 25, Part 2, 694.
16. *OR*, Vol. 27, Part 2, 704.
17. Alexander L Holley, *A Treatise on Ordnance and Armor* (New York: D. Van Nostrand, 1865); ALBG file 14-19; *Photographic History of the Civil War*, 163; Col. Berkeley R. Lewis, *Notes on Ammunition of the American Civil War, 1861-1865* (Richmond: The William Byrd Press, Inc., 1959), 19; *OR*, Vol. 36, Part 2, 485; *OR*, Vol. 5, 731.
18. *OR*, Vol. 29, Part 2, 671.
19. *OR*, Vol. 18, 189.
20. *OR*, Vol. 21, 37.
21. "Confederate Artillery Service." *SHSP*, Vol. 11, 108–109.
22. *OR*, Series 3, Vol. 1, 274, 309; Dale Hikes, untitled history paper, 9/61 (ALBG file 14-19); Artillery and Ammunition of the Civil War, 143.
23. *OR*, Vol. 25, Part 2, 795; Vol. 27, Part 2, 676; Vol. 40, Part 1, 670.
24. *Artillery and Ammunition of the Civil War*, 165; *OR*, Vol. 27, Part 1, 872.
25. *OR*, Vol. 21, 1,048.
26. *Artillerist's Manual*, 183; *Artillery and Ammunition of the Civil War*, 194; *Grape and Canister*, 551.
27. *The Ordnance Manual for the Use of the Officers of the Confederate States Army*, 67; *Artillerist's Manual*, 180–181.

28. *The Guns at Gettysburg*, chapter five, endnote #69.
29. *OR*, Vol. 27, Part 1, 1,000, 1,035; Sgt. Horace K. Ide (Dr. Elliott W. Hoffman, ed.), *The First Vermont Cavalry in the Gettysburg Campaign* (Gettysburg Magazine #14, Morningside House, Inc., 1996), 14.
30. *OR*, Vol. 27, Part 1, 891; *The Guns at Gettysburg*, 80–81; Joshua Chamberlain, *The Passing of the Armies* (Dayton: Morningside Bookshop, 1974), 213.
31. *The Ordnance Manual for the Use of the Officers of the Confederate States Army*, 319; *The Field Manual for the Use of the Officers on Ordnance Duty*, 90.
32. *The Civil War Diary of Josiah Gorgas*, 25–26.
33. *The Field Manual for the Use of the Officers on Ordnance Duty*, 90, 95–96.
34. *The Ordnance Manual for the Use of the Officers of the Confederate States Army*, 328–329; *The Field Manual for the Use of the Officers on Ordnance Duty*, 98–99.
35. *Summary of Ordnance and Ordnance Stores on Hand in the Artillery Regiments, 2nd Quarter Ending June 30, 1863* (National Archives, Washington, D.C.) (Record Group 156, Microfilm Publication M1281, Roll #1, Vol. 2), 17–21.
36. *OR*, Vol. 27, Part 1, 242; *The Union Cavalry in the Civil War*, Vol. 1, 311; J. Boone Bartholomees Jr., *Buff Facings and Gilt Buttons*, (Columbia, S.C.: University of South Carolina Press, 1998), 63.
37. *OR*, Vol. 25, Part 2, 820.
38. Erna Risch, *Quartermaster Support of the Army 1775-1939* (Wash. D. C.: Center of Military History - U. S. Army, 1989), 379; *Artillerist's Manual*, 395; *Artillery and Ammunition of the Civil War*, 194.
39. U.S. War Dept., *Instruction for Field Artillery*, 1st published 1861 (Greenwood Press, Publishers, New York, Reprint 1968), 49.
40. John D. Billings, *Hardtack and Coffee* (Boston: George M. Smith & Co., 1887), 329; *OR*, Ser. 3, Vol. 4, 889; Stephen Starr, *The Union Cavalry in the Civil War* (Baton Rouge: Louisiana University Press,1979), Vol. 1, 309–310; Jennings Wise, *The Long Arm of Lee* (Lincoln: University of Nebraska Press 1991), Vol. 2, 922; *Summary of Ordnance and Ordnance Stores on Hand in the Artillery Regiments, 2nd Quarter Ending June 30, 1863* (National Archives, Washington, D.C.) Record Group 156, Microfilm Publication M1281, Roll #1, Vol. 2, 20–21; Quartermaster Support of the Army 1775-1939, 377.
41. *Instruction for Field Artillery*, 47–48; *Artillery and Ammunition of the Civil War*, 194.
42. *OR*, Vol. 27, Part 3, 842.
43. *OR*, Vol. 42, Part 2, 581.
44. *The Guns at Gettysburg*, 158–159.
45. *OR*, Vol. 27, Part 2, 677.
46. *The Ordnance Manual for the Use of the Officers of the Confederate States Army*, 154–155.
47. *OR*, Vol. 27, Part 2, 611.
48. *OR*, Vol. 27, Part 2, 302, 304.
49. *Hardtack and Coffee*, 186, 324, 328–329.
50. *Hardtack and Coffee*, 327–328.
51. *BP*, Vol. 1, 387.
52. *Personal Recollections of the Civil War*, 147–148.
53. *Hardtack and Coffee*, 281–282.
54. *OR*, Vol. 27, Part 1, 879.
55. *OR*, Vol. 27, Part 3, 231.
56. *Hardtack and Coffee*, 281, 291–293.
57. *OR*, Vol. 27, Part 3, 524.
58. *OR*, Vol. 27, Part 3, 542, 569; *The Union Cavalry in the Civil War*, Vol. 1, 444.

Chapter V: Artillery Ammunition

1. Exhibit at GNMP
2. *OR*, Vol. 42, Part 2, 575; *Artillerist's Manual*, 156–157.
3. *OR*, Vol. 27, Part 1, 583.

4. Robert H. Gruber, *Summary Statements of Quarterly Returns of Ordnance and Ordnance Stores on Hand in Regular and Volunteer Army Organizations 1862-1867, 1870-1876* (National Archives Microfilm Publications Pamphlet Describing M1281, 1984), 4.

5. *OR*, Series 3, Vol. 3, 935.

6. *Summary of Ordnance and Ordnance Stores on Hand in the Artillery Regiments, 2nd Quarter Ending June 30, 1863* (National Archives, Washington, D.C. Record Group 156, Microfilm Publication M1281, Roll #1, Vol. 2); *OR*, Vol. 29, Part 2, 413.

7. *OR*, Vol. 46, Part 2, 772.

8. *Notes on Ammunition of the Civil War, 1861-1865*, 27; *OR*, Vol. 21, 195.

9. *OR*, Vol. 46, Part 2, 575-76.

10. *Field Artillery Weapons of the Civil War*, 115, 231.

11. *Grape and Canister*, 538; *Artillerist's Manual*, 250.

12. *Artillerist's Manual*, 165.

13. *OR*, Vol. 42, Part 2, 575.

14. *OR*, Vol. 46, Part 2, 772.

15. Capt. Edwin B. Dow, 6th Maine Battery, *N. Y. Times* article dated June 29, 1913, page 6 (ALBG file 6 MA6).

16. *Grape and Canister*, 540; *Artillerist's Manual*, 256; *Field Artillery Projectiles*, 17; *BP*, Vol. 2 , 814.

17. Cushing of Gettysburg, 236.

18. Harry W. Pfanz, *Gettysburg—Culp's Hill and Cemetery Hill* (Chapel Hill: The University of North Carolina Press, 1993), 255.

19. Editors of Time-Life Books, *Arms and Equipment of the Confederacy* (Alexandria, Time-Life Books, 1996), 283.

20. *"Old Ginger Fingers."* Gettysburg Compiler, Dec. 27, 1898 (ALBG file 8-19).

21. *OR*, Vol. 29, Part 2, 391.

22. *OR*, Vol. 33, 676.

23. *Artillerist's Manual*, 269 (footnote).

24. *BP*, Vol. 1, 407.

25. *The Field Manual for the Use of the Officers on Ordnance Duty*, 22.

26. *Field Artillery Projectiles*, 19.

27. *Artillerist's Manual*, 155; *Notes on Ammunition of the American Civil War, 1861-1865*, 15.

28. *Lee's Lieutenants* (New York, Charles Scribner's Sons, 1944), Vol. 3, 780.

29. *OR*, Vol. 20, Part 2, 111–112.

30. *Field Artillery Projectiles*, 18.

31. *Introduction to Field Artillery Ordnance 1861-1865*, 26.

32. *OR*, Vol. 46, Part 2, 772.

33. Oliver Otis Howard, *Autobiography of Oliver Otis Howard* (New York: The Baker & Taylor Co., 1907), Vol. 1, 438.

34. Alexander Hunter, "Sharpsburg, A High Private's Sketch of." *SHSP*, Vol. 11, 15.

35. F. W. Hackley, *Civil War Ordnance* (3-page paper, ALBG "Ordnance" file).

36. *Field Artillery Projectiles*, 297.

37. *Artillerist's Manual*, second edition, revised and enlarged, 124; *Field Artillery Weapons of the Civil War*, 111; *The Ordnance Manual for the Use of the Officers of the Confederate States Army*, 524; *Field Artillery Projectiles*, 322.

38. *A Treatise on Ordnance and Armor*, ALBG File 14-19; *The Eleventh Corps at Gettysburg*, 31.

39. *Field Artillery Weapons of the Civil War*, 113; *Field Artillery Projectiles*, 159; *The Handbook of Artillery for the Service of the United States*, Part 14, Item #9.

40. *OR*, Vol. 38, Part 1, 122; *Field Artillery Weapons of the Civil War*, 113; *Introduction to Field Artillery Ordnance 1861-1865*, 161.

41. *Introduction to Field Artillery Ordnance 1861-1865*, 126; *Field Artillery Weapons of the Civil War*, 113; *Field Artillery Projectiles*, 158.

42. *OR*, Vol. 11, Part 1, 303; Vol. 21, 195, 210, 466; Vol. 38, Part 1, 121, 487; Vol. 27, Part 1, 1026;Vol. 40, Part 2, 292.
43. *OR*, Vol. 11, Part 3, 237.
44. *OR*, Series 3, Vol. 3, 108.
45. "Confederate Artillery Service." *SHSP*, Vol. 11, 107.
46. *OR*, Vol. 29, Part 2, 413–414.
47. *The Field Manual for the Use of the Officers on Ordnance Duty*, 38.
48. "Confederate Artillery Service," *SHSP*, Vol. 11, 105.
49. *Artillerist's Manual*, 11; *The Handbook of Artillery for the Service of the United States*, Part 8, Item #30.
50. *Artillerist's Manual*, 223–224.
51. *Notes on Ordnance of the American Civil War 1861-1865*, 10.
52. *The Ordnance Manual for the Use of the Officers of the Confederate States Army*, 467; *Artillerist's Manual* , second edition, revised and enlarged, 451.
53. *Grape and Canister*, 543; *Field Artillery Projectiles*, 435; *Introduction to Field Artillery Ordnance 1861-1865*, 40; *The Handbook of Artillery for the Service of the United States*, Part 10, Item #14.
54. *Field Artillery Projectiles*, 435.
55. "Confederate Artillery Service." *SHSP*, Vol. 11, 104–105.
56. *Grape and Canister*, 542-4; *Notes on Ammunition of the American Civil War,1861-1865*, 19; *Field Artillery Projectiles*, 300.
57. *Field Artillery Projectiles*, 299; *Introduction to Field Artillery Ordnance 1861-1865*, 30.
58. *Battles and Leaders of the Civil War*, 358.
59. *OR*, Vol. 27, Part 1, 937.
60. *OR*, Vol. 27, Part 1, 1,026; Vol. 11, Part 3, 242.
61. *OR*, Vol. 27, Part 1, 754–755.
62. *OR*, Vol. 47, Part 1, 907; Vol. 21, 211.
63. *OR*, Vol. 21, 207.
64. *Artillerist's Manual*, 22.
65. "Confederate Artillery Service." *SHSP*, Vol. 11, 107.
66. *Fighting for the Confederacy*, 248.
67. *OR*, Vol. 25, Part 1, 260.
68. *OR*, Vol. 33, 676.
69. *OR*, Vol. 21, 748.
70. *OR*, Vol. 40, Part 1, 669–670.
71. *OR*, Vol. 28, Part 2, 388.
72. *OR*, Vol. 25, Part 2, 795.
73. *OR*, Vol. 27, Part 2, 459.
74. Attack and Die, 59; *OR*, Vol. 27, Part 2, 458-9; David Martin, *Gettysburg, July 1* (Conshohocken, PA: Combined Books, 1995), 282.
75. *OR*, Vol. 11, Part 3, 362.
76. *OR*, Vol. 11, Part 3, 362; Vol. 5, 67.
77. *OR*, Vol. 29, Part 2, 421.
78. *OR*,Vol. 27, Part 1, 241, 364–365, 895; Part 2, 458, 612; Edward Longacre, *The Man Behind the Guns—A Biography of General Henry Jackson Hunt* (A.S. Barnes & Co., Inc., 1977), 178.
79. *The Guns at Gettysburg*, 57; *OR* Vol. 27, Part 1, 751, 879; *OR*, Vol. 27, Part 1, 873–874, 879.
80. Fighting for the Confederacy, 246; *Grape and Canister*, 443; *OR*, Vol. 27, Part 2, 612.

Chapter VI: Artillery Operations

1. *A Diary of a Battle*, xi.
2. *Instruction for Field Artillery*, 2.
3. *Grape and Canister*, 535; Rory Muir, *Tactics and the Experience of Battle in the Age of Napoleon* (New Haven: Yale University Press, 1998), 46.

4. *Tactics and the Experience of Battle in the Age of Napoleon*, 193.
5. Richard Holmes, *Acts of War* (New York: The Free Press, 1986), 231; Bandy, Freeland, & Bearss, eds., Samuel Stouffer, Arthur A. Lumsdaine, Marion Harper Lumsdaine, Robin M. Williams, Jr., M. Brewster Smith, Irving L. Janis, Shirley A. Star, Leonard S. Cottrell, Jr., *The American Soldier, Combat and its Aftermath* (Princeton: Princeton University Press, 1949), Vol. 2, 83.
6. *The Gettysburg Papers*. 2 Vols. (Morningside Bookshop, 1978), Vol. 1, 346.
7. Donald L. Smith, *The Twenty-Fourth Michigan* (Harrisburg: The Stackpole Co., 1962), 64; Edwin B. Coddington, *The Gettysburg Campaign, a Study in Command* (New York: Charles Scribner's Sons, 1968), 508.
8. *OR*, Vol. 27, Part 1, 785; Tactics and the Experience of Battle in the Age of Napoleon, 38.
9. *Tactics and the Experience of Battle in the Age of Napoleon*, 193.
10. Earl J. Hess, *The Union Soldier in Battle* (University Press of Kansas, 1997), 28–29.
11. *Attack and Die*, 124.
12. *BP*, Vol. 1, 432–433.
13. *The Gettysburg Papers*, Vol. 1, 345–346.
14. *Fighting for the Confederacy*, 245–246.
15. *OR*, Vol. 27, Part 2, Page 603, 605.
16. *OR*, Vol. 27, Part 2, 675.
17. Col. G.F.R. Henderson, *The Science of War* (Longmans, Green and Co. Ltd, 1927), 261.
18. *Fighting for the Confederacy*, 245.
19. *Fighting for the Confederacy*, 245.
20. *The Eleventh Corps at Gettysburg*, 31.
21. *Battles and Leaders of the Civil War*, Vol. 3, 371–372.
22. *OR*, Vol. 27, Part 1, 238.
23. *OR*, Vol. 27, Part 2, 610.
24. *Fighting for the Confederacy*, 246; E. P. Alexander, *Military Memoirs of a Confederate* (Charles Scribner's Sons, 1907), 418.
25. *BP*, Vol. 2 , 812-3.
26. *Fighting for the Confederacy*, 250–251.
27. *OR*, Vol. 27, Part 1, 372.
28. *Battles and Leaders of the Civil War*, 371–372.
29. Captain William L. Ritter, "Maryland Artillery-Sketch of the Third Battery." *SHSP*, Vol. 11, 116.
30. *OR*, Vol. 42, Part 2, 576.
31. *OR*, Vol. 42, Part 2, 574–575.
32. *Regimental Strengths and Losses*, 234; *Battle Tactics of the Civil War*, 167.
33. *Battle Tactics of the Civil War*, 166.
34. *Artillerist's Manual*, second edition, revised and enlarged, 358; *Grape and Canister*, 150.
35. *Fighting for the Confederacy*, 251.
36. E. P. Alexander, "Causes Of The Confederate Defeat At Gettysburg." *SHSP*, Vol. 4, 109.
37. *OR*, Vol. 27, Part 1, 870.
38. *The Eleventh Corps at Gettysburg*, 31–32.
39. *The Eleventh Corps at Gettysburg*, 70.
40. *OR*, Vol. 27, Part 2, 624.
41. *OR*, Vol. 42, Part 2, 575–577; *Artillerist's Manual*, 403.
42. *OR*, Vol. 42, Part 2, 576–577.
43. *The Gettysburg Papers*, Vol. 1, 346.
44. *Cushing of Gettysburg*, 68; *The Field Manual for the Use of the Officers on Ordnance Duty*, 127; *Artillerist's Manual*, 183, 250.
45. *Attack and Die*, 61.
46. *OR*, Vol. 42, Part 2, 576.
47. *OR*, Vol. 27, Part 1, 356–357.
48. *Artillery and Ammunition of the Civil War*, 233.

49. *OR*, Vol. 27, Part 1, 1,045; *Artillery and Ammunition of the Civil War*, 234.

50. *The Gettysburg Papers*, Vol. 1, 372-3.

51. *Grape and Canister*, 443; *OR*, Vol. 27, Part 1, 243;Vol. 27, Part 2, 354.

52. *Artillery and Ammunition of the Civil War*, 234.

53. *OR*, Vol. 42, Part 2, 578.

54. *OR*, Vol. 2, 99.

55. *Instruction for Field Artillery*, 2.

56. *OR*, Vol. 42, Part 2, 578; *Artillerist's Manual*, 405.

57. *The Guns at Gettysburg*, 239–240; *The Handbook of Artillery for the Service of the United States*, Part 1, Section 8, On Field-Guns and Batteries.

58. *Artillerist's Manual*, 257; Artillery and Ammunition of the Civil War, 225; *The Guns at Gettysburg*, 242.

59. *Cushing of Gettysburg*, 249.

60. *Artillerist's Manual*, 260; *The Field Manual for the Use of the Officers on Ordnance Duty*, 129.

61. *Arms and Equipment of the Confederacy*, 285.

62. *Arms and Equipment of the Confederacy*, 285.

63. *Summary of Ordnance and Ordnance Stores on Hand in the Artillery Regiments, 2nd Quarter Ending June 30, 1863* (National Archives, Washington, D.C.) Record Group 156, Microfilm Publication M1281, Roll #1, Vol. 2; *The Guns at Gettysburg*, 104; *The Gettysburg Papers*, Vol. 2, 773.

64. *Artillerist's Manual*, 251.

65. *Artillerist's Manual*, second edition, revised and enlarged (Dayton: Morningside, 1991), 203.

66. *Artillerist's Manual*, 251.

67. John J. Pullen, *The Twentieth Maine* (Phila. & New York: J.B. Lippincott Company, 1957), 49.

68. *The Guns at Gettysburg*, 104; The Gettysburg Papers, Vol. 2, 773.

69. *Civil War Collector's Encyclopedia*, 24; *The Ordnance Manual for the Use of the Officers of the Confederate States Army*, 467; *The Handbook of Artillery for the Service of the United States*, Part 15, Miscellaneous; Gettysburg–Culp's Hill and Cemetery Hill, 189.

70. Schenck, A.D., *Material for Field Artillery* (1886), 16.

71. *Personal Recollections of the Civil War*, 147.

72. " Maryland Artillery-Sketch of the Third Battery." *SHSP*, Vol. 11, 190.

73. *Personal Recollections of the Civil War*, 83.

74. *Artillerist's Manual*, 257; *The Handbook of Artillery for the Service of the United States*, Part 2, Section 1, Pointing Guns and Howitzers.

75. *OR*, Vol. 11, Part 3, 242; Vol. 21, 216.

76. *Artillerist's Manual*, 223.

77. *Artillerist's Manual*, 58.

78. *The Ordnance Manual for the Use of the Officers of the Confederate States Army*, 465.

79. *OR*, Vol. 27, Part 1, 885.

80. *Diary of a Battle*, 249.

81. *OR*, Vol. 27, Part 1, 883–884.

82. *OR*, Vol. 27, Part 1, 449; George Stewart, *Pickett's Charge* (Greenwich CT: Fawcett Publications, Inc., 1963), 137.

83. *Artillerist's Manual*, 404.

84. *Notes on Ordnance of the American Civil War 1861-1865*, 15.

85. *Artillerist's Manual*, 155; *Grape and Canister*, 550.

86. *OR*, Vol. 21, 828.

87. *The Eleventh Corps at Gettysburg*, 36–37.

88. *Artillerist's Manual*, 404.

89. *OR*, Vol. 42, Part 2, 578–579.

90. *The Eleventh Corps at Gettysburg*, 38.

91. *OR*, Vol. 27, part 1, 689. [There is confusion as to which battery is involved in this incident. Osborn claimed it was Norton's Battery H, First Ohio Light Artillery that left the field. His

account was most likely connected with McCartney's account of Edgell's First New Hampshire leaving ammunition on the ground. Edgell relieved Norton in the same position.]

92. *The Guns at Gettysburg*, 119; Ironmaker to the Confederacy: Joseph R. Anderson and the Tredegar Iron Works, 130.
93. *OR*, Vol. 27, Part 3, 600.
94. *Grape and Canister*, 427; *BP*, Vol. 1, 229.
95. *BP*, Vol. 1, 228.
96. *BP*, Vol. 1, 428.
97. *Pickett's Charge*, 125.
98. *The Twentieth Maine*, 25–26.
99. Jacob Hoke, *The Great Invasion* (New York: Thomas Yoseloff, New Edition, 1959), 364–365.
100. *Personal Recollections of the Civil War*, 178.
101. *Artillerist's Manual*, 249; *OR*, Vol. 11, Part 2, 261.
102. John Worsham, "The Second Battle of Manassas. Account of it by One of Jackson's Foot Cavalry." *SHSP*, (article from the Times Dispatch, October 23, 1904), Vol. 32, 85.
103. *The Union Soldier in Battle*, 18–19.
104. *The Gettysburg Papers*, Vol. 1, 341.
105. *The Twentieth Maine*, 52.
106. *Fighting for the Confederacy*, 253.
107. *The Guns at Gettysburg*, 130; *OR*, Vol. 27, Part 1, 706.
108. *BP*, Vol. 3, 1,360–1,361.
109. Peter S. Carmichael, *Lee's Young Artillerist, William R. J. Pegram* (Charlottesville: University Press of Virginia, 1995), 103.
110. *Battles and Leaders of the Civil War*, Vol. 3, 365[footnote].
111. *The Gettysburg Papers*, Vol. 2, 735.

Chapter VII: Artillerymen

1. *Instruction for Field Artillery*, 107.
2. *OR*, Vol. 42, Part 2, 581.
3. *OR*, Vol. 27, Part 2, 432.
4. *Personal Recollections of the Civil War*, footnote 83–84.
5. *OR*, Vol. 46, Part 1, 970.
6. *The Union Soldier in Battle*, 113.
7. *BP*, Vol. 2, 1,156–1,157.
8. *OR*, Vol. 27, Part 2, 381.
9. *The Eleventh Corps at Gettysburg*, 36.
10. *The Eleventh Corps at Gettysburg*, 38.
11. *The Union Soldier in Battle*, 92.
12. *The Guns at Gettysburg*, 131.
13. *A Diary of a Battle*, 408.
14. Douglas Southall Freeman, *Lee's Lieutenants*, Vol. 3, 179.
15. *BP*, Vol. 3, 1,364.
16. *OR*, Vol. 27, Part 2, 320.
17. *Battles and Leaders of the Civil War*, 361–362.
18. *Fighting for the Confederacy*, 251.
19. *Lee's Lieutenants*, Vol. 3, 179.
20. *Fighting for the Confederacy*, 245.
21. *OR*, Vol. 27, Part 2, 351–352.
22. *Fighting for the Confederacy*, 336.
23. E. P. Alexander, "Causes Of The Confederate Defeat At Gettysburg." *SHSP*, Vol. 4, 110.

Chapter VIII: Summary

1. *Fighting for the Confederacy*, 251.
2. Edward Hagerman, *The American Civil War and the Origins of Modern Warfare* (Indiana University Press, 1988), 94–95.
3. David Gregg McIntosh, "Review Of The Gettysburg Campaign." *SHSP*, Vol. 37, 136–137.
4. *Pickett's Charge*, 149.
5. *Pickett's Charge*, 148–149; *OR*, Vol. 27, Part 1, 380.
6. *OR*, Vol. 27, Part 2, 435.
7. *A Diary of a Battle*, 245; *OR*, Vol. 27, Part 2, 352.
8. *Pickett's Charge*, 148.
9. *Battles and Leaders of the Civil War*, 373-4.
10. *OR*, Vol. 27, Part 1, 480.
11. *Gettysburg Papers*, Vol. 2, 751.
12. *OR*, Vol. 27, Part 1, 884.
13. *OR*, Vol. 27, Part 1, 750.
14. *OR*, Vol. 27, Part 1, 750.
15. *OR*, Vol. 27, Part 1, 884.
16. *The Eleventh Corps at Gettysburg*, 78–79.
17. T. M. R. Talcott, "The Third Day At Gettysburg." *SHSP*, Vol. 41, 46.
18. E. P. Alexander, "Causes Of The Confederate Defeat At Gettysburg." *SHSP*, Vol. 4, 104–105
19. *Battles and Leaders of the Civil War*, 372-3; *OR*, Vol. 27, Part 1, 885.
20. David Gregg McIntosh, "Review Of The Gettysburg Campaign." *SHSP*, Vol. 37, 138.
21. *The Eleventh Corps at Gettysburg*, 44.
22. Maj. Justus Scheibert, of the Prussian Royal Engineers, "Leading Confederates On The Battle Of Gettysburg." *SHSP*, Vol. 5, 92–93.
23. *Fighting for the Confederacy*, 277–278.

Epilogue

1. *Civil War Collector's Encyclopedia*, 114–115.
2. *OR*, Vol. 36, Part 3, 888–889.
3. Perry D. Jamieson, Crossing the Deadly Ground (Tuscaloosa: The University of Alabama Press, 1994), 20, 78; *Artillery and Ammunition of the Civil War*, 163.
4. *Crossing the Deadly Ground*, 79, 82.
5. Boyd L. Dastrup, *The Field Artillery* (Greenwood Press, Wesport, CT, 1994), 37-43; *Crossing the Deadly Ground*, 83-4, 128; Konrad F. Schreier, Jr., *U.S. Army Field Artillery Weapons-1866 to 1918* (Periodical Journal of America's Military Past Vol. XXIV, Summer 1997, No. 2, Whole No. 79), 20.

Glossary

Battery wagon A support vehicle used to service the guns. It was packed with an assortment of equipment, supplies, and a variety of tools needed to keep the battery operational.

Bolt Solid shot used in rifled cannon.

Bore The cylinder-shaped hole at the muzzle where the ammunition is introduced.

Bormann fuse A time device consisting of a soft metal disk on a threaded cylinder and screwed into the shell. The fuse burn time was determined by cutting the thin metal at the appropriate graduated mark, exposing the fuse powder.

Bourrelets Two oversized iron bands encircling the body of the projectile—one was near the top of the round and one near the bottom. Bourrelets reduced machining time for the projectile's final dimension and also reduced friction with the bore.

Breech The rear-end of the barrel.

Breechloader A weapon loaded from the rear.

Breech sight A brass sight marked with degrees of elevation and an adjustable bar to line up and aim with the muzzle sight.

Bronze A metal composed of 90 percent copper and 10 percent tin. Howitzers, Napoleons, and James guns were made of bronze.

Bursting charge The small powder charge used to detonate shell or case shot.

Caisson A two-wheeled support vehicle, containing two ammunition chests and a spare wheel, pulled by a limber and accompanying the artillery piece.

Canister Close-range ammunition consisting of a tin can loaded with lead or iron balls packed in sawdust.

Cartridge bag The cloth bag containing the propellant charge of the projectile.

Cascabel The bulb-shaped extension at the breech.

Case shot An explosive projectile loaded with lead or iron balls symmetrically held in place by pitch or sulfur melted into the cavity.

Cast iron The prime metal for making projectiles and many artillery barrels. Its hardness and brittleness were good for projectiles but not beneficial for making cannons.

Chase The tapered portion of the gun barrel from the trunnions to the muzzle.

Combination fuse This timing device contained both an adjustable self-igniting time fuse and a percussion fuse. The projectile detonated from the percussion fuse if its impact was sooner than the burn of the time fuse.

Concussion fuse Used primarily for spherical ammunition, this chemical fuse was designed to explode from the shock of it hitting an object.

Deviation The variations in the trajectories of like projectiles fired under the same conditions.

Dish The convex shape of spokes which gave elasticity to the wheel and absorbed the shock.

Drift The left or right deviation of a projectile from its intended path.

Elevating screw The screw mechanism under the breech that raises and lowers the barrel to change the range.

Enfilade Firing a gun to sweep the length of an enemy line.

Field artillery Weapons small enough to maneuver through difficult terrain and keep up with a moving army and its rapid changes. Field artillery included mounted and horse artillery.

Forge Support vehicle for a battery. The limber chest of a forge carried smith's supplies and tools.

Friction primer An ignition device for the gun, it was a small brass tube inserted in the vent and communicated fire to the propellant charge.

Fuse A device for detonating explosive projectiles.

Fuse plug A wooden or threaded metal device for holding the fuse in the projectile.

Gaining twist A varying rate of spiral in rifled guns to reduce the initial shock on the projectile. A gaining twist started at its slowest rate in the rear of the bore and increased towards the muzzle.

Grapeshot The earlier version of canister, it contained an arrangement of layered iron balls, fewer and larger than in canister, held together by iron plates and a threaded bolt at the center.

Greek fire An incendiary shell fired from cannons.

Gunner's level A metal device used to indicate the perpendicular of an artillery piece. It was rarely used in the field artillery.

Handspike A heavy wooden implement inserted in the two pointing rings at the trail to direct the barrel's aim or maneuver the gun.

Hot shot A solid projectile, after being heated to a white or red-hot temperature, it was fired at wooden structures or ships. Splintering wood made it more combustible and, after a time, the smoldering debris ignited to a flaming fire.

Howitzer A short-barreled artillery piece used primarily for firing hollow projectiles. It had a powder chamber in the rear of the barrel with a diameter smaller than that of the bore.

Initial velocity The speed of the projectile when it left the barrel.

Lanyard A heavy cord attached to a wooden hand-grip and, at the other end, a hook for attachment to the friction primer to fire the gun.

Limber A two-wheeled support vehicle, containing one ammunition chest, that pulled the artillery piece or a caisson or other support vehicles.

Muzzleloader A weapon loaded from the front of the barrel.

Oblique fire Shooting at a target in an angular fashion.

Pendulum hausse A brass sight which rested in a cradle at the rear of the barrel and used an adjustable slider and graduated scale to achieve proper range. The pendulum hausse was free-swinging and weighted with lead at the bottom to obtain a vertical line with the earth which allowed the gunner to aim properly.

Percussion fuze A fuse that detonated from contact.

Piece The general term referring to an artillery weapon.

Pointing a piece Aiming the weapon.

Pointing rings The two iron rings attached to the trail for use with the handspike to aim or maneuver the piece.

Priming wire The pointed heavy-wire tool used to clear debris from the vent or puncture the powder bag.

Prolonge A heavy rope, wound around two brackets on the trail, used to pull the piece.

Propellant charge The gunpowder quantity used to deliver the projectile to the target.

Quadrant A tool, rarely used in the field, that measured the degree of elevation of the barrel in relation to the perpendicular and used in conjunction with the Table of Fire.

Recoil The backward reaction of a fired weapon.

Ricochet firing Method used for spherical-shaped ammunition allowing a bouncing effect across open terrain to gain range or rattle the enemy.

Rifling Spiral lands, raised portions, and grooves which imparted the spin on the projectile.

Sabot For smoothbores, a wooden disk for joining the powder cartridge to the projectile and securing the ball's position. For rifled guns, a component that changed shape to grab the rifling and impart the spin.

Shell An explosive projectile which uses its body, rather than containing balls, to fragment and inflict damage.

Shot A solid projectile used for battering or fired into targets with depth.

Smoothbore A barrel without lands and grooves in the bore.

Spherical projectile Round shot or shell.

Spiking a gun Deliberate attempt to disable the piece temporarily with a spike or similar object and prevent communicating fire to the powder charge.

Sponge-rammer The implement used to clean the bore and insert ammunition in the barrel.

Table of Fire The Table of Fire, pasted inside the limber lid, listed the degrees of elevation, ranges, and times of flight for various projectiles; used to calculate accuracy of fire.

Tangent scale A brass sight shaped with steps. Each step was marked with designated degrees of elevation to obtain specific ranges.

Thumbstall A protective leather accouterment, was used to close the vent.

Tow Chopped hemp rope used for stuffing the voids between projectiles packed in ammunition chests.

Tow hook A tool with an iron thirteen-inch long hook for grabbing and pulling out tow material. A small hammer was also attached to repair sabot straps and fixed ammunition.

Trail The wooden section of the cannon carriage that rests on the ground or attaches to the limber.

Trajectory The curved flight path of a projectile.

Trunnions Cylinder-shaped protrusions on both sides of the barrel to cradle and secure the barrel in the gun carriage.

Twist The degree of rotation on a projectile.

Velocity The speed of a projectile in motion.

Vent The opening at the rear of the barrel that communicated the fire to the powder charge.

Windage The difference between the bore diameter of the gun and the diameter of the projectile.

Wrought iron An easily welded or forged iron that was strong, malleable and made an excellent material for cannon barrels

Bibliography

Alexander, Edward Porter (Gary W. Gallagher, ed.). *Fighting for the Confederacy* (Chapel Hill: The University of North Carolina Press, 1989).

_____. *Military Memoirs of a Confederate* (Charles Scribner's Sons, 1907).

_____. "Confederate Artillery Service" *Southern Historical Society Papers* (Richmond, VA, February-March, 1883),Vol. 11, Nos. 2–3.

_____. "Causes Of The Confederate Defeat At Gettysburg." *Southern Historical Society Papers*, Vol. 4, 104–05, 109–10.

Bandy, Freeland, & Bearss, eds. *The Gettysburg Papers*. 2 Vols. (Morningside Bookshop, 1978), Vol. 1.

Bartholomees, J. Boone Jr. *Buff Facings and Gilt Buttons* (Columbia, SC: University of South Carolina Press, 1998).

Billings, John D. *Hardtack and Coffee* (Boston: George M. Smith & Co., 1887).

Broun, W. LeRoy, Prof. "The Red Artillery. Confederate Ordnance, the Difficulty in Supplying It." *Southern Historical Society Papers*, Vol. 26, 368, 372.

Brown, Kent Masterson. *Cushing of Gettysburg* (The University Press of Kentucky, 1993).

Bruce, Robert V. *Lincoln and the Tools of War* (Bobbs Merrill Company, Inc., 1956).

Busey, John & David Martin, *Regimental Strengths and Losses at Gettysburg* (Hightstown, NJ: Longstreet House, 1986).

Carmichael, Peter S. *Lee's Young Artillerist, William R. J. Pegram* (Charlottesville: University Press of Virginia, 1995).

Chamberlain, Joshua. *The Passing of the Armies* (Dayton: Morningside Bookshop, 1974).

Clark, Victor S. *History of Manufactures in the United States, 1860-1893* (New York: Peter Smith,1929 edition, reprinted 1949), Vol. 2.

Coddington, Edwin B. *The Gettysburg Campaign, a Study in Command* (New York: Charles Scribner's Sons, 1968).

Crum, Herb S. ed. *The Eleventh Corps at Gettysburg, The Papers of Major Thomas Osborn, Chief of Artillery* (Edmonston Publishing, Inc., Hamilton, NY).

Dastrup, Boyd L. *The Field Artillery* (Greenwood Press, Westport, CT, 1994).

Dew, Charles B. *Ironmaker to the Confederacy: Joseph R. Anderson and the Tredegar Iron Works* (New Haven: Yale University Press, 1966).

Dickey, Thomas S. & Peter C. George. *Field Artillery Projectiles* (Mechanicsville, VA: Arsenal Publication II, 1993).

Dow, Edwin B., Capt. 6th Maine Battery, *N. Y. Times* article dated June 29, 1913, page 6 (ALBG file 6 MA6).

Downey, Fairfax. *The Guns at Gettysburg* (New York: David McKay Company, Inc., 1958).

Freeman, Douglas Southall. *Lee's Lieutenants* (New York: Charles Scribner's Sons, 1944), Vol. 3.

Gettysburg Compiler, Dec. 27, 1898, author unknown. *"Old Ginger Fingers"* (Assoc. of Licensed Battlefield Guide Files), file 8-19.

Gibbon, John. *Artillerist's Manual,* 1860 reprint (Glendale, NY: Benchmark Publishing Co., Inc. 1970).

_____. *Artillerist's Manual,* second edition, revised and enlarged (Dayton, OH: Morningside, 1991).

_____. *Personal Recollections of the Civil War* (Dayton, OH: Press of Morningside Bookshop, 1978).

Gorgas, Josiah, Col. Chief of Ordnance (Prepared under). *The Ordnance Manual for the Use of the Officers of the Confederate States Army* (1st Edition, Press of Morningside Bookshop, 1976).

Griffith, Paddy. *Battle Tactics of the Civil War* (Yale University Press, 1989).

Gruber, Robert H. *Summary Statements of Quarterly Returns of Ordnance and Ordnance Stores on Hand in Regular and Volunteer Army Organizations 1862-1867, 1870-1876* (National Archives Microfilm Publications Pamphlet Describing M1281, 1984).

Hackley, F. W. *Civil War Ordnance* (Assoc. of Licensed Battlefield Guide Files), "Ordnance" file.

Hagerman, Edward. *The American Civil War and the Origins of Modern Warfare* (Indiana University Press, 1988).

Hazlett, James C., Edwin Olmstead, M. Hume Parks, *Field Artillery Weapons of the Civil War* (Newark: University of Delaware Press, second edition, 1988).

Hazlewood, M. W., Capt. "Pickett's Men in the Gettysburg Charge." *Southern Historical Society Papers,* Vol. 23, 232.

Henderson, G.F.R., Col. *The Science of War* (Longmans, Green and Co. Ltd, 1927).

Hess, Earl J. *The Union Soldier in Battle* (University Press of Kansas, 1997).

Hikes, Dale. Untitled history paper (Assoc. of Licensed Battlefield Guide Files, 9/61) file 14-19.

Hoke, Jacob. *The Great Invasion* (New York: Thomas Yoseloff, New Edition, 1959).

Holley, Alexander L. *A Treatise on Ordnance and Armor* (New York: D. Van Nostrand, 1865), Assoc. of Licensed Battlefield Guide Files, file 14-19.

Holmes, Richard. *Acts of War* (New York: The Free Press, 1986).

Howard, Oliver Otis. *Autobiography of Oliver Otis Howard* (New York: The Baker & Taylor Co., 1907), Vol. 1.

Hunt, O. E. ed. *Photographic History of the Civil War* (Secaucus: The Blue and the Grey Press, 1987), Vol. 3.

Hunter, Alexander, "Sharpsburg, A High Private's Sketch of." *Southern Historical Society Papers,* Vol. 11, 15.

Ide, Sgt. Horace K. (Dr. Elliott W. Hoffman, ed.), *The First Vermont Cavalry in the Gettysburg Campaign* (Gettysburg Magazine #14, Morningside House, Inc., 1996).

Jamieson, Perry D. *Crossing the Deadly Ground* (Tuscaloosa: The University of Alabama Press, 1994).

Johnson, Robert U. & Clarence C. Buel, eds. *Battles and Leaders of the Civil War,* 4 Vols. (Century Company, 1884-89, Reprint, New York: Thomas Yoseloff, 1956), Vol. 3.

Jones, Archer. *Civil War Command and Strategy* (New York: The Free Press, 1992).

Ladd, David L. & Audrey J. eds. *The Bachelder Papers—Gettysburg in Their Own Words* (Dayton: Morningside House, Inc., 3 Vols: Vols. 1 & 2, 1994, Vol. 3, 1995).

Lewis, Col. Berkeley R. *Notes on Ammunition of the American Civil War, 1861-1865* (Richmond: The William Byrd Press, Inc., 1959).

Longacre, Edward. *The Man Behind the Guns—A Biography of General Henry Jackson Hunt* (A.S. Barnes & Co., Inc., 1977).

Lord, Francis A. *Civil War Collector's Encyclopedia* (Secaucus, Castle, div. of Book Sales, Inc., 1963).

Luvaas, Jay, Dr. & Col. Harold W. Nelson, eds. *The U.S. Army War College Guide to the Battle of Gettysburg* (Carlisle, PA: South Mountain Press, Inc., 1986).

Mallet, J. W., "Work of the Ordnance Bureau of the War Department of the Confederate States, 1861–5." *Southern Historical Society Papers*, Vol. 37, 8.

Martin, David. *Gettysburg, July 1* (Conshohocken, PA: Combined Books, 1995).

McIntosh, David Gregg, "Review Of The Gettysburg Campaign." *Southern Historical Society Papers*, Vol. 37, 136–38.

McWhiney, Grady and Perry Jamieson. *Attack and Die* (The University of Alabama Press, 1982).

Melton, Jack W. Jr. & Lawrence E. Pawl, *Introduction to Field Artillery Ordnance 1861-1865* (Kennesaw Mountain Press, 1994).

Muir, Rory. *Tactics and the Experience of Battle in the Age of Napoleon* (New Haven: Yale University Press, 1998).

Munden, Kenneth W. & Henry Putnam Beers, *The Union* (Published for the National Archives and Records Administration by the National Archives Trust Fund Board, 1986).

Naisawald, L. Van Loan. *Grape and Canister* (New York: Oxford University Press, 1960).

National Archives. Washington, D.C., *Summary of Ordnance and Ordnance Stores on Hand in the Artillery Regiments, 2nd Quarter Ending June 30, 1863* (National Archives, Washington, D.C.) Record Group 156, Microfilm Publication M1281, Roll #1, Vol. 2).

Nevins, Allan, ed. *A Diary of a Battle*, The Personal Journals of Col. Charles S. Wainwright 1861–1865 (Gettysburg, PA: Stan Clark Military Books, 1962 Reprint).

Nye, Wilbur Sturtevant. *Here Come the Rebels* (Baton Rouge: Louisiana State University Press, 1965).

Peterson, Harold Leslie. *Notes on Ordnance of the American Civil War 1861-1865* (Wash. D.C., The American Ordnance Association, 1959).

Pfanz, Harry W. *Gettysburg—Culp's Hill and Cemetery Hill* (Chapel Hill: The University of North Carolina Press, 1993).

Pickett, LaSalle Corbell. *My Soldier* (New York: The S.S. McClure Co.,1908), McClure's Magazine Vol. XXX, Nov. to April, 1907-1908.

Pullen, John J. *The Twentieth Maine* (Phila. & New York: J.B. Lippincott Company, 1957).

Ripley, Warren. *Artillery and Ammunition of the Civil War* (New York: Promontory Press, 1970).

Risch, Erna. *Quartermaster Support of the Army 1775-1939* (Wash. D. C.: Center of Military History - U. S. Army, 1989).

Ritchie & Dunnavant, publishers. *The Field Manual for the Use of the Officers on Ordnance Duty* (Ritchie & Dunnavant, 1862. Reprinted by Thomas Publications, 1984).

Ritter, William L., Captain. "Maryland Artillery—Sketch of the Third Battery." *Southern Historical Society Papers*, Vol. 11, 116, 190.

Roberts, Joseph. *The Handbook of Artillery for the Service of the United States*, 5th edition, revised and enlarged (New York: D. Van Nostrand, 1863).

Scheibert, Justus, Maj. of the Prussian Royal Engineers. "Leading Confederates On The Battle Of Gettysburg." *Southern Historical Society Papers*, Vol. 5, 92–93.

Schenck, A.D. *Material for Field Artillery* (1886).

Schreier, Konrad F., Jr. *U.S. Army Field Artillery Weapons—1866 to 1918* (Periodical Journal of America's Military Past, Vol. XXIV, Summer 1997, No. 2, Whole No. 79).

Scott, James K. P. *The Artillery at Gettysburg* (Assoc. of Licensed Battlefield Guide Files), file 4-19A.

Smith, Donald L. *The Twenty-Fourth Michigan* (Harrisburg, The Stackpole Co., 1962).

Stark, Wayne. Civil War Cannon Costs (Internet Address: http://www.cwartillery.org/art-cost.html).

Starr, Stephen. *The Union Cavalry in the Civil War* (Baton Rouge: Louisiana University Press, 1979), Vol. 1.

Stewart, George. *Pickett's Charge* (Greenwich CT: Fawcett Publications, Inc., 1963).

Stouffer, Samuel, Arthur A. Lumsdaine, Marion Harper Lumsdaine, Robin M. Williams Jr., M. Brewster Smith, Irving L. Janis, Shirley A. Star, Leonard S. Cottrell Jr. *The American Soldier, Combat and its Aftermath* (Princeton: Princeton University Press, 1949), Vol. 2.

Switlik, M. C. *The More Complete Cannoneer* (Museum and Collector Specialties Co., 3rd edition, 1990).

Talcott, T. M. R., "The Third Day At Gettysburg." *Southern Historical Society Papers*, Vol. 41, 46.

Time-Life Books, eds. *Arms and Equipment of the Confederacy* (Alexandria: Time-Life Books, 1996).

U.S. Army Military Museum, West Point, N.Y. Small Arms display.

U.S. Government Printing Office, *Report of the Joint Committee on the Conduct of the War*, Vol. 4 (Wilmington, NC: Broadfoot Publishing Company, 1999).

U.S. War Department, *Instruction for Field Artillery*, 1st published 1861 (New York: Greenwood Press, Publishers, Reprint 1968).

U.S. War Department, *The War of the Rebellion: A Compilation of the Official Records of the Union and Confederate Armies*, 70 vols.

Vandiver, Frank E. ed. *The Civil War Diary of Josiah Gorgas* (University AL: University of Alabama Press, 1947).

Williams, William Bradford. *History of the Manufacture of Explosives for the World War, 1917-1918* (Chicago: University of Chicago Press, 1920).

Winslow, Richard E. III. *General John Sedgwick* (Novato, CA: Presidio Press, 1982).

Worsham, John, "The Second Battle of Manassas. Account of it by One of Jackson's Foot Cavalry." *Southern Historical Society Papers* (article from the Times Dispatch, October 23, 1904), Vol. 32, 85.

Index

CPSIA information can be obtained at www.ICGtesting.com
Printed in the USA
BVOW07s1643220414

351182BV00003B/14/P